Tracing Your West Indian Ancestors

Second expanded edition

Guy Grannum

PUBLIC RECORD OFFICE

Public Record Office Readers' Guide No. 11

First edition published by the Public Record Office in 1995
Second edition first published in 2002 by

Public Record Office
Kew
Richmond
Surrey
TW9 4DU
www.pro.gov.uk

Front cover illustrations: workers on a sugar plantation, Barbados, 1949 (INF 10/44); tourists arriving at the customs pier, Bridgetown, Barbados, 1955 (INF 10/39).
Back cover illustration: Map of the Caribbean, *c.* 1750 (CO 700/WestIndies12)

Printed in Great Britain by Antony Rowe, Chippenham, Wiltshire

Contents

Illustrations   ix
Preface   xi
Acknowledgements   xii
Glossary   xiii

Introduction   1

1   FIRST STEPS   6
     1.1 Who are the West Indians?   6
     1.2 How do I start my research?   7
     1.3 My ancestor was a slave. Where do I start?   10
          1.3.1 Records to start your research with   10
          1.3.2 Surnames   12
     1.4 What can I find on the internet?   16
     1.5 What does the Church of Jesus Christ of Latter-day Saints hold? 18
     1.6 Is there anything I should know about using archives and libraries? 19
     1.7 How do I make best use of the Public Record Office?   20

2   RECORDS OF THE COLONIAL OFFICE   23
     2.1 Original correspondence   24
     2.2 Entry books   25
     2.3 Acts   25
     2.4 Sessional papers   26
     2.5 Government gazettes   26
     2.6 Miscellanea   26
          2.6.1 *Blue Books of Statistics*   26
          2.6.2 Naval office returns   29
          2.6.3 Newspapers   29
     2.7 Registers of correspondence   29
     2.8 Registers of out-letters   31

3   MIGRATION TO THE WEST INDIES   33
     3.1 Emigration: general records   33
          3.1.1 Passenger lists   33
          3.1.2 Passports   34
          3.1.3 Naturalization   34
     3.2 Indentured servants   37
     3.3 Transportation   38

3.4	Slave trade	39
3.5	Liberated Africans	40
3.6	East Indians	41
3.7	American loyalists	43
4	**LIFE CYCLE RECORDS**	**45**
4.1	**Records of births, marriages and deaths**	**45**
	4.1.1 Church registers	46
	4.1.2 Slave registers	47
	4.1.3 Civil registers	47
4.2	**Censuses and other listings**	**48**
4.3	**Wills and grants of administration**	**50**
	4.3.1 Local records	50
	4.3.2 Prerogative Court of Canterbury	51
5	**LAND AND PROPERTY RECORDS**	**54**
5.1	**Land grants**	**54**
5.2	**Maps and plans**	**55**
5.3	**Plantation records**	**55**
6	**MILITARY AND RELATED RECORDS**	**60**
6.1	**Army**	**61**
	6.1.1 Records of service	62
	6.1.2 Other records	66
	6.1.3 West Indian regiments	67
	6.1.4 Records of West Indian regiments	71
	6.1.5 Militia	75
6.2	**Royal Navy**	**76**
	6.2.1 Records of service	76
	6.2.2 Other records	77
	6.2.3 Royal Naval Reserve	78
	6.2.4 Royal Naval Volunteer Reserve	78
	6.2.5 Naval dockyards	79
6.3	**Royal Marines**	**80**
	6.3.1 Records of service	80
	6.3.2 Other records	80
	6.3.3 Colonial marines	81
6.4	**Royal Air Force**	**81**
	6.4.1 Records of service	82
	6.4.2 Other records	84
6.5	**Merchant navy**	**84**
	6.5.1 Records of service	84
	6.5.2 Other records	87

7	SLAVES	88
	7.1 Slave Registry and the Slave Compensation Commission (T 71)	88
	7.1.1 Slave Registry	89
	7.1.2 Slave Compensation Commission	90
	7.2 Other records	92
	7.2.1 Colonial Office returns	92
	7.2.2 Reports of protectors of slaves	93
	7.2.3 Manumissions (grants of freedom)	93
	7.2.4 Acts on the status, condition and treatment of slaves	95

| 8 | THE COLONIAL CIVIL SERVANT | 97 |

9	MIGRATION FROM THE WEST INDIES	102
	9.1 Migration to the United Kingdom	102
	9.2 West Indian migration outside the United Kingdom	111
	9.2.1 Records of the Foreign Office	113
	9.2.2 Immigration records	114
	9.2.3 Registers of births, marriages and deaths	115

10	BRITISH WEST INDIES RESOURCES	118
	10.1 British West Indies, general	119
	10.2 Anguilla	121
	10.3 Antigua and Barbuda	123
	10.4 Bahamas	125
	10.5 Barbados	128
	10.6 Bay Islands	131
	10.7 Belize (formerly British Honduras)	131
	10.8 Bermuda	133
	10.9 British Virgin Islands	134
	10.10 Cayman Islands	136
	10.11 Dominica	137
	10.12 Federation of the West Indies	139
	10.13 Grenada	140
	10.14 Guyana (formerly British Guiana)	142
	10.15 Jamaica	144
	10.16 Leeward Islands	147
	10.17 Montserrat	148
	10.18 Nevis	151
	10.19 St Christopher (St Kitts)	153
	10.20 St Lucia	156
	10.21 St Vincent and the Grenadines	159
	10.22 Tobago	161
	10.23 Trinidad	163
	10.24 Turks and Caicos Islands	165
	10.25 Windward Islands	166

11   RECORDS OF THE NON-BRITISH WEST INDIES   167
    11.1 Cuba   167
    11.2 Denmark   169
    11.3 Dominican Republic (formerly Santo Domingo)   169
    11.4 France   170
    11.5 Haiti (formerly Saint-Domingue)   170
    11.6 Honduras   171
    11.7 Netherlands   171
    11.8 Panama   172
    11.9 Spain   173
    11.10 Sweden   173
    11.11 United States of America   173

Useful addresses   175
Bibliography   178
Index   190

Illustrations

                                                                    Page

Frontispiece Map of the Caribbean, 1904 (CO 700/WestIndies52).   ii

Figure 1 Photograph of the West Indies Cricket Team who toured in England   2
in 1906 (COPY 1/500, registered 21 August 1906).

Figure 2 Trinidad: Slave register, 1813. Return of slaves on Forest Plantation   14
(T 71/501, fo 29).

Figure 3 Jamaica: Petition of Sarah Bonner, free quadroon, for rights and   25
privileges, November 1783 (CO 140/66, p. 57).

Figure 4 Dominica: *Government Gazette*, 1865, list of patients in the infirmary 27
(CO 75/1, p. 226).

Figure 5 Dominica: *Government Gazette*, 1920, list of trade licences issued   28
(CO 75/14, p. 35).

Figure 6 Guyana: *Blue Book of Statistics*, 1890, list of government pensioners   30
(CO 116/259, pp. O1–2).

Figure 7 Bahamas: certificate of naturalization for Theophanis George   35
Tiliacos, Greek, certificate number O275, 19 May 1923
(HO 334/249).

Figure 8 St Vincent: list of Indians disembarked from the *Newcastle*, 1867,   42
and the estates they were indentured to (CO 264/9, p. 63).

Figure 9 Barbados: death notices announced in *The Liberal*, Wednesday 30   48
August 1854 (CO 33/12, fo 117).

Figure 10 Cayman Islands: census of heads of households, 1802   49
(CO 137/108, fo 272).

Figure 11 Barbados: will of Fearnot Cox dated 30 July 1784, showing slaves   52
being bequeathed to family members (PROB 37/897)

Figure 12 Grenada: plan of Georgetown, 1765 (CO 700/Grenada5).   56

Figure 13 St Lucia: return of relief paid to persons in distress following   58
the great hurricane of August 1831 (T 1/4396, paper 6312/33).

Figure 14 Roll of the Bermuda Volunteer Rifle Corps   65
who were attached to the Lincolnshire Regiment
(CO 318/336, War Office, 24 November 1915).

Figure 15 Roll of 5th battalion of the British West Indies Regiment   70
comprising men mainly from British Honduras (Belize)
(CO 318/340, War Office, 28 October 1916).

Figure 16 Roll of West Indian RAF recruits who trained in Canada   83
(AIR 2/6876).

Figure 17   Seamen's papers for Edward Valentine Browne, born in   86
                  Montserrat, discharge number R755406 (BT 372/2403).

Figure 18   Barbados: slave register, 1826 (T 71/537, p. 148).   91

Figure 19   Antigua: list of slaves manumitted, January to March 1823   94
                  (CO 7/14).

Figure 20   Application form of Walter Belfield Grannum for the post of   98
                  Medical Superintendent, Barbados Lunatic Asylum, 1916
                  (CO 28/289, fo 69).

Figure 21   Guyana: *Blue Book of Statistics*, 1890, staff in the judicial 100
                  department (CO 116/259, pp. M64–5).

Figure 22   1901 census for the family of Walter Belfield Grannum born in 104
                  Barbados (RG 13/1517, fo 52).

Figure 23   Passenger list for SS *Antilles*, arrived Plymouth, 8 May 1955 106
                  (BT 26/1332).

Figure 24   Certificate of registration for Eva Juliet Borough, born Jamaica, 107
                  certificate number R1/174547, issued 2 September 1971
                  (HO 334/1817).

Figure 25   Panama: list of British West Indians in the Lunatic Asylum,   112
                  Canal Zone, Panama, 1918 (CO 318/346, Foreign Office,
                  25 April 1918).

Figure 26   Curacao: return of births registered at the British Consul, 1950 116
                  (FO 907/5, p. 32)

Figure 27   Martinique: list of vacated sugar estates, May 1794 (WO 1/31,   168
                  p. 367).

Preface

I joined the Public Record Office in 1988, and from 1991 have been advising researchers on how to make the best use of the PRO. I started tracing my West Indian ancestors at about the same time and soon became aware that there were no general guides to help me like those familiar to researchers of ancestors in the UK, America, Australia and Canada. Increasing numbers of people were visiting or writing to the PRO for help in tracing their Caribbean ancestors; as there was no literature to guide them, *Tracing Your West Indian Ancestors* was written to fill this neglected area. The aim of the guide is to describe the most important records in the Public Record Office for the study of West Indian family history. These sources can also be used to study the social, economic and military history of the British West Indies from the time of their settlement in the 16th century to the 20th century.

Since the publication of the first edition in 1995 there have been significant changes to the Public Record Office, notably that the office in Chancery Lane has closed and the records transferred to Kew or to the Family Records Centre in Islington. Many records have been recently released which are important for studying West Indian families in the West Indies and those who have migrated to Britain. For example, new accessions include records of service for soldiers, air crew and sailors who served in the First World War; merchant seamen's services, 1913–1972; registers from the Chaplain of the Fleet; and certificates of registrations of citizens and the colonies to 1987.

The guide has been completely revised and many chapters have been expanded, especially those on military services (which now include information on the British West Indies Regiment and the Royal Air Force), plantation records, slave records, and migration both to Britain and to non-British countries. I have consolidated the information for each country, included brief notes on the country's history and events which have affected the records, and expanded archive addresses and the bibliography.

Following feedback from users of the first edition I have included a chapter which provides guidance on genealogical research in relation to West Indian families. Finally, as there has been significant growth in the World Wide Web as a research tool, I have included useful internet resources. For researchers wishing to make use of the PRO, we have made available our catalogue and other online resources (such as copies of selected documents, and exhibitions) on our web site at <www.pro.gov.uk>.

Guy Grannum
September 2002

Acknowledgements

To Mrs Mary Pym, my grandmother, who sparked my interest in my ancestry.

I would like to thank Karen Grannum, Mandy Banton, Sheila Knight, Diana Shelley and numerous members of the Caribbean mailing list for their support and advice in the production of this guide.

Glossary

The records in the PRO for the study of the West Indies and West Indians have many terms which are now obsolete or have changed their meaning and may now be considered offensive. Although I have tried to use modern words I have on occasion had to use colonial words. It may be useful, therefore, if I provide a short list of some of the more common words and terms which you will find in this guide and in the records:

Coolie Asian Indian labourer

Creole Someone born in the West Indies or parts of North and South America. In the British West Indies the term is used for Black and white inhabitants.

East Indian Someone from the Indian sub-continent. Large numbers of Asian Indians migrated to the West Indies between 1834 and 1920 (see **3.6**).

Emancipate To free from slavery. In the British West Indies slaves were emancipated on 1 August 1834 under the Abolition of Slavery Act 1833.

Ethnicity and colour Colonial and government officials were fairly consistent in their use of terms for colour and ethnicity since they had social and legal meaning (in the West Indies). It should usually be clear from the context of the record which ethnic groups were being referred to.

Asian Someone from the Indian sub-continent. The nineteenth century documents usually use the word 'coolie'. Chinese West Indians were usually called Chinese.

Black Someone not of white European descent. If Black is found in context with other ethnic terms, for example Asian, Indian or coloured, then it means a person of African descent.

Coloured Someone not of white European descent. If coloured is found in context with other ethnic terms, for example Black, Indian or Asian, it means a person of mixed ethnic ancestry and more usually someone of mixed African and European ancestry. The term 'mulatto' is often used instead of 'coloured'.

Indian Until 1834 Indian meant indigenous Amerindian or of Amerindian descent, but after 1834, with the migration of Asian Indian labourers, Indian usually meant someone from the Indian subcontinent. Nineteenth century documents often refer to Asian Indians as 'coolies'.

Negro African or a person of African descent.

White   Someone of 'pure' European descent, although in many colonies someone who was 1/16th Black was legally white.

Many colonial authorities graded slaves and free people according to their ethnic origin. The terms varied slightly from country but the common usage in Jamaica was:

Mulatto   The child of a white and a Black (1/2 Black, one Black parent). The term 'mulatto' was more commonly used to describe someone of mixed European and African descent

Quadroon   The child of a white and a mulatto (1/4 Black, one Black grandparent).

Mustee   The child of a white and a quadroon; sometimes also called mustifino or octoroon (1/8 Black, one Black great-grandparent).

The child of a white and a mustee was white, by Jamaican law (1/16 Black, one Black great-great-grandparent).

Sambo   The child of a mulatto and a Black (3/4 Black, a single white grandparent).

The child of a sambo and a Black was Black (7/8 Black, one white great-grandparent).

Manumission   Legally freed from slavery (see **7.2.3**).

Maroon   From 'cimarrones' (Spanish for wild or unruly), maroons were Spanish runaway slaves who settled in the mountains of Western Jamaica and fought the British. Their numbers were later increased by British runaway slaves.

West Indians   Originally a West Indian could be someone who was born, or was settled in the West Indies, or someone based in the UK who had interest in the West Indies, such as an absentee proprietor or merchant. Later it was only used to describe people born or settled in the West Indies.

West Indies   Chain of volcanic and coral islands from Florida in North America to Venezuela in South America. For administrative reasons the British government included Bermuda, British Honduras (Belize) and British Guiana (Guyana) as West Indian possessions.

Introduction

When I first came to London in 1982 I knew nothing about my ancestry and thought it would be interesting to try to research my family history. I have an unusual surname and thought it would be easy! I searched the birth, marriage and death indexes and wills for England and Wales and found references to my father and his brothers and sisters, my grandfather (no mention of his brothers), and his father's marriage, and that was it. There are virtually no other Grannums listed until the 1950s.

I mentioned this to my grandmother and she remembered that my great-grandfather was listed in *Who's Who*; he isn't, although he is in *Who Was Who*. The entry said that he was born in Barbados, as were his brother and father (both are also listed); all were colonial civil servants.

From records at the PRO, making use of the Church of Jesus Christ of Latter-day Saints resources, publications, newspapers and for a brief time employing a researcher in Barbados, I have now traced my Barbadian Grannum family back to the 1730s. However, I still have not managed to get back further to a place of origin (Barbados was uninhabited when colonized by the British in 1627).

There are a great many Grannums around the world. In common with many West Indians they have migrated to Britain, other West Indian Islands, Latin America, United States, Canada and Australia. They are a mixture of Europeans and African-Caribbeans, having descended from European settlers, slaves and the children of slave owners and their slaves. They served in the armed forces, colonial civil service, local colonial government, the merchant navy, and some were imprisoned.

Much has been written on family history for most of the former British Empire, especially South Africa, Canada, the United States of America, New Zealand and Australia. Very little has been written about the British West Indies or the other British colonies in Central and South America. The British West Indies are among a chain of islands spreading from Florida to Venezuela. They contain a diverse population of indigenous Amerindians, and the descendants of Dutch, Spanish, African, British, Portuguese, Chinese, Danish, Swedish, Indian and French settlers. This small group of islands was important to the development of Britain's empire during the sixteenth to eighteenth centuries. The wealth created by the plantations encouraged the banking and insurance industries and, it is said, sparked Britain's industrial revolution.

Figure 1   Photograph of the West Indies Cricket Team who toured England in 1906 (COPY 1/500, registered 21 August 1906). The team arrived in Southampton on 4 June 1906 on RMS *Trent* (see passenger list in BT 26/277) and included H B G Austin (Barbados), C K Bancroft (Barbados), Burton (Guyana), G Challenor (Barbados), L Contantine (Trinidad), Cumberbatch (Trinidad), P Goodman (Barbados), A R Harrigan (Trinidad), Layne (Barbados), G C Learmond (Trinidad), C S Morrison (Jamaica), R Ollivierre (St Vincent), J R Parker (Guyana) and S Smith (Trinidad). Constantine, Learmond, Goodman and Burton also played in the first West Indies cricket tour of England in 1900 (see two photographs of the team in COPY 1/446, registered 18 June 1900; passenger list in BT 26/168, RMS *Trent* arrived in Southampton 6 June 1900).

This guide aims to aid research in the British Dependent Territories and former colonies of Antigua, Bahamas, Barbados, Bermuda, Cayman Islands, Dominica, Grenada, Jamaica, Montserrat, Nevis, St Christopher (St Kitts), St Lucia, St Vincent, Tobago, Trinidad, Turks and Caicos Islands, and the British Virgin Islands, together with Guyana (formerly British Guiana) and Belize (formerly British Honduras). It is not intended to be a guide to general genealogical sources and techniques nor is it meant to stand on its own.

I have included short references for further reading in each chapter, with comments or page references where appropriate. You will find fuller details about these books in the **Bibliography** at the back. Some of these books may be hard to find in the United Kingdom as many are published in the USA and the Caribbean.

Website addresses are given in full in the relevant chapter and are only repeated in the **Bibliography** if they form part of the book or journal publisher's address.

I have referred to relevant chapters of Amanda Bevan's *Tracing Your Ancestors in the Public Record Office* throughout the guide. The PRO also has information leaflets on many of the subjects covered in this guide, which can be obtained in person from the PRO or online at <www.pro.gov.uk>; they cannot be sent by post.

When Europeans first discovered the West Indies at the end of the fifteenth century, most of the islands had indigenous populations. The Portuguese and Spanish enslaved many of these indigenous Amerindians to work on their plantations and gold mines in South America; many more were wiped out through disease and invasion. Some Amerindians still survive in the Caribbean, such as in Dominica, but most did not survive European settlement.

The Americas were 'beyond the line', that is they lay outside the territorial limits of European treaties, so disputes in the Americas did not invalidate peace treaties in Europe. While the Spanish attempted to keep other European powers out of America, the gold of the Spanish Main acted as a lure to adventurers and pirates. During the seventeenth and eighteenth centuries the Spanish gradually lost their hold on the Caribbean and Latin and North America. The Portuguese settled in Brazil, the French and English colonized fragments of North America and many of the West Indian islands, and the Dutch settled Surinam and some islands, as well as enjoying a brief spell in Brazil. The Danes and Swedes also colonized some of the islands.

Regular territorial disputes and European wars meant that islands frequently changed hands from one power to another. On islands captured by Britain from the Spanish, French and Dutch, there was little or no attempt to expel all the non-British. During the French Revolution and the Spanish-American independence wars many refugees fled to 'friendly' British islands. These non-British populations would also have had their slaves and servants.

Labour was necessary for the settled islands to prosper and many thousands, free and unfree, were transported from Europe. From the 1650s the most significant change in the populations was the mass transportation of slave labour from the West Coast of Africa. The Spanish and Portuguese were already using African labour in Latin America, but the numbers enslaved escalated once the Dutch, French and British islands realised the necessity of a large unskilled work force, used to tropical climate, food and diseases, to maintain their plantations.

It has been estimated that more than eleven million Africans were transported to the New World, with an estimated 1.6 million Africans sent to the British West Indies. By the mid eighteenth century most of the British islands had Black populations which far exceeded the white population. It is not possible to identify the origin of the Black populations as very poor records were kept and, even where ethnic origins are noted, these are often the names of the areas of departure from Africa rather than the true ethnic group.

When slavery was abolished in the British colonies many colonies, notably Trinidad and British Guiana, suffered severe labour problems. Trinidad had established various schemes before 1834 to encourage labour, such as the immigration of Chinese labourers in 1806. Other people encouraged to settle were disbanded soldiers from the West India Regiments, Black colonial marines who enlisted in America during the War of 1812, East Indians (from the Indian subcontinent), liberated Africans freed from illegal slavers, and Portuguese from Madeira and the Azores.

The study of genealogy in the West Indies relies on the same sources as used in Britain: parish records, legal records, military service, census returns, tax returns, wills, maps, private correspondence and newspapers. However, the PRO does not hold the domestic records of colonial governments or the more important records for West Indian family research, such as church records and wills; these are held locally in the country's archives and register offices (see **Chapter 10** for further information). The PRO does hold numerous references to people who lived in the West Indies, such as adventurers who planted sugar cane, slaves who toiled the land, soldiers and sailors who fought in the Napoleonic Wars, transported criminals, and Asian Indians who emigrated as indentured labourers.

Many West Indian countries were captured from or ceded by other European powers and records of their pre-British history may survive in provincial and national archives of other European countries. For example, Guyana was Dutch, St Lucia, Grenada, Dominica and St Vincent were French, Trinidad was Spanish, and for eighty years St Christopher was jointly shared by both Britain and France. At various times the British also temporarily occupied islands held by other European powers, and the records in the PRO may contain information about their inhabitants.

Further reading

Curtin, *Atlantic Slave Trade*
Dunn, *Sugar and Slaves*
Edwards, *History of the British West Indies*
Fage, *History of Africa*
Higman (ed.), *General History of the Caribbean, Vol. VI*
Louise (ed.), *History of the British Empire*
Lovejoy, *Transformations in Slavery*
Lucas, *Historical Geography of the British Colonies: The West Indies*

First steps

This book is not intended to be a guide to general genealogical sources or techniques but you may find it useful to have some general guidance to help start your research. There are many published guides to family history and your local library may have some. I have listed some guides at the end of this chapter; unfortunately, there are only a few for the British West Indies (see **1.2**). However, research techniques and records are very similar whether you are carrying out family history research in the UK, Canada, the United States or the Caribbean.

1.1 Who are the West Indians?

The majority of people in the West Indies are immigrants. Caribs and other indigenous Amerindians still live on many of the islands and in Central and South America, but these are now minority populations, having been reduced by war, disease and forced migration.

West Indians are a diverse population comprising British, Dutch, Spanish, French, Portuguese, African (from a wide variety of countries and ethnic groups), Danish, American, German, Lebanese, Chinese and East Indian migrants. They are a mixture of voluntary (planters, merchants, adventurers, economic migrants, indentured servants and discharged soldiers), involuntary (transported prisoners and slaves) and displaced migrants (refugees from American colonial wars, from religious persecution, liberated Africans and fugitive slaves). Although people often refer to West Indians as if they are a single group, they are not: each country has its own cultural identity based on history, language, religion and ethnic makeup.

There has also been much migration between the islands and with Africa, Europe and North, Central and South America. It cannot be assumed that your ancestors came directly from the 'mother' country to the West Indies. For example, an English family in Jamaica may have reached there after first settling in Barbados, then migrating to South Carolina, and then arriving in Jamaica as loyalists following the American Revolution. An African family in Trinidad may not be a product of West Indian slavery but may be descended from a freed refugee from Georgia, USA, who enlisted with the British forces during the War of 1812.

To use an extreme but possible example, an African family in Trinidad could have been descended from a slave who moved with his owner from Barbados to Jamaica and who later ran away and joined the maroons (see **Glossary**). A descendant was captured during the Maroon War against the British in 1796 and transported to Nova Scotia and was one of the black settlers to Sierra Leone in 1800. A son enlisted in the West Indies Regiment, was discharged and then settled in Trinidad.

1.2 How do I start my research?

There is no set way to go about tracing your family but you should always start with what you know about yourself, your parents, brothers, sisters, aunts, uncles and grandparents etc. Try to collect as much information as possible on the dates of births, marriages and deaths and locations. If dates are unknown try to approximate and for births try to find out the order of siblings. Talk to your family and relatives, identify people in family photographs and how they fit into your family, and collect or copy documentary evidence such as certificates of baptism, births and marriages, family bibles, wills and personal correspondence. Listen to family tales and oral traditions which if not totally factual may have some truth in them – these may have sparked your interest in your family in the first place!

At some point your research will take you beyond your immediate family and you will need to visit archives and libraries. To do this you need to know which island your family came from and ideally which parish. It will have a significant bearing on the sources you need to research if you also know their religious denomination, ethnic group, status, occupation and the approximate dates they lived in that country.

The next step after collecting family papers and speaking with family members is to search civil registration records of births, marriages and deaths in the countries where your family lived. These records are held by each country's registration office or archive, although many have been filmed by the Church of Jesus Christ of Latter-day Saints (LDS) and can be ordered through your nearest Family History Centre (see **1.5**). These records will usually provide addresses and the names of one or both parents, depending on the event, and ages may be recorded on marriage and death records, which will help approximate dates of birth. State registration for each country started at different times from the late nineteenth century, and before then you will need to check church records, which are arranged by parish and then by church or chapel. Many early church records have been deposited with the registration offices or other archives but most are still held by the individual churches. Again, many have been microfilmed by the LDS. Before the early 1800s the Anglican Church was the predominant church in the older British West Indian islands; the former French and Spanish colonies were predominantly Catholic. Increasingly from the late eighteenth century various non-conformist denominations, for example Moravian, Baptist and Methodist, established chapels.

There are a few points to bear in mind:

- Britain does not hold the locally created records of her dependencies or former colonies, although some records for the Dutch West India Company's administration of British Guiana have been transferred to the PRO. Some locally created records have ended up in private hands and many have been deposited in archive services throughout the world. However most are to be found, if they survive, in the archives and other depositories in the relevant country.

- The records are not centralized and each country has its own archives, libraries and registry offices.

- Local records can be incomplete, having suffered from neglect, poor record keeping practices, war and tropical environment, such as hurricanes, humidity and insects, fire, earthquakes and volcanoes.

- Records are not always written in English: those countries which were conquered and ceded to Britain still used Dutch, Spanish or French in legal documents for many years afterwards. French-based patois is still widely spoken in Grenada, the Grenadines and Trinidad, and in St Lucia and Dominica it is known as Kwéyòl (Creole).

- Slaves were the personal property of their owners. They had very few rights and were rarely recorded by the church or state. It can be extremely difficult tracing descendants of slaves during the period of slavery before 1834 but there are some sources which can help (see **1.3**).

- The name someone was known by was not necessarily the name officially recorded at birth and could be a pet name, alias or second name.

- Surnames were not standardized: officials wrote the name as they heard it and often people could not read or write and could not check what was written. Therefore, when looking for families you need to check surname variations.

- Marriage did not always precede the birth of children. Common-law marriage was common in the West Indies and any children of these relationships were usually registered with the mother's name. At some point in the child's life he or she might have adopted the father's name and therefore might marry and die under a different name from that they were born with. This can cause problems as the father of common-law relationships is not usually recorded on the birth certificate, the mother is not recorded on the children's marriage certificates, and neither are recorded on the death certificate. You need to use other records to trace such relationships such as wills and private correspondence.

- Write everything down and include the source such as family bible, certificate and spoken word. If it is from an archival record, note the archive and the full reference. You may need to recheck your information or pass the information on. Also record sources you have used even if the results proved negative because this information can be very important in itself and will help you not to repeat the exercise.

- Respect people's wishes. If they do not want to give you information do not press them.

- And last but no means least – check original material whenever possible as errors may have crept into indexes or transcripts.

The culmination of your research may be to find the country of origin for your ancestor. Christopher Columbus first discovered the West Indies in 1492 and, with the exception of a minority of surviving indigenous Amerindians, West Indians are all immigrants. You may be lucky enough to find clues to the homeland for your first West Indian ancestor, in which case you may be able to start researching archives in that country. If your ancestor migrated before the nineteenth century you may also need to know from which town, village or parish he or she left because most of the records were generated by the church or local authorities rather than centralized by the state. However, not all countries recorded events in legal documents and you may need to research oral evidence and traditions.

1.2.1 Further reading

I have found three guides for West Indian genealogy.

Mitchell, *Jamaican Ancestry*
Porter, *Jamaican Records: Research Manual*
Salazar, *Love Child: Genealogist's Guide* <www.candoo.com/projects/lovechild.html>
Crooks, *Ancestors*, is a novel based on genealogical research.

The following guides relate mainly to British genealogy. However, the sources and research techniques for West Indian genealogy are very similar and these will provide some guidance on how to start your family history (see **1.3** for guides on African-American genealogy)

Blatchford, *Family and Local History Handbook*
Chapman, *Tracing Your British Ancestors*
Cole, *Tracing Your Family Tree*
Colwell, *Teach Yourself Tracing Your Family History*
Family Tree Magazine
Fowler, *Joys of Family History*

Galford, *Essential Guide to Genealogy*
Genealogists' Magazine
Greenwood, *Researcher's Guide to American Genealogy*
Grenham, *Tracing Your Irish Ancestors*
Herber, *Ancestral Trails*
Hey, *Oxford Guide to Family History*
Pelling and Litton, *Beginning Your Family History*
Reader's Digest, *Explore Your Family's Past*
Rose and Ingalls, *Guide to Genealogy*
Scottish Record Office, *Tracing Your Scottish Ancestors*
Sinclair, *Tracing Your Scottish Ancestors*
Stephenson, *Writing Your Family History*
Titford, *Succeeding in Family History*

1.3 My ancestor was a slave. Where do I start?

Descendants of African slaves make up the majority of populations on most West Indian countries. On the British islands, slavery became an established form of labour from the 1640s when Dutch merchants from Brazil introduced sugar cane into Barbados. Sugar farming was physically demanding and mentally monotonous. Africans were used to tropical conditions, food and disease, and were considered more suitable for this unpleasant form of agriculture than white indentured servants who had previously made up the labour market.

However, if you have African ancestors you cannot assume that they were slaves as many Africans migrated to the West Indies from the 1830s and many Africans freed from illegal slavers also settled in the West Indies.

Slaves were personal property who could be bought, sold, gifted, inherited and bequeathed, according to the whims of their owner. Personal records of slaves are limited, they could not possess property, and in some British colonies they were actively discouraged from attending church.

1.3.1 Records to start your research with

Until the establishment of slave registries from 1814 (see **7.1**), most records of slaves, their births and deaths, are to be found among the personal papers of their owners and records relating to their owners and plantations. Many of the sources for slaves will be discussed in greater detail in **Chapter 7**, under records of the Colonial Office (**Chapter 2**), slave trade (**3.5**), American Loyalists (**3.8**), births, marriages and deaths (**4.1**), wills (**4.3**) and plantation records (**5.3**).

Useful sources for information relating to slaves include:

- Deeds and registers of property.

- Mortgage and transfer indentures and deeds.

- Manumission registers and deeds – legal documents freeing slaves, who were often the children of slaves by their owners' and other favoured slaves (**7.2.3**).

- Wills bequeathing slaves to family and friends (**4.2**).

- Acts legally manumitting slaves by ordinance or by the legislative council (**7.2.3**).

- Notices in newspapers and gazettes for auctions and runaways (**2.6.3**).

- Records of the slave registry and Slave Compensation Commission (see below and **7.1**).

- Church records. Although the baptism of slaves was actively discouraged in the Protestant colonies this did occur and from the early nineteenth century local legislation was relaxed to permit baptism. There are very few references to slave marriages and many slave burials were unrecorded as they occurred on the plantation. It was uncommon for child slaves to be baptised, but when this did occur the mother was usually recorded along with the owner.

- Plantation records such as punishment books, stock books, inventories, correspondence, accounts, purchases, loss books, and journals or diaries (**5.3**).

- Reports of protectors of slaves, which include punishments, criminal cases, manumissions, baptisms and marriages (**7.2.2**).

Most of these records are to be found locally, if they survive, in the relevant country's archive or register office, but copies of some of these types of documents are found in the PRO.

The owner or plantation will be found in most of these records, which will help identify family or estate papers for further clues. Often racial information is given, for example 'Black' or 'Negro' for predominantly African slaves and 'coloured' or 'mulatto' for slaves of mixed racial ancestry. Some colonies had a grading scale of 'whiteness' denoting the proportion of European to African blood. The term 'Creole' is often found which means someone born in the West Indies. Occasionally ethnic origin may be recorded but often this is not accurate, having been based on information provided either by one of the merchants in the chain from the forts and trading posts (factories) in Africa, the officials on the ships or the merchants selling the slaves on the islands. Often this may be where the slave was transported from rather than his or her true origin.

The most important records for information on slaves in the PRO are those of the Colonial Office (see **Chapter 2**), the slave registry and the Slave Compensation Commission (**Chapter 7**). Colonial Office records relating to slaves are numerous and include reports of slave rebellions, reports of protectors of slaves, inhabitants of workhouses, slaves granted their freedom, numbers of slaves being imported, and registration of slaves. Colonial newspapers contain notices of runaways, which name the slave and often give a brief physical description, and notices for slave auctions.

The records of the central slave registry (see **7.1**) are in the series T 71, for the period 1812 to 1834 (when slavery was abolished), although most do not start until 1817. The registers are arranged by colony and most are arranged by parish and then alphabetically by owner or estate; most also contain indexes to owners.

The registers contain much information on the slaves and their owners. For slaves they give at least name, age, colour and country of origin. The information given in the registers differs between colonies. Most registers list slaves by sex and age but some, such as those for St Lucia and Trinidad, are arranged by family and record other family members such as brothers, sisters, and cousins if on the same return. Mothers are occasionally noted in the returns but fathers are rarely recorded. After the first registration most colonies only note increases (births, inheritance and purchase) and decreases (deaths, bequests, sales and manumissions) in their numbers of slaves. Some, such as Bermuda, list all slaves.

1.3.2 Surnames

It is commonly believed that slaves took the surname of their owner, and that this will help in identifying records for family history. Although this did occur, it was not always the case. British slave law denied slaves surnames because they had no legal father and they were the property of their owner. A good example of this can be found in the baptismal entries of slaves where usually only their first name is given.

However, from a brief examination of church baptismal records for the period after 1834, following the abolition of slavery, it seems that most former slaves already possessed titles or surnames. There was no established way for slaves and free people to have a surname. It is possible that on freedom former slaves found that they needed a surname for personal or legal reasons, for example when baptised or married, or to purchase or rent land or property, or for employment.

An analysis of the Barbados baptism registers shows that most surnames used by slaves and former slaves were ones that were common on that island. Slaves may have retained surnames from earlier owners which were carried by their descendants from one owner to the next. Gutman, in *The Black Family in Slavery and Freedom*, shows that American slaves were often known by the name of their original owner, who was not necessarily their last owner. A brief examination of manumission returns and the 'Book of Negroes' compiled by the British military authorities in 1783 of Black refugees from the American Revolution (PRO 30/55/100, no 10427) shows that few slaves possessed the same surnames as their owners. The Guy Carleton Branch of the United Empire Loyalists' Association of Canada has indexed this list.

Surname practices of slaves and freedmen and women is complicated and can have several origins:

- The surname of the owner – chosen or used by the slave or given it by an official as a locative or paternal name, for example William, of Jordan's estate, may become William Jordan.

- The surname of the original or former owner – chosen by the slave, or used by the new owner to differentiate between slaves with the same first name. For example, Eliza Redman on John Ellis's estate may have come from a Redman owner and Eliza may have retained Redman as a surname on freedom.

- The surname of the father – who could be the owner, a white employee, a slave on the plantation/household, or a slave from another plantation/household. The children of slaves by their owner or white overseers often took their father's surname and this is shown in manumission registers and wills.

- The mother's surname – since slaves could rarely marry children often took the mother's surname, for example the slave registers for St Lucia and Trinidad, show slaves listed in families with the children having the surname of their mother. Children might later adopt their father's name.

- The last name – many slaves had more than one forename. Usually this was to differentiate between several slaves with the same name, for example an owner might have on the estate a Tom, Tom William, Thomas and Thomas Edward. It is possible that Tom William later became known as Tom William(s) and Thomas Edward, Thomas Edward(s). It is also possible that the last forename was the surname of a previous owner.

- Chosen – for official and legal reasons. Such surnames may have been chosen from influential, prominent or popular individuals or families.

29.

The Return of Ambrose Linhaud for the Plantation called *Forest* in the Quarter called Chaguanas, a Cocoa Plantation owned by the Heirs or

Names	Surnames	Colour	Employment	Age	Stature		Country
			List of Families of Slaves on the Plantation Forest				
			Family of Harriott				
Othello	Harriott	Negro	Labourer	55	5 4	8½	African Ibo
Clarissa	Harriott	Negro	None	45	5	3	Creole of Martinique
Prince	Harriott	Negro	None	5	3	2½	Creole of Demerary
Gill	Harriott	Negro	None	3	2	8	Creole of this Island
			Family of Murray				
Juba	Murray	Negro	Labourer	45	5	7	African Moco
Juliet	Murray	Negro	Labourer	40	4	10	African Ibo
Sam	Murray	Negro	Labourer	19	5	7	Creole of Demerary
			General List of Male Slaves on the Plantation Forest				
Polydore	Linhaud	Negro	Driver	60	5	11	Creole of Anguilla
Fortune	Lamb	Negro	Labourer	38	5	7½	African Congo
Mercury	Gombo	Negro	Labourer	30	5	7	African Chamba
Gift	Caprara	Negro	Labourer	31	5	5	African Congo
Cook	Vincent	Negro	Labourer	42	5	3½	African Mandingo
Lothario	Christian	Negro	Labourer	65	5	4	African Ibo
Bob	Richard	Negro	Labourer	66	5	3	African Moco
Sunday	Palmiste	Negro	None	61	5	9½	African Chamba
Joe	Miller	Negro	Labourer	44	5	1½	African Mandingo
Brutus	Minge	Negro	Labourer	29	5	6	African Ibo

The whole number of Slaves on the said Plantation Forest is Seventeen. A true Return

Carried to Folio 799. Henry Murray

The Return of Luce Alou for the Plantation called *Saint Dediz* in the Quarter called St Ann, a Coffee Plantation owned by

			General List of Male Slaves on the Plantation Saint Dediz				
Louis	Sebre	Negro	Labourer	32	5 ft	9	African Quaqua
			General List of Female Slaves on the Plantation Saint Dediz				
Marie	Louise	Negro	Labourer	28	4	11	African Mandingo

The whole number of Slaves on the said Plantation Saint Dediz is Two A true Return

Carried to Folio 800 Henry Murray

Figure 2   Trinidad: Slave register, 1813. Return of slaves on Forest Plantation (T 71/501, fo 29).

29

42

legal Representatives of the late Captain John Harriot deceased of which the said Ambrose Lindsaid is in Possession as Manager.

Marks	Relations	Corrections	
		1815	1816
Country marks on the forehead & Temples		5.8½ Comboes	
A scar on the left Ancle	Wife of Othello Harriett	5.3½ Comboes	
No marks	Son of Othello & Clarissa Harriett	3.7	3.9
No marks	Son of Othello & Clarissa Harriett	3.2½	3.5
Country marks on both Temples		Dead	
A scar on the Right Side	Wife of Juba Murray		
No marks (two scars under the left breast Comboes) Son of Juba & Juliet Murray			
No marks		5. Mo. Comboes	
Country marks on the breast		Sold in Febr 803 Portfig:	
Country marks on both Cheeks, breast &c			
Disfigured by Venereal		5.5½ Comboes	
Country marks on both Cheeks		5.3½ Comboes	
Lame of the left hand		Ditto	
Country marks on Temples (Comboes)		5.3½ Comboes	
Country marks on face & head (Comboes)			
Wants the great toe of the right foot			
No marks (scars on the nose & left Comboes)		5.7½ Comboes	

Amb Lindsaid 5. April 1813   Henry Murray

Lucea Alow of which the said Lucea Alow is in Possession

| No marks | | Manumitted | |

No marks
Lucea Alow her + Mark 27th March 1813.

Henry Murray

- Given – by the church or by a government official for official and legal records. This is likely to be the case for liberated Africans freed from illegal slavers who only had their African name.

It is interesting to note that surnames of slaves and former slaves reflect those in common use in the parish or in the country, rather than being made up or exotic ones as is common for first names.

1.3.3 Further reading

I have not found any guides for African-Caribbean genealogy but these African-American guides provide useful clues and insights.

Beasley, *Family Pride: Tracing African-American Genealogy*

Burnard, 'Slave naming patterns'

Burroughs, *Black Roots*

Gutman, *Black Family in Slavery and Freedom*

Handler and Jacoby, 'Slave names and naming in Barbados'

Howell, *How to Trace Your African-American Roots*

Jamison, *Finding Your People*

Johnson, Cooper and Rosen, *Student's Guide to African American Genealogy*

Rose, *Black Genesis*

Staff, *African-American Genealogy Workbook*

Streets, *Slave Genealogy*

Woodtor, *Finding a Place Called Home: Guide to African-American Genealogy*

Young, *Afro-American Genealogy*

Afro-American Historical and Genealogical Society, PO Box 73086, Washington, DC 20056-3084 <www.rootsweb.com/~mdaahgs/>

1.4 What can I find on the internet?

The internet is an extremely useful resource for family historians, containing personal family histories, databases of primary and secondary sources, reading lists, archive and library catalogues, digital images of documents, discussion groups, introductions to family history, guides to sources and genealogical groups.

The first place to start for quick hits is by using your favourite search engines. Start with a simple search, such as your surname or country, and such terms as 'family history' or 'genealogy' or 'ancestry'. If you get too many hits you can add the country of origin, or restrict the search to a specific ancestor. If you get too few, try just the surname. Because each search engine has indexed different sites in different ways you should try several search engines. This approach should reveal family historians with an interest in your surname. However, most family history data is held in databases which cannot be found using the normal web based search engines and you will need to search these databases directly from the compilers' sites.

There are many useful sites, far too many to include here, and the number continues to grow. However, I have included a few useful sites in the relevant chapters of the guide. Please note that web site addresses may change and it is important to verify family history information with the original sources.

<www.afrigeneas.com> A specialist web site concentrating on sources and guidance for African-Americans

<www.ancestry.com> Commercial site with free and chargeable databases to a wide variety of sources

<www.ccharity.com/> Christine's African-American Genealogy Website

<www.centrelink.org> Caribbean Amerindian Centrelink, a web site for those interested in Indigenous Amerindians of the Caribbean area such as Caribs, Arawaks and Tainos.

<www.cyndislist.com/> A popular genealogical gateway, comprising research tools and links to over 50,000 genealogical web sites. <www.cyndislist.com/hispanic.html> gateway to resources for Hispanic, South American and Caribbean family history

<www.familyrecords.gov.uk> A collaborative gateway to British government departments and agencies who hold primary genealogical resources. The contributors include the Public Record Office, the Family Records Centre, the Public Record Office of Northern Ireland, National Archives of Ireland, and the Office of National Statistics

<www.familysearch.com> Church of Jesus Christ of Latter-day Saints' online resources. A searchable database to the International Genealogical Index, submitted family histories, library catalogue and Family History Centre addresses

<www.familytreemaker.com> Commercial site hosted by Family Tree Maker. Contains many databases of names contained in their CD-ROM publications.

<www.genuki.org.uk> The United Kingdom and Ireland Genealogical Information Service. A handbook on British genealogy and a gateway to British Internet resources

<groups.google.com> Holds archives of newsgroups the contents of which can be searched

<www.pro.gov.uk> The Public Record Office's web site containing an online catalogue, information leaflets and other useful information relating to the PRO and how to make best use of its resources

<www.rootsweb.com> A genealogical gateway to web based groups, discussion lists and online resources

<www.rootsweb.com/~caribgw> Caribbean Genealogical Web Project contains country-based resources and links to useful websites. Guyana is under the South American GenWeb Project at <www.rootsweb.com/~sthamgw>, and Belize under the North American GenWeb Project at <www.rootsweb.com/~nrthamgw>

Discussion groups and newsgroups

<www.rootsweb.com/~caribgw/mailinglist.html> Home page of the Caribbean-L mailing list

<soc.genealogy.west-indies> Also hosts the Caribbean-L mailing list and may be available through your Internet Service Provider news server

1.4.1 General guides on using the internet for family history

Christian, *The Genealogist's Internet*
Crowe, *Genealogy Online*
Hawgood, *Internet for Genealogy*
Helm and Helm, *Genealogy Online for Dummies*
Kemp, *Virtual Roots*
McClure and Wilcox, *Guide to Online Genealogy*
Peacock, *Good Web Guide to Genealogy*

1.5 What does the Church of Jesus Christ of Latter-day Saints hold?

The Church of Jesus Christ of Latter-day Saints (LDS), also known as the Mormons, has microfilmed many records which can be used by family historians. These include parish registers, registers of wills, civil registration returns, censuses, military records and publications.

They have indexed many millions of birth, baptismal and marriage events from parish registers and submitted entries by their members, which have been published as the International Genealogical Index (IGI) and various Vital Records Listings. The

IGI is a most important resource, it is arranged geographically and there is a section for the Caribbean. However, at present most entries for the British West Indies relate to Barbados families, but it is continuously added to.

They also have other computerized and online resources. All of these can be seen at their Family History Centres, which if not actually housed at your nearest Centre can be ordered from their main library in Utah. The IGI and many other resources are also available on their website <www.familysearch.com>. You can also check their library holdings for every country by the type of record and the location of every Family History Centre.

1.6 Is there anything I should know about using archives and libraries?

Most archives and libraries will not carry out research for you. You will need either to visit or arrange for someone to visit on your behalf, which may mean employing a local researcher.

Before visiting an archive or arranging for research to be carried out decide what you are looking for and the types of records which may hold that information. Most archival material is not indexed or catalogued beyond the title and asking for information on a specific individual will not usually be fruitful. The records may also be arranged according to who created them rather than by parish, subject or person. For official records they are then usually filed by date.

Contact the archive to find out if they are likely to hold the material you want and if they have any other relevant material. Ask about opening hours, location, facilities and access conditions as well. For example, what kind of identification do you need, do you need to book, is there a fee and does it close at lunchtime? If you use a tape recorder or computer ask whether these are allowed and whether power points are available.

When using primary sources you should use a graphite pencil. You may be asked not to use an eraser in case documents are damaged.

Many popular records, such as registers of baptisms, marriages, burials and wills, have been microfilmed to preserve them and you may find that the Church of Jesus Christ of Latter-day Saints has copies which can be ordered through one of their Family History Centres (see **1.5**).

1.7 How do I make best use of the Public Record Office?

The PRO holds the records of central government departments and the courts of law of the United Kingdom, England and Wales. In general terms the records are arranged first by the department which created, inherited or transferred the records to the PRO and, second, by the series, which often represents the type of document, for example musters, government gazettes or correspondence, or records of an internal department or division. The records are then usually arranged chronologically or sequentially by former departmental file references.

Each document has a unique three-part reference. The first part is the **Department** code, for example CO for the Colonial Office, BT for the Board of Trade, and PC for the Privy Council, according to the department which created it. The second part is the **Series** number, which represents the series within the department code. The third and final part is the **Piece** number, which represents the individual document. For example the description book for those who enlisted in the 5th West India Regiment, 1811–1817, is WO 25/656, and the 1951 electoral register for Barbados is CO 32/124.

To identify the department and series, consult the online catalogue <catalogue. pro.gov.uk> or the printed *Current Guide to the Holdings of the PRO*. There is no overall index to records of the PRO. The catalogue describes each record title, the detail of which varies greatly from a brief description such as 'minutes' to a detailed description of individual letters within a document. The catalogue has a very powerful search engine and you should read the help notes to the catalogue, together with its tips and suggestions, to make best use of it. You cannot usually search for names unless the record of the family or individual makes up a whole file or the description contains more than the document title, for example when the catalogue describes individual letters or papers in a piece.

Very few documents are currently available online. There is a programme to digitize and make available popular genealogical series such as registered copy wills (PROB 11) and censuses of England and Wales for 1841 to 1901. In addition, images from the PRO's online exhibitions and news items are available. Most images can be seen using PRO Online <www.pro-online.pro.gov.uk> and for the censuses at <www.census.pro.gov.uk>.

The PRO has two offices: all documents, with the exception of the censuses for England and Wales 1841–1891 are held at PRO, Kew. The censuses for England and Wales 1841–1901, non-conformist registers, miscellaneous overseas registers of births, marriages and deaths, and registered wills and administrations granted by the Prerogative Court of Canterbury can be seen at the Family Records Centre (FRC). The Office of National Statistics is also located at the FRC and holds the indexes to births, marriages and deaths for England and Wales from 1837.

Public Record Office
Kew, Surrey
TW9 4DU
Tel: 020 8392 5200
Fax: 020 8392 5286
<www.pro.gov.uk>

Opening hours:
Monday	9 a.m. to 5 p.m.
Tuesday	10 a.m. to 7 p.m.
Wednesday	9 a.m. to 5 p.m.
Thursday	9 a.m. to 7 p.m.
Friday	9 a.m. to 5 p.m.
Saturday	9.30 a.m. to 5 p.m.

Note that documents may be ordered till 4 p.m. on Mondays, Wednesdays and Fridays; till 4.30 p.m. on Tuesdays and Thursdays; from 9.30 a.m. to 12 noon and from 1.30 p.m. to 3 p.m. on Saturdays.

The PRO is closed on public holidays, on Saturdays preceding a public holiday and for annual stocktaking (usually for one week in December).

You do not need an appointment but you will need to obtain a reader's ticket. To do so when you first visit the PRO please bring with you formal documentary proof of identity. Citizens of Britain and the Republic of Ireland will need to provide a valid cheque card or driver's licence. If you are not a British citizen you will need to bring your passport or national identity card. If you do not have any of these forms of identity, please contact the PRO for advice before visiting. Without a valid reader's ticket you cannot order documents. You do not need one to visit the Family Records Centre.

Family Records Centre
1 Myddelton St
London EC1R 1UW
Tel: 020 8392 5200
Fax: 020 8393 5286
<www.pro.gov.uk>
<www.familyrecords.gov.uk>

Opening hours:
Monday	9 a.m. to 5 p.m.
Tuesday	10 a.m. to 7 p.m.
Wednesday	9 a.m. to 5 p.m.

Thursday	9 a.m. to 7 p.m.
Friday	9 a.m. to 5 p.m.
Saturday	9.30 a.m. to 5 p.m.

The FRC is closed on public holidays and Easter and Christmas weekends.

The PRO does not undertake research. If you are unable to visit, the PRO maintains a list of independent professional researchers who for a fee may undertake research on your behalf. Please write enclosing a stamped addressed envelope for researchers on a particular topic; the list is also available on the PRO's website at <www.pro.gov.uk/research/irlist/default.htm>. Researchers also advertise their services in family history magazines and directories, and on genealogical websites.

You may use only graphite pencils in the PRO reading rooms. Pens of any kind are not allowed. You may use personal computers, typewriters and tape recorders in most of the reading rooms. The rules are available at <www.pro.gov.uk/about/access/rules.htm>.

1.7.1 Some general genealogical guides to the Public Record Office

Bevan, *Tracing Your Ancestors*
Colwell, *Dictionary of Genealogical Sources*
Colwell, *Family Roots*
Colwell, *Family Records Centre*
Cox, *New to Kew?*

2 Records of the Colonial Office

The most important records for the study of the West Indies and West Indians are those of the Colonial Office and its predecessors. The term 'Colonial Office', as used in the PRO and this guide, refers to the various departments which at different times had oversight of the colonies. These include the various secretaries of state, the Lords of Trade and Plantations, the Board of Trade, various committees of the Privy Council, and the Colonial Office. See Thurston's *Records of the Colonial Office* and the PRO catalogue under departmental code CO for a full description of the history and the records of the Colonial Office.

The records of the Colonial Office relating to individual colonies are arranged according to the type of document: original correspondence, entry books, acts, sessional papers, government gazettes, miscellanea (*Blue Books of Statistics*, naval office returns and newspapers), registers of correspondence, and registers of out-letters. These are the records received or created by the Colonial Office rather than the records of colonial governments; where they survive, these are held in the appropriate country's archives. Chapter 10 lists Colonial Office series for each colony, together with examples of genealogical sources which can be found among Colonial Office records.

Not all records of the Secretary of State relating to the West Indies are in Colonial Office records and some are in State Papers, Domestic series (various SP series, arranged by monarch). References to these documents are found in the *Calendar of State Papers, Domestic* (which end in 1704) and *Calendar of Home Office Papers* (1760–1775). There are typescript calendars in the Map and Large Document Reading Room for part of the intervening period. The document descriptions on the online catalogue often describe individual letters.

Many of the records described below may survive in the relevant country's archives, for example incoming letters from the Colonial Office, other West Indian governments and other British government departments, drafts of outgoing letters, draft and printed copies of the *Blue Books*, sessional papers, acts and government gazettes. Many are also published, for example newspapers, government gazettes, *Blue Books*, sessional papers and departmental reports and acts, and it is possible that copies may be available in national, academic and specialist libraries.

2.1 Original correspondence

These are despatches (letters) and reports received by the Colonial Office from the governor and correspondence with other bodies concerning a particular colony. Until 1951 each colony or administrative unit has separate original correspondence series. Until 1800 the correspondence is arranged by date of despatch. From 1801 until 1926 the volumes are arranged first by the governor's despatches, then by letters from UK government departments, and finally by letters from individuals. From 1926 the correspondence is in subject files.

Published reference books for these records are the *Calendar of State Papers, Colonial, America and West Indies, 1574–1739,* and *Journals of the Board of Trade and Plantations, 1704–1782*. Selected correspondence is described in Ragatz's *Guide to the Official Correspondence of the Governors*. Unpublished reference is through the registers of correspondence which are described in **2.7** and the chronological indexes, 1815–1870, in CO 714.

The papers are mostly of an official and administrative nature. The following types of records are found, and although they do not occur for every colony they give an idea of the usefulness of these records: petitions (also known as memorials), tax lists, censuses (most are statistical but some give the name of the head of household with the numbers of women, children, servants and slaves), colonial civil servants' application forms, land grants, newspapers (which sometimes give announcements of births, marriages and deaths), lists of prisoners, returns of government slaves, lists of manumitted slaves, and records of the local courts such as chancery, petty sessions and vice admiralty sessions.

From 1873 and increasingly from the 1890s the original correspondence series have been extensively weeded, and are described in the registers (**2.7**) as 'destroyed under statute'. Most surviving papers, especially from 1926, tend to be of a purely administrative nature demonstrating the type of work carried out by the Colonial Office or those which set precedent in colonial affairs and in the colonies. There are few papers concerning individuals, such as petitions and applications, unless they raise an important or interesting matter.

Drafts of these letters, usually without the enclosures, may survive in the relevant country's archives.

As the West Indian countries became independent, diplomatic relations with Britain and matters of British nationality and citizenship, were dealt with by the Commonwealth Office (DO series) until 1967, and the Foreign and Commonwealth Office (FCO series) from 1967 (see **9.2.1** and the catalogue for information). The records of the Colonial Office finish in 1967 following its merger with the Foreign Office and governors' correspondence is to be found in FCO series.

2.2 Entry books

These record outgoing correspondence from the Colonial Office to governors and government departments. They also contain instructions, petitions, letters, reports, and commissions, and include details of patents for grants of land. Before 1700 they record letters received as well as letters despatched. Entry books were superseded in 1872 by the registers of out-letters (**2.8**). Enclosures are rarely entered in full. The original out-letters, together with enclosures, may survive in the relevant country's archives.

2.3 Acts

These are copies of local acts and ordinances. For family historians they can include private acts of naturalization in the colony, sales of land to recover debt, grants of manumission, appointments of office holders, and names of people transported or deported from the colony. Acts are listed in CO 5/273–282 (1638–1781) and CO 383 (1781–1892).

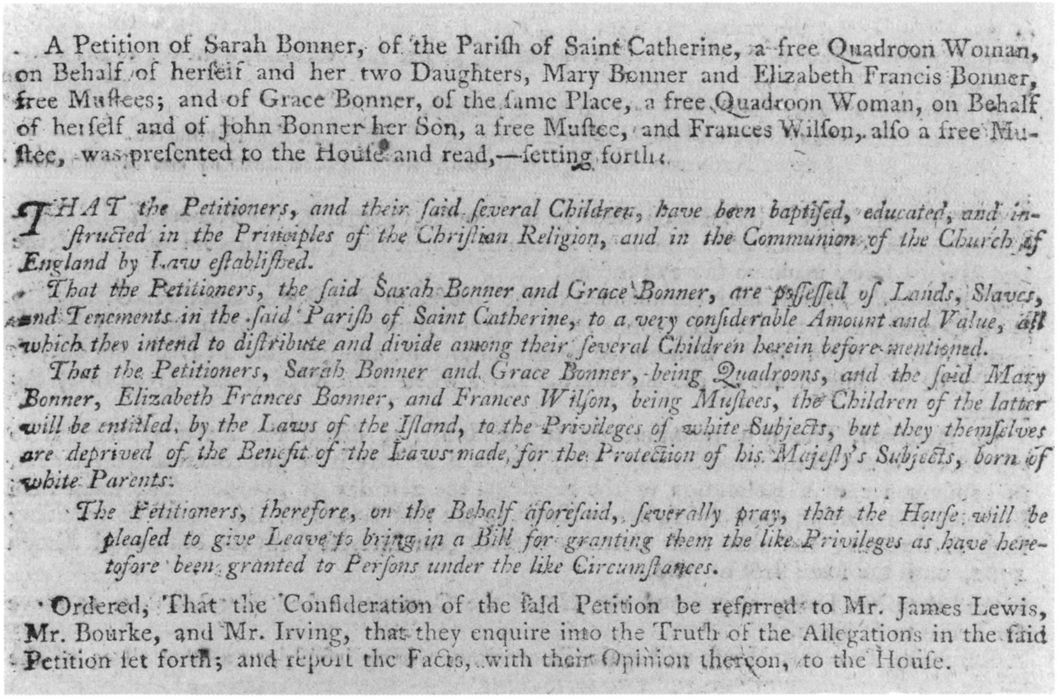

A Petition of Sarah Bonner, of the Parish of Saint Catherine, a free Quadroon Woman, on Behalf of herself and her two Daughters, Mary Bonner and Elizabeth Francis Bonner, free Mustees; and of Grace Bonner, of the same Place, a free Quadroon Woman, on Behalf of herself and of John Bonner her Son, a free Mustee, and Frances Wilson, also a free Mustee, was presented to the House and read,—setting forth:

THAT the Petitioners, and their said several Children, have been baptised, educated, and instructed in the Principles of the Christian Religion, and in the Communion of the Church of England by Law established.

That the Petitioners, the said Sarah Bonner and Grace Bonner, are possessed of Lands, Slaves, and Tenements in the said Parish of Saint Catherine, to a very considerable Amount and Value, all which they intend to distribute and divide among their several Children herein before mentioned.

That the Petitioners, Sarah Bonner and Grace Bonner, being Quadroons, and the said Mary Bonner, Elizabeth Frances Bonner, and Frances Wilson, being Mustees, the Children of the latter will be entitled, by the Laws of the Island, to the Privileges of white Subjects, but they themselves are deprived of the Benefit of the Laws made for the Protection of his Majesty's Subjects, born of white Parents.

The Petitioners, therefore, on the Behalf aforesaid, severally pray, that the House will be pleased to give Leave to bring in a Bill for granting them the like Privileges as have heretofore been granted to Persons under the like Circumstances.

Ordered, That the Consideration of the said Petition be referred to Mr. James Lewis, Mr. Bourke, and Mr. Irving, that they enquire into the Truth of the Allegations in the said Petition set forth; and report the Facts, with their Opinion thereon, to the House.

Figure 3 Jamaica: Petition of Sarah Bonner, free quadroon, for rights and privileges, November 1783 (CO 140/66, p. 57).

2.4 Sessional papers

These are the proceedings of the executive and legislative councils which formed the government of each colony. They touch upon all matters raised by the local government, such as petitions to the assembly, grants of manumission of slaves and appointments. They also contain annual reports of the departments of colonial governments, but the PRO does not hold complete collections.

2.5 Government gazettes

These are official newspapers produced by most colonies. Early gazettes were, along with newspapers, the only way local populations could keep up with the events in Britain and Europe, such as wars, royal affairs and proceedings of Parliament.

For family and local historians the gazettes can provide a wealth of information. Examples include: birth, marriage and death notices, including occasional obituaries of notable people; notices of proceedings and sales of property in the courts of chancery and petty sessions; lists of people applying for liquor, dog and gun licences; lists of jurors, druggists (chemists or pharmacists), constables, voters, solicitors, nurses, medical practitioners and militia; notices of sales of land; public appointments, leave of absence and resumption of duty; notices relating to cases of intestacy, guardianship and wills; notices on applications for naturalization; inquests into shipwrecks; ships entering and clearing port, sometimes with the names of first class passengers; lists of people paid parish relief; and tax lists.

2.6 Miscellanea

Miscellanea series contain primarily *Blue Books of Statistics*. For some colonies they also contain naval officers' returns and newspapers.

2.6.1 Blue Books of Statistics

These annual volumes begin about 1820 and continue until the mid-1940s. They contain statistical information about each colony, such as population, education, religion and economy. They also include names of public employees arranged by department, with their salary, date of appointment and the names of government pensioners.

(226)

TABLE E.

Patients who have left the Infirmary cured or relieved during 1865.

Name.	age	Native Country.	Residence.	Occupation.	Date of admission.	Left cured.	Left Relieved.	Diseases and Remarks.
					1864.	1865.		Extensive ulceration of the
Solitude Celestin	50	Dominica	Barouie	Labourer	Aprl. 20	June 24		leg amputation below the knee.
Gustave Bonaparte	20	do	W. House	do	May 27	Feb. 12		Severe ulcerat'n of the leg
Charles	21	do	do	do	June 24	Mar. 2		Ulceration of the foot
John Pierre	35	do	Mel. Hall	do	July 29	Apr. 24		Stricture
Joseph George	22	do	Roseau	do	Augst 30		Mar. 15	Epeliptic Fits
Whitfield	19	do	Canef Est	do	Sept. 13	Mar. 6		Ulcer of the leg [with f'ver
Laurent	24	do	Roseau	Groom	Oct 26	Sept. 2		Inflammation of the eyes
Thomas Valle	40	do	do	Boatman	Novr. 11	Jan. 26		rheum affect'n of the back
Pierre African	50	Africa	Cur. Rest	Labourer	Novr. 26	" 7		Abscess of the hand
John Baptiste	40	Dominica	St Joseph	do	Decr. 3	" 6		Ulcer of the foot
Prince Lewis	16	do	M. Wallis	do	Decr. 2		Feby. 8	Frac. of leg, admittnd for relief the fracture having been neglected
George Train	51	England		Sailor	Decr. 16	" 4		Intermittent Fever
Avriette	20	Dominica	Roseau	Labourer	" 18	" 16		Fever &c.
Elizabeth St. Rose	24	do	Roseau	do	" 30	June 24		Ulcer of the toe
Caroline Baptiste	50	do	Geneva Estate	do	1865. Jany. 7		Jany 24	Rolapsus Uteri
George William	21	do	Barouie	do	" 12	Feb. 15		Dropsy [head
Henry	31	Madras	Bal Town	do	" 15	" 6		Fever, with severe pain of
Maria	6	Mart'que			" 15	" 6		Cough
Angelle	3				" 15	" 6		Worms
Louisa Sam	37	Dominica	Roseau	W'woman	" 18	April 2		Inflammation of the eyes
Andria	24	do	do	Labourer	" 25	Mar. 26		Abscess of the breast
Jule	14	do	Gomier	do	" 30	April 2		Dropsy
Alfred Bellot	21	do	Newtown	Carpenter	Feby. 7	Mar. 19		Inflammation of the eyes
Louisa Louis	46	do	Couliabre	Labourer	" 9	May 29		Ulcer of the foot
William George	60	do	River Est	do	" 11	Mar. 2		Pain in the chest
Rose J. Philip	17	do	Roseau	do	" 12	May 11		Ulceration &c
Sophia	12	do	Campbell	do	" 18	" 14		Ulcer of the foot
Amelia Paul	13	do	Pt Michel	do	" 22	Mar. 6		Head & face severely injured by accident Sugar Mill
Jane Johnson	25	do	Roseau	H. Servant	" 23	Sep. 18		Ulceration of the foot
Henry Cooper	25	England		Sailor	" 23	Feb. 24		Sprained Arm
Pierre Billy	25	Dominica	Bell Vue	Labourer	" 27	Mar. 6		Fractured wound of the back by a bayonet
Elie Aladdin	48	Mart'que	Layou	do	" 27	" 14		Ulcer of the foot
Leger Bernard Degazon	50	do	Roseau		" 27	April 3		Tumour of the neck—operation performed
Jean	50	Dominica	do	Labourer	March 5	" 27		Apoplexy
Louison George	50	do	Belvidere	do	" 8	July 15		Ulcer of the Scrotum
Josephine	24	do	Gomier	do	" 22	May 18		Rheumatic pains, swelling of the leg
Jeremie	14	do	Roseau V.	do	" 28	" 6		Gor'd in the thigh by an ox
Sammie	30	Madras	Roseau	do	" 29	pril 6		Pains in the back & side from a fall
Tasie Moise	16	Dominica	do	do	April 2		Apr 21	Dropical swelling—removed from the Infirmary to her friends
Mary Jno Lewis	50	do	do	do	" 2	April 18		Dysentery
Andrea African	50	Africa	M prosper	do	" 4	June 19		Affection of the eyes
William	12	Dominica	River Est	do	" 6	Oct. 23		Ulceration of the toe
Pascal	64	do	Roseau	Baker	" 19		May 4	General Debility
Stephen	12	do	Antrim V	Labourer	" 19	ay 21		Fingers crushed in a sugar mill
Nicholas Pascal	22	do	Grandbay	do	" 22	" 6		Ulcer of toe
Daniel	20	do	do	do	" 23	" 18		Ulcer of leg
Ellen	49	do	Roseau	do	" 25	Sep. 23		Rheumatism
Henry	13	do	Souffriere	do	" 26	Aug. 23		idiopathic Tetanus
Mary Ann	30	do	Roseau	do	" 27		June 27	Affection of the womb
Sophia	60	Africa	Mahaut	do	May 3		May 21	Prolapsus uteri
John Pierre	24	Dominica	P Ruperts	do	" 4	June 15		Ulcer of the toe
Barnes	14	do	Ma'uchrie	do	" 13	July 1		Severe sprain of knee joint
Nelson	20	do	Chk. Hall	do	" 15		May 20	Finger broken
Jean	25	Gu'loupe	Roseau	do	" 16	June 10		Rheumatic pains

Figure 4   Dominica: *Government Gazette*, 1865, list of patients in the infirmary (CO 75/1, p. 226).

OFFICIAL GAZETTE, MONDAY, FEBRUARY 16, 1920.   35

List of TRADE LICENCES issued by the Treasurer from 1st August 1919 to 31st January 1920.

To whom granted.	Description of Licence.	Locality.	Date of Expiry.
Adrien Lelia	Huckster	Pte. Michel	
Alfred Anastasie	,,	Portsmouth	
Ambrose Evanah		,,	
Do.	6th Class Trade	,,	30 June 1920.
Andrew Garfield	,,	,,	
Anthony Frarcillia	Huckster	Old Street	
Augustin James	6th Class Trade	La Roche	
Baron A. A.	,,	Belle Hall	
Bank, The Colonial	Banker's	Long Lane	31 Decr. 1920.
Bank of Canada, The	,,	Old Street	Do.
Bellony Mary [Royal	Huckster	Portsmouth	
Benjamin Erene		Capuchin	
Bertrand John A.	6th Class Trade	St. Joseph	
Bertrand Elmira	,,	Hillsbro' St.	
Blanchard G. W.	,,	Market St.	
Bruno Knight	Huckster	Salisbury	
Birmingham Brenda	,,	Tete Morne	
Birmingham Anestine	,,	Picodeau	
Carbon Edwill	,,	Boetica	
Casey Ethel	,,	Portsmouth	
Charles Virginia	,,	Upper Lane	
Coipel Angelina	6th Class Trade	Brantridge	
Dickson, D. D.	5th Class Trade	Londonderry	
Destouche Roderick	,,	Pte. Michel	
Doram Elizabeth	Huckster	Marigot	
Ducreay Elmira	,,	Granby Street	
Dumas E. F.	,,	Church St.	
Dupigny Margaret	6th Class Trade	New Street	
Duverney Felicia	,,	New Town	
Edwards Marion	Huckster	Market St.	
Emanuel Moses J.	6th Class Trade	Portsmouth	
Emanuel Rosaline	,,	Balahou Town	
Eusebe Peter A.	Huckster	La Roche	
Fontaine Joseph B.	,,	Bagatelle	
Firmin John	,,	Soufriere	
Florent Clementine	,,	Granby St.	
Fraser Virginia	6th Class Trade	Layou	
Germain Virginia	,,	Granby Street	
Griffith Alcina	Huckster	River Street	
Hall James	,,	New Town	
Joseph Luvenia	,,	Upper Lane	
Jacob Fanny	,,	Grand Bay	
James Elizabeth	6th Class Trade	New Street	
James Elize	,,	Marigot	
Johnson Antoine	,,	New Town	
Johnson Valentine	Huckster	,,	
John Baptist Etheline	,,	Lake Road	30 June 1920.
Joseph Paul	6th Class Trade	Mahaut	
Lecointe Ernestine	,,	Pte. Michel	
Leonard William	,,	High Street	
Magloire Beatrice	,,	Fond Canie	
Michel Mrs. Aaron	Huckster	Market St.	
Morancie Matilda	,,	New Street	
Myler Jessie	,,	Ship Street	
Mondesire Angustine	6th Class Trade	St. Sauveur	
Noel Nixon	,,	Morne Jaune	
O'Brien Mary	Huckster	Old Street	
Phillip, C. G.	,,	,,	
Pierre Ismenie	6th Class Trade	Colihaut	
Roberts Ann R.	,,	Granby Street	
Rossi Laura	Huckster	King's Lane	
Royer Mary	,,	Clifton	
Ryan Matilda	,,	Gt. Marlbro' St.	
Samuel George	,,	New Town	
Scotland Elfreda	,,	Castle Bruce	
Serrant Mary	,,	New Town	
Shillingford, E. P. &	6th Class Trade	Loubiere	
Shillingford Bros. [Co	,,	Balahou Town	
Shillingford St. Geo.,	,,	Salisbury	
Stedman Felicienne	Huckster	Carse O'Gowrie	

Figure 5   Dominica: *Government Gazette*, 1920, list of trade licences issued (CO 75/14, p. 35).

2.6.2 Naval office returns

Customs returns taken at colonial ports. They record the names of incoming and outgoing vessels, the master, the owner, port of registry, tonnage, number of crew, type of goods, and the previous and next port.

2.6.3 Newspapers

An incomplete series of newspapers received by the Colonial Office during the 1830s to 1850s. They are similar in format and content to government gazettes (**2.5**).

The British Library Newspaper Library (see **Useful addresses**) contains collections of colonial newspapers. The newspaper catalogue can be searched online at <prodigi.bl.uk/nlcat/>.

2.7 Registers of correspondence

Registers of correspondence are bound volumes which record correspondence received by the Colonial Office and its predecessors. Between 1703 and 1759 manuscript calendars of the correspondence of the Board of Trade are found in the General Registers (CO 326/1–51). From 1759 to 1782 a single, annual, calendar was produced (CO 326/52–74). Between 1822 and 1849 all incoming correspondence was entered in a series of registers arranged by groups of colonies (CO 326/85–358).

In 1849 the Colonial Office introduced a system of registration whereby every incoming letter was allocated a number in the Daily Register (CO 382), which started with '1' each year. Details of the letter were then entered in a register for the colony. There is a series of these registers of correspondence, which run until 1951, for each colony.

Until 1926 the following details were noted in columns: date of registration, registered number (taken from the daily register), name of the correspondent, date of letter, letter number, subject of letter and a brief précis, related correspondence, action taken and remarks. The cross-references contained in the registers are abbreviated and usually refer to other correspondence recorded in the same register. For example, 'Gov' refers to governors' despatches, 'MO' to Miscellaneous Offices, and 'C' to individuals beginning with 'C'. A table of abbreviations is given in Thurston pp. 399–400.

Other information may be stamped into the register, such as 'destroyed under statute', if the letter has been destroyed; 'printed for Parliament', with the date (these are in the

O 1   PENSIONS.   PENSIONS.   O 2

Name	Amount of the Pension in Sterling (£ s. d.)	Authority under which the Pension is granted.	Service for which Pension is granted.	Date from which the Pension has been paid.	Amount of Emolument when last employed in the Public Service. (£ s. d.)	Age of Pensioner on 31st Dec., 1890.	Cause of Retirement. (a)
Alexander Ferguson							
PENSIONS.	70 0 0	Ordinance 11, 1888	Minister of St. Luke's Parish	Mar. 1, 1868	500 0 0	60	Ill-health.
SUPERANNUATION ALLOWANCES. (a.)							
J. McSwiney	96 0 0	Ditto	Sheriff of Berbice & Stipendiary Magistrate	April 1, 1868	(b) 750 0 0	83	16 years of service.
George Fox	210 0 0	Ditto and No. 4 of 1861	Principal of Queen's College	May 16, 1872	500 0 0	77	21 do.
D. Shier	480 0 0	Ordinance 22, 1860	Medical Inspector of Estates' Hospitals.	Aug. 25, 1873	1,000 0 0	75	24 do.
N. J. Darrell	105 0 0	Ordinance 12, 1875	Commissary of Taxation...	Oct. 1, 1875	375 0 0	76	14 do.
N. T. Veasey	180 0 0	Ditto	Harbour Master, Georgetown	Sep. 29, 1875	500 0 0	75	13 do.
James Elliott	45 0 0	Ditto	Keeper, New-Amsterdam Prison	April 11, 1876	187 10 0	72	Ill-health.
J. Goring	38 6 8	Ditto	Post Office Letter Carrier	April 7, 1877	83 6 8	62	Do.
Mary Munro	17 10 0	Ditto	Matron of Georgetown Prison	Jan. 1, 1878	62 10 0	79	14 years of service.
N. L. Bradwaite	204 3 4	Ditto	Aid-Waiter, Customs	Jan. 11, 1879	291 13 0	81	35 do.
E. B. Bhose	170 0 0	Ditto	Consulting Interpreter and Curate of St. Patrick's.	April 1, 1879	500 0 0	62	Abolition of office of Consul. Interpr.
J. G. Austin (b)	253 17 8	Ditto	Immigration Agent General	Nov. 4, 1879	(c) 1,500 0 0	78	11 years of service.
J. S. Hackett	660 0 0	Ditto	Surgeon to Berbice Hospital, and District Medical Officer.	May 1, 1879	1,000 0 0	66	33 do.
Horace E. Wickham	310 0 0	Ditto	Rector of St. Peter's Parish	May 26, 1880	500 0 0	67	31 do.
H. W. Austin	800 0 0	Ditto	Comptroller of Customs ...	July 1, 1881	1,000 0 0	71	15 do.
A. Hitchins	72 0 0	Ditto	Curate of St. Paul's Parish	Jan. 26, 1881	300 0 0	75	12 do.
Samuel Johnstone	150 0 0	Ditto	Clerk, Immigration Department	April 1, 1883	250 0 0	64	30 do.
F. A. Van Holst	88 0 0	Ditto	Aidwaiter, Customs, Berbice	July 1, 1883	200 0 0	73	22 do.
A. T. Hubbard	204 3 4	Ditto	Weigher and Gauger, Colonial Bonded Warehouses.	July 1, 1884	291 13 4	81	34 do.
J. J. Large	84 0 0	Ditto	Curate of St. Luke's	Jan. 1, 1884	300 0 0	54	Ill-health.
H. P. Plummer	560 0 0	Ditto	Stipendiary Magistrate	Feb. 1, 1884	800 0 0	65	35 years of service.
F. J. Wyatt	576 0 0	Ditto	Rector of St. George's	Jan. 1, 1884	900 0 0	63	32 do.
J. C. Lang	105 0 0	Ditto	Commissary of Taxation...	Nov. 2, 1884	375 0 0	52	Ill-health.
Samuel Manning	198 0 0	Ditto	Curate, Trinity Parish	Jan. 1, 1886	300 0 0	68	38 years of service.
T. R. Milner	250 0 0	Ditto	Rector, St. Michael's	Mar. 16, 1885	500 0 0	61	25 do.
D. M. Gallagher	884 0 0	Ditto	Assistant Receiver General, Berbice	Aug. 1, 1886	600 0 0	57	29 do.

REMARKS.

(a) Superannuation Allowance is calculated at the rate of one-sixtieth of the average Salary for the three years preceding the date of retirement, in the case of Officers joining the Service after the passing of Ordinance 12 of 1875, and at a like rate on the Salary at the date of retirement in the case of those Officers who were in the Service before the passing of that Ordinance, and is available to every public servant drawing a salary of £30 and upwards after ten years of service and 55 years of age.

(b) At the date of Mr. J. G. Austin's retirement, he held the office of Colonial Secretary of Hong Kong.

REMARKS.

(a) Under this head—whose years of service are given as the cause of retirement—the Officer at the date of his retirement had attained the age of 55.

(b) £450 of this from Imperial Funds.

(c) Superannuation allowed on average between salaries of £1,000 and £1,500 for the last three years of service.

Figure 6   Guyana: *Blue Book of Statistics*, 1890, list of government pensioners (CO 116/259, pp. O1–2).

House of Commons Sessional Papers); 'printed for the Colonial Office', with a colony and number noted (to be found in Colonial Office Confidential Print series); and 'secret' (these papers are often filed in CO 537). The letter was then given a minute sheet on which were written similar details as in the register; this was used by Colonial Office officials to make comments. Draft replies may be attached to the letter. If a letter from another government department has been destroyed it may be possible to find a copy in the records of that department.

Until 1926 the registers are arranged first by the governor's despatches, then by letters from British government departments, and then by letters from individuals. Increasingly from 1868 the 'individuals' section may be used as an index to individuals and subjects mentioned in the correspondence. At the end of each register there is often a list of printed material received from the colony, such as acts, *Blue Books*, and sessional papers.

It is important to note that the registers are arranged by the date the Colonial Office received the letter, but the original correspondence is filed by the date of the letter.

In 1926 a series of annual subject files was introduced and each colony was allocated a block of file numbers. The registers continue in the same series as before but they are arranged in file number order. There is usually a key to the files in the front of each volume. The registers give a brief description of each letter filed under the subject, the date and name of sender, and the action taken. If the letter was destroyed or printed this will also be recorded.

2.8 Registers of out-letters

There is a series of registers of out-letters for each colony. They continue from the entry books (**2.2**), starting in 1872 and finishing in 1926. These are compiled in the date order of the outgoing correspondence from the Colonial Office. The registers are arranged first by governor, then government department, and finally by the individual with whom the Colonial Office was corresponding. They record the name of recipient, date of despatch, number of despatch, a brief description, and the registered number of the letter to which it was the reply. Unlike the entry books, these give only a précis of each outgoing letter. If a draft copy survives it will be in the appropriate original correspondence series.

Further reading

PRO information leaflets
Acts of the Privy Council, Colonial Series

Andrews, *Guide to Materials for American History*
Bell and Parker, *Guide to British West Indian Archive Materials*
Calendar of State Papers, Colonial, America and West Indies
Journals of the Board of Trade and Plantations
Pugh, *Records of the Colonial and Dominions Offices*
Ragatz, *Guide to the Official Correspondence*
Redington and Roberts (eds.), *Calendar of Home Office Papers*
Thurston, *Records of the Colonial Office*
Walne (ed.), *Guide to Manuscript Sources*

3 Migration to the West Indies

3.1 Emigration: general records

3.1.1 Passenger lists

Very few passenger lists survive in the PRO before 1890. The British government did not register people emigrating from these shores or arriving in the West Indies, and until the First World War it was not necessary for emigrants to have passports.

Licences to pass beyond the seas (E 157) include registers of passengers going to America and the West Indies between 1634 and 1639, and in 1677. Port Books 1565–1798 (E 190) are customs accounts and often include names of passengers. The Privy Council registers (PC 2) contain many petitions and letters of people emigrating to, or already settled in, the colonies. These and other Privy Council papers relating to the colonies 1613–1783 are described in Acts of the Privy Council, Colonial Series.

Between 1773 and 1776 a register (T 47/9–12) was made of emigrants going from England, Wales and Scotland to the Americas. Information provided includes: name, age, occupation, reason for leaving the country, last place of residence, date of departure and destination. A card index is available in the Research Enquiries Room at Kew. T 47/9–11 is listed in Michael Tepper's, *Passengers to America*. Many early passenger lists are also found in Colonial Office original correspondence series (**2.1**). Passenger lists in the PRO before 1890 do not contain much information relating to the emigrant apart from their name, where they sailed from and the intended destination of the ship. Many of these sources have been published and are included in the bibliography. Colonial newspapers and government gazettes occasionally give the names of first class passengers in the shipping intelligence sections.

Between 1890 and 1960, the Board of Trade kept passenger lists of people leaving from British ports to places outside Europe and the Mediterranean. These passenger lists (BT 27) are arranged by date, by port of departure and by ship. Information given in the passenger lists includes the name, age and occupation of each passenger, and, from the 1920s, often the place of residence in Britain. There are no passenger lists after 1960. There are no indexes of passengers, but for the period 1906 to 1951, if you know the name of the ship and an approximate date of sailing, you can identify the port and month from the registers in BT 32. Unfortunately for some periods not all ports are included. It is possible that inwards passenger lists may survive in the relevant country's archives. The PRO does not hold any passenger lists of people who travelled by aeroplane.

3.1.2 Passports

Until the First World War it was not necessary to have a passport in order to emigrate. Early passports were issued to merchants, and to government and court officials to ensure safe conduct in foreign countries. SP 44/411 is an entry book of passes issued between 1697 and 1784. Later registers (FO 610) run from 1795 to 1948: they are arranged chronologically by date of issue and give the passport number, name of the applicant and destination. There are indexes (FO 611) for the period 1851–1861 and 1874–1916 which give the name, passport number and date of issue.

The colonial secretary also issued passports to people wishing to go to the colonies. Correspondence relating to passes issued between 1796 and 1818 is in CO 323/97–116; later correspondence is in the relevant country series. Most of the earlier passes seem to have been issued to Dutch planters and business men wishing to return to the recently captured colonies of Surinam and Demerara; Demerara was later ceded to Britain as a state of British Guiana.

Under the Colonial Regulations of 1868 governors were authorized to issue passports for foreign travel to people naturalized in the colonies. Interestingly, it was not until 23 September 1891 that governors were told they could issue passports to British born subjects, although many colonies had already been doing this. These registers if they survive are in the relevant country.

3.1.3 Naturalization

Until 1962 subjects in British colonies were also British citizens and did not need to naturalize. Citizenship conferred specific rights, subject to certain restrictions, which varied over time. These rights included the right to vote, inherit or bequeath property, serve in a public office, protection by the British crown and government in foreign countries, and on occasion exemption from some taxes.

Foreign subjects in the British colonies did not need to naturalize to reside or work there but, if they wanted rights such as the vote, they did. Until 1914 naturalization could be granted by local act or by the legislature, details of such grants may be found in the relevant country's acts or sessional paper series. Correspondence and memorials relating to naturalizations may be found in original correspondence and sessional papers series. Notices of naturalizations are often published in government

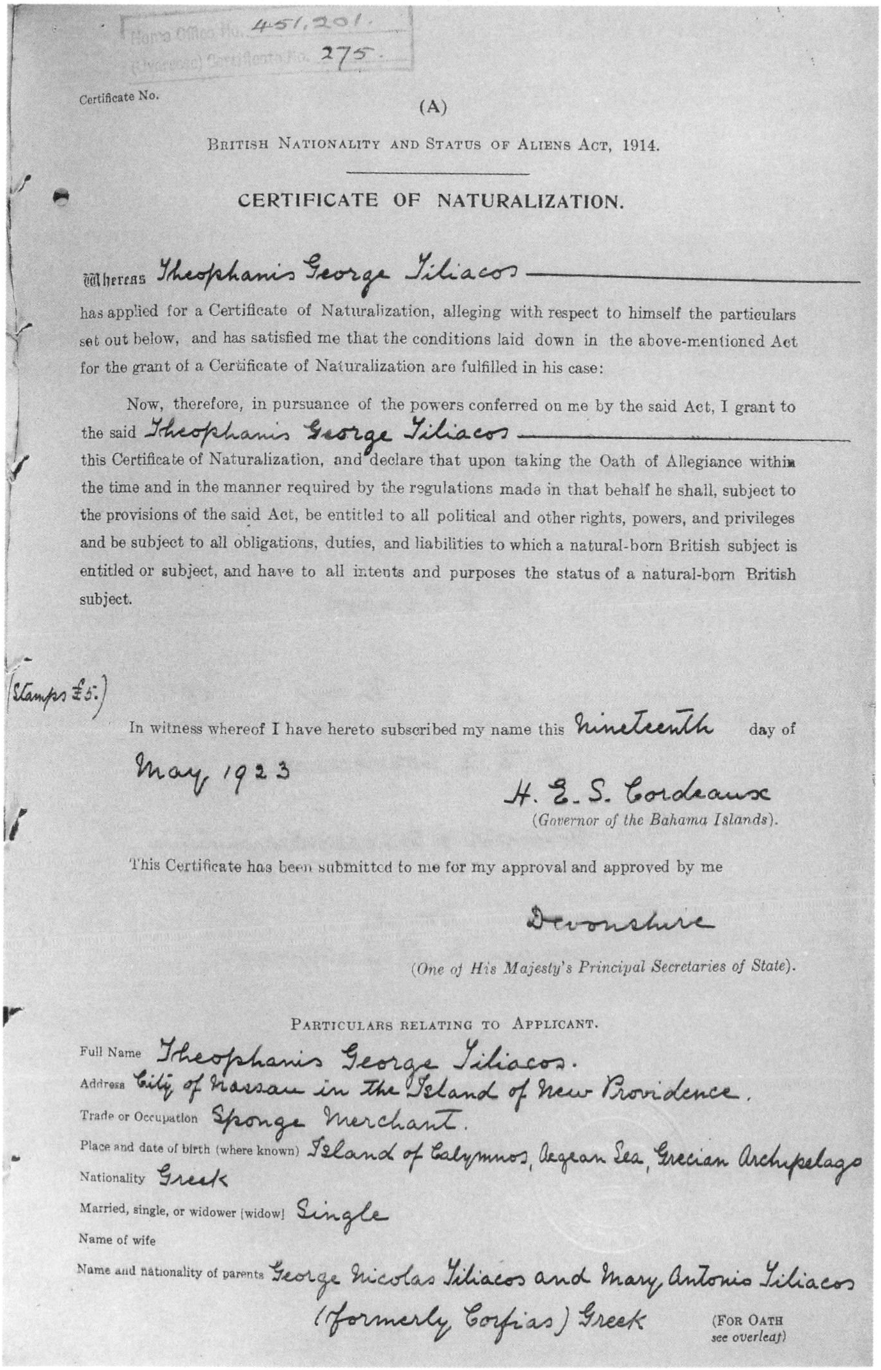

Home Office No. 451,201.
(Overseas) Certificate No. 275.

Certificate No.

(A)

British Nationality and Status of Aliens Act, 1914.

CERTIFICATE OF NATURALIZATION.

Whereas Theophanis George Tiliacos

has applied for a Certificate of Naturalization, alleging with respect to himself the particulars set out below, and has satisfied me that the conditions laid down in the above-mentioned Act for the grant of a Certificate of Naturalization are fulfilled in his case:

Now, therefore, in pursuance of the powers conferred on me by the said Act, I grant to the said Theophanis George Tiliacos this Certificate of Naturalization, and declare that upon taking the Oath of Allegiance within the time and in the manner required by the regulations made in that behalf he shall, subject to the provisions of the said Act, be entitled to all political and other rights, powers, and privileges and be subject to all obligations, duties, and liabilities to which a natural-born British subject is entitled or subject, and have to all intents and purposes the status of a natural-born British subject.

(Stamps £5.)

In witness whereof I have hereto subscribed my name this nineteenth day of May, 1923

H. E. S. Cordeaux
(*Governor of the Bahama Islands*).

This Certificate has been submitted to me for my approval and approved by me

Devonshire
(*One of His Majesty's Principal Secretaries of State*).

Particulars relating to Applicant.

Full Name Theophanis George Tiliacos.
Address City of Nassau in the Island of New Providence.
Trade or Occupation Sponge Merchant.
Place and date of birth (where known) Island of Calymnos, Aegean Sea, Grecian Archipelago
Nationality Greek
Married, single, or widower (widow) Single
Name of wife
Name and nationality of parents George Nicolas Tiliacos and Mary Antonio Tiliacos (formerly Corfias) Greek

(For Oath *see overleaf*)

Figure 7 Bahamas: certificate of naturalization for Theophanis George Tiliacos, Greek, certificate number O275, 19 May 1923 (HO 334/249). Correspondence and testimonials relating to the naturalization is in CO 23/293, fos 106–22.

gazettes. Enrolled grants of naturalizations may be found in deeds or patent registers in the country's archive or register office.

Under the British Nationality and Status of Aliens Act 1914, naturalizations in the colonies needed to be first approved by the colonial secretary and then by the home secretary. A Colonial Office circular of 28 April 1915 (CO 854/51) describes the regulations for the granting of naturalizations by the non-self-governing colonies. The governor was to first send the completed, but unsigned, certificate of naturalization to the colonial secretary, together with testimonials. If the application was approved it was signed by the home secretary and returned to the governor, who then signed and dated it and ensured that the applicant took the oath of allegiance. A copy of the certificate, with the oath endorsed, was then sent to the colonial secretary who forwarded it to the home secretary for registration.

These naturalizations are indexed in the annual British *Parliamentary Papers*, 1844–1961, which provide the certificate number and, until 1936, a Home Office paper number. Home Office indexes to 1980 are available at the PRO, and some have been annotated to show change of name, revoked naturalizations and changes to nationality. These colonial naturalizations are indexed at the end of the indexes in the overseas section and have an 'O' prefix. The certificates to 1987 are in HO 334, arranged by certificate number. The certificates contain the following information: full name, address, trade or occupation, place and date of birth, nationality, marital status, name of spouse and children if applicable, and the names and nationality of parents. Naturalization certificates after 1987 and indexes after 1980 are held by the Home Office, Immigration and Nationality Directorate (see **Useful addresses**).

The Home Office papers for colonial naturalizations have not survived but correspondence and memorials, especially in cases of doubt, are often found in the relevant original correspondence series. Copies of the correspondence and duplicate certificates may also survive among the records of the governor's secretary's office, immigration office or register office in the relevant country.

It is important to note that these certificates relate to the naturalization of foreign subjects and are not registrations of citizenship ('R' certificates) introduced in 1948 for Commonwealth British subjects who applied for British citizenship. These 'R' certificates applied initially to people from the self-governing countries of the Commonwealth, such as India, Pakistan and Australia but were extended to all colonial subjects in 1962 (see **Chapter 9** for further information on these certificates).

3.1.4 *Further reading*

PRO information leaflets
Acts of the Privy Council, Colonial Series
Bevan, *Tracing Your Ancestors*, Chapters 12, 13 and 14
Coldham, *Complete Book of Emigrants*
Coldham, *Emigrants from England*
Dobson, *Directory of Scots Banished*
Dobson, *Directory of Scottish Settlers*
Dobson, *Original Scots Colonists*
Filby and Meyer (eds), *Passenger and Immigration Lists Index*. A bibliographic guide to 500,000
    names taken from published passenger lists to America in the seventeenth to nineteenth
    centuries. From 1982 there are annual supplements of some 150,000 names each.
Games, *Migration*
Hotten, *Original Lists*
Kershaw and Pearsall, *Immigrants and Aliens* (especially Chapter 5 on naturalization)
Tepper, *Passengers to America*

3.2 Indentured servants

Once the West Indies were settled there was a high demand for cheap labour. This was
met initially by indentured servants from Britain, and then later by African slave
labour. Indentured servants were shipped to the colonies by agents who arranged a
transport fee through colonial merchants. They were transported free but had to serve
a period of seven to ten years. After their period of servitude they were supposed to
be allotted ten acres of land, but in the more densely populated islands, such as
Barbados, this did not always occur. The PRO does not hold lists of indentured
servants, and where they survive they are to be found in county record offices,
especially for London, Liverpool and Bristol where the agents resided.

Indentured servitude was later restored following the abolition of slavery in 1834,
with new groups of apprenticed migrants, mainly from India (see **3.6**).

3.2.1 *Further reading*

Clark and Souden, *Migration and Society*
Coldham, *Bristol Registers*
Galenson, *White Servitude*
Kaminkow and Kaminkow, *List of Emigrants*
Virtual Jamestown <jefferson.village.virginia.edu/vcdh/jamestown/bristol.search.html> a
    database of indentured servants transported from Bristol to the American colonies in the
    seventeenth century.

3.3 Transportation

From 1615 until the loss of the mainland American colonies in 1783 many thousands of people were sentenced to transportation, or had death sentences commuted to transportation, and were shipped to the American colonies. Many of these, especially in the early to mid seventeenth century, were transported to the West Indies, but most records do not state the final destination. Transportation was for ten years as most of the colonies forbade longer sentences. Merchants arranged for shipment of transportees and, if on arrival in the colonies they were not already allocated an estate to work on, they were put up for auction.

State Papers, Domestic (SP series) contain correspondence and petitions concerning transportation and lists of reprieved people. Up to 1704 these are calendared in the *Calendar of State Papers, Domestic*. Lists of people to be transported occur in the Patent Rolls (C 66), the Treasury Papers (T 1, 1747–1772) and the Treasury Money Books (T 53, 1716–1744). Until 1745 the Treasury papers are described in the *Calendar of Treasury Books and Papers*.

Trials and verdicts of cases tried by the assize circuits are among various ASSI series. Governors' despatches and colonial entry books also describe cases and policy concerning transportation. Other records, such as quarter sessions papers, transportation bonds and landing certificates, may be found in UK county record offices. *Tracing Your Ancestors* and Baker's *Introduction to Legal History* explain the history of the different courts (**3.3.1**).

From 1783 other destinations were sought and Australia became Britain's next penal settlement. However, between 1824 and 1853 convicts were sent to Bermuda to build the naval base on Ireland Island; the convicts were able to return once their sentence had been served. Lists of convicts on the Bermuda hulks are in HO 8 and records of baptisms, 1826–1946, and burials, 1826–1848, for the naval base, Ireland Island, are in ADM 6/434–436.

3.3.1 Further reading

PRO information leaflets
Baker, *Introduction to Legal History*
Bevan, *Tracing Your Ancestors*, Chapter 40
Calendar of State Papers, Colonial, America and West Indies
Calendar of State Papers, Domestic
Calendar of Treasury Books
Calendar of Treasury Books and Papers
Calendar of Treasury Papers

Coldham, *Bonded Passengers to America*
Coldham, *Complete Book of Emigrants*
Coldham, *Emigrants in Chains*
Hawkings, *Criminal Ancestors*
Oldham, *Britain's Convicts*

3.4 Slave trade

Slavery became established in the British colonies from the 1640s when Dutch merchants from Brazil introduced sugar cane. Sugar farming created a monoculture which was physically demanding and required large numbers of labourers. Africans, used to tropical climates, diseases and food, were considered more suitable than white indentured labourers. It has been estimated that some 1.6 million slaves were transported to the British West Indies between 1640 and 1808, when slave trade to British colonies was abolished.

The slave trade was essentially a triangular trade in which merchants traded British goods for slaves from trading settlements and forts on the West Coast of Africa. These slaves were then traded for goods, such as sugar, rum and molasses in the West Indies. Before 1698 the Company of Royal Adventurers of England, trading with Africa and its successors, monopolized the British slave trade. The various African companies administered British possessions on the West coast of Africa until 1833 when the government bought the company and its West African forts and settlements. The records of the African companies are in T 70. These records include details of payment for shipments of slaves, names of employees of the African companies and of their agents in Africa and the West Indies, and general correspondence.

Most of the records relating to the slave trade in the PRO consist of petitions from merchants, statistics of imported slaves and navy office returns in the records of the Colonial Office. Details of the crews of slaving vessels can be found in the ships' musters in BT 98, although very few survive before 1800.

Until 1808 there are no lists of slaves transported from Africa in the PRO, and any after that date exist because slave ships had been seized for illegally transporting slaves. The slaves then became forfeited to the crown (**3.5**).

3.4.1 Further reading

Donnan, *Documents of the Slave Trade*
Eltis, Behrendt, Richardson and Klein, *Transatlantic Slave Trade* – a database on CD-ROM
Eltis, *Rise of Atlantic Slavery*

Klein, *Atlantic Slave Trade*
Tattersfield and Fowles, *Forgotten Trade*
Thomas, *Slave Trade*
Walvin, *Black Ivory*
Walvin, *Britain's Slave Empire*
Walvin, *Slave Trade*

3.5 Liberated Africans

The slave trade was abolished on 1 May 1807 (Abolition of the Slave Trade Act 1807), although vessels which sailed before that date could under certain circumstances trade until 1 March 1808. Any vessels seized under the 1807 and subsequent acts for illegally carrying slaves were taken as prize, the master was fined and the slaves became forfeited to the crown. This meant that they became government slaves and many were enlisted into the Royal Navy or the army, especially the West India Regiments and the Royal African Corps.

From 1808 Sierra Leone became the centre for British suppression of the slave trade on the west coast of Africa and many liberated Africans settled there. Two Sierra Leone censuses include details of liberated Africans living there in 1831 (CO 267/111) and 1833 (CO 267/127). In the 1840s many liberated Africans emigrated to Jamaica and other West Indian islands. Correspondence concerning this emigration, petitions and some passenger lists are in CO 267, for example a nominal list of liberated Africans with their ages who left for Port Antonio, Jamaica, on the *Morayshire* and the *Amity Hall* in 1848 is in CO 267/203. Nominal lists of liberated Africans who left for St Lucia and Jamaica on the *Una* in January 1849, for Jamaica on the *Etheldred*, 29 May 1849, and for Trinidad on the *Agnes*, 28 May 1849 are in CO 267/207.

The trials of illegal slavers were held at vice-admiralty courts in Africa, the West Indies, Havana and Rio de Janeiro. Under various treaties with slave trading powers, such as the Netherlands, Portugal, Spain and Brazil, ships of these and other nations could be sentenced at Mixed Commission Courts. Proceedings, and other papers relating to illegal slave trading are found mainly among the records of the Foreign Office, especially those of the Slave Trade Department (FO 84) and the Mixed Commission Courts.

The primary court was held at Sierra Leone (HCA 49/97, 1808–1817 and FO 315, 1819–1868). The other courts were at Cape Town (FO 312, 1843–1870), Havana (FO 313, 1819–1869), Jamaica (FO 314, 1843–1851), and Rio de Janeiro (FO 129/3–13, 15, 1819–1861, and FO 131/1–11, 1820–1885). These records include registers of slaves liberated, crew lists and log books of captured ships, and correspondence with the Admiralty and Foreign Office. Other records can be found in the papers of the

Admiralty (ADM 1), the Slave Trade Adviser of the High Court of Admiralty (HCA 37), colonial customs returns (CUST 34), Colonial Office original correspondence series (especially for Sierra Leone, CO 267), and the Treasury (T 1).

3.5.1 Further reading

Howell, *Royal Navy and the Slave Trade*
Lloyd, *Navy and the Slave Trade*
Ward, *Royal Navy and the Slavers*

3.6 East Indians

When slavery was abolished the newly freed slaves had to serve a period of four years for their former masters which was known as apprenticeship. When apprenticeship ended in 1838 in colonies with available land, such as Trinidad, St Vincent and British Guiana, many freed slaves left their owners to establish their own smallholdings. As a result, many colonies suffered severe labour shortages and petitioned the crown to help relieve this problem. Chinese labourers were employed in Trinidad from 1806, and later migrant workers from other West Indian islands, liberated Africans, Portuguese from Madeira and the Azores, and to a lesser extent labourers from France and Germany, were encouraged.

The largest group of migrants were Asian Indians from the Indian subcontinent, who are often referred to in the records as East Indians or 'coolies'. Policy papers concerning their recruitment, with reports and correspondence relating to welfare and employment in the colonies, are found among appropriate colonial correspondence series, CO 323 and CO 318. CO 318 contains documents devoted to Indian labour for the period 1843–1873. These are continued in CO 323, and later in the Immigration Department records CO 571, 1913–1920. From the 1870s the records of the Land Board and Emigration Department, CO 384–CO 386 (registers in CO 428), include information on Chinese and Indian emigration. CO 384 and CO 385 include surgeons' reports for emigrant ships which sometimes list births and deaths. Other papers record ships commissioned to sail from Madras and Calcutta with the numbers of Indians on board. Some lists of these emigrants may be found in the colonial correspondence and government gazettes.

Several enquiries into the state of Indian labour were published in the British *Parliamentary Papers*. Reports of the various local bodies who administered and reported on apprenticed labour may be found in the appropriate country's archives.

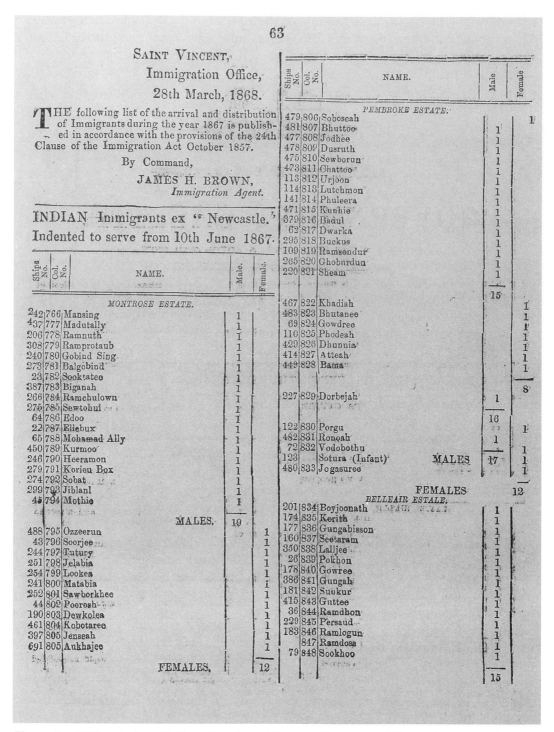

Figure 8 St Vincent: list of Indians disembarked from the *Newcastle*, 1867, and the estates they were indentured to (CO 264/9, p. 63).

The Indian subcontinent was administered by the East India Company and from 1858 by the India Office. The records of these organizations are held by the British Library, Oriental and India Office Collections (see **Useful addresses**). The records of the agents who arranged for the transportation of Indians to the West Indies may survive in the National Archives of India (see **Useful addresses**).

3.6.1 Further reading

Cumpston, *Indians Overseas*
Dabydeen and Samaroo, *Across the Dark Waters*
Lai, *Chinese in the West Indies*
Ramdin, *Arising from Bondage*
Saha, *Emigration of Indian Labour*
Saunders, *Indentured Labour*
Thomas, *Indians Overseas*
Tinker, *New System of Slavery*
J. S. Ferreira's 1999 *Preliminary Bibliography on Portuguese Immigration to the Americas, with Special Emphasis on the Caribbean* can be found on <freepages.genealogy.rootsweb.com/~portwestind/research/sources/ferreira_biblio.htm>

3.7 American loyalists

During and after the American War of Independence 1775–1783, many people lost their land and possessions because of their loyalty to the British crown. Many loyalists fled to Britain, Nova Scotia and the West Indies, in particular to the Bahamas, Dominica and Jamaica. Correspondence regarding these refugees to the West Indies can be found in original correspondence and sessional papers series, for example CO 23/25, fo 131 lists 52 loyalist households who arrived in the Bahamas in 1784.

Under the Treaty of Peace (1783) and the Treaty of Amity (1794) loyalists were able to claim compensation for their losses. The records of Treasury Commissioners investigating claims, with pension and compensation lists, are in T 50, 1780–1835; T 79, 1777–1841; AO 12, 1776–1831; and AO 13, 1780–1835. Correspondence and petitions regarding relief and compensation can be found in T 1. In 1783 East Florida was ceded to Spain, and loyalists, made similar claims; many left for the Bahamas and Jamaica. The records of the East Florida Claims Commission are in T 77; T 77/19 relates to claims made by the settlers in the Bahamas.

Former slaves of Americans who fought for the British cause were allowed to remain free; many of these Black loyalists who escaped to Nova Scotia and England became the initial settlers of Sierra Leone. The 'Book of Negroes' (PRO 30/55/100, no 10427) compiled by British military authorities in 1783 lists Black refugees in New York before they left for Nova Scotia. Sierra Leone was established in 1787 by a group of philanthropists as a settlement for freed slaves from Britain and the West Indies. The proceedings and other papers of the Committee for the Relief of Poor Blacks, 1786–1787, are among the papers in T 1/631–638, 641–647. Four hundred poor Blacks, together with some English women, were transported as the first settlers to Sierra Leone and a list of those at Plymouth, 16 February 1787, is in T 1/643, no 487.

The settlement did not survive and in 1791 a group of Black loyalists from Nova Scotia was encouraged to settle. A list of the Blacks of Birch Town, Nova Scotia, who gave their names for Sierra Leone, November 1791, is in CO 217/63, fos 361–366. Their numbers increased with the arrival in 1800 of Jamaican maroons, who had been expelled from Jamaica for Nova Scotia in 1796.

3.7.1 Further reading

PRO information leaflets
Braidwood, *Black Poor and White Philanthropists*
Brown, 'American Loyalists in Jamaica'
Coldham, *American Loyalist Claims*
Walker, *Black Loyalists*

4 Life cycle records

These are the primary sources for a family historian which record the major events in the lives of individuals: birth, marriage and death, including censuses and wills.

4.1 Records of births, marriages and deaths

Before the registration of births, marriages and deaths by the state (known as civil registration) these events were recorded by religious authorities. The Church of England was the primary church in the older British colonies until the early 1800s when other Christian churches were established, such as Methodist, Moravian and Baptist. In the colonies ceded from France and Spain the Catholic church was more important. Church registers recorded baptisms, rather than births, and burials rather than deaths. Other religions and Christian denominations are represented in the West Indies and may record other life events as part of their ceremonies.

Before the establishment of the Diocese of Jamaica and Barbados in 1824 the Bishop of London had jurisdiction over the West Indian Anglican churches but this responsibility was limited to the appointment and management of the clergy (see Manross, *Fulham Papers*, for more information). No registers or Bishops' Transcripts were sent to London although copies of a few registers for the Bahamas, 1721–1728, and St George's, Nevis, 1716–1723, are in the Lambeth Palace Library (see **Useful addresses**).

The governor had responsibility for much of what would be considered in Britain as being the rights of the church, such as the creation and disposal of parishes, issuing marriage licences, probate of wills, and overseeing public morals. There were no church courts, which in England and Wales dealt with moral offences. In the West Indies moral offences were regulated by the justices of the peace, although it was often unclear which such offences could be tried at the quarter sessions. (For more information on the legal system in England and Wales, see *Tracing Your Ancestors* and Baker's *Introduction to Legal History*, details in **Bibliography**).

Some colonies passed local legislation to regulate such offences, for example in 1722 Barbados passed an act to 'regulate the punishment of such crimes and vices as are cognisable in the ecclesiastical courts and for suppressing vice and profanities'. This act permitted the Bishop's commissary authority to act against offending clergy but reinforced the justices' jurisdiction over lay people.

4.1.1 Church registers

Registers of baptisms (births), marriages and burials (deaths) may be deposited in the country's archive or registry office, but many are still held by the individual church, which you will need to contact for access to its registers. Many registers have been microfilmed by the Church of Jesus Christ of Latter-day Saints (LDS) and can be accessed via their family history centres. Some returns, especially for Barbados, have been indexed in the LDS's International Genealogical Index (see **1.5**). A few early eighteenth century returns are found among the governors' despatches in the PRO and these are listed under the relevant country in **Chapter 10**.

Early registers usually only describe the date of the event and the names. For example, baptisms may only give the names of child and parents. If the mother was unmarried the register usually only gives her name, and the child was registered with her surname. Status of slaves and free Black people is usually given, such as 'free coloured' or 'adult Negro'. Slaves were often baptised as adults and the baptismal entries usually only show the owners and not the parents. Marriage entries give marital status.

Later registers from the mid nineteenth century usually contain more information, for example the address and father's occupation. Baptismal entries may also give date of birth and mother's maiden name; Catholic registers usually give the name of godparents and possibly any relationship to the child. Marriage entries usually give the name and occupation of the parties' fathers and record whether they are dead. Burials may give age at death and cause of death.

Until the late eighteenth century slaves are rarely recorded in the church registers. In the Protestant colonies owners were discouraged from baptising their slaves, although many were baptised. Slaves tended to be baptised as adults and the registers do not give ages or parentage, although the owner is recorded as his or her permission was needed. Many slaves chose to be baptised with a Christian name different from their slave name, and this new name was used by the slave especially if he or she became free; owners may also have used the new name in their lists of slaves.

Marriage between slaves was extremely rare and the few examples I have seen occurred during the 1820s. Many plantation slaves were buried without Christian rites on the plantation. Slaves in more urban areas and household slaves were more likely to be buried in churchyards or separate slave cemeteries, or possibly in the grounds of the house. Slaves may be recorded in the usual baptism and burial registers, which were normally arranged chronologically by event, but they may be recorded at the end of the registers or even in separate registers.

Slaves were chattel, which meant that they were the personal property of their owner. Most of the events which affected their lives were plantation affairs, and records of births and deaths were events that would be recorded by their owner, if at all. On plantations, slaves had a value according to their occupation, sex and age, and were often listed with livestock. These records are private records and are described further in **5.3**.

4.1.2 Slave registers

An important source for the period 1812 to 1834, and the most important for slaves, is the slave registers in T 71, which were compiled to established legally held slaves (**7.1**). They can provide information not only on slaves but also their owners, and most free people of modest means would have owned at least one slave as a domestic servant or to hire out. The registration was carried out approximately every three years and lists changes from the previous register. Slave births and deaths are recorded, which will help give the approximate date of the event. Changes in ownership are shown in the registers, for example on the death of an owner slaves were often bequeathed to family members, on marriage slaves were transferred as property from wife to husband, as a dowry, and slaves were often gifted to children when they left home. Many registers are indexed, while others are arranged alphabetically by plantation, or name of the registered holder. The registers in T 71 are duplicates which were forwarded to the Slave Registry in London from 1821, and the originals may survive in the relevant country archive.

4.1.3 Civil registers

Civil registration, the recording of births, marriages and deaths by the state, was begun by all of the British West Indian colonies at different times from the mid nineteenth century. Occasionally different events were registered at different times, for example in Barbados registration of births started in 1890, and of deaths in 1925. The PRO does not hold any civil registration returns, which should be found in the relevant registry office and many are available through the LDS (see **1.5**).

The registers tend to be detailed, for example registers of births give name, sex, name of mother and her maiden name, and the name and occupation of father. Some countries such as Barbados and Guyana allowed baptismal names to be added later, and the Bahamas asked for colour. Marriage registers usually provide name, marital status, occupation, age, address and the father's name and occupation; the entry usually shows whether the father is deceased. Death registers will give address, name, sex, age, occupation and cause.

Newspapers and colonial gazettes sometimes have notices of births, marriages and deaths, especially of prominent citizens.

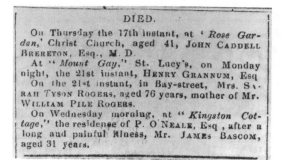

DIED.

On Thursday the 17th instant, at ' *Rose Garden*,' Christ Church, aged 41, JOHN CADDELL BRERETON, Esq., M. D.

At " *Mount Gay*," St. Lucy's, on Monday night, the 21st instant, HENRY GRANNUM, Esq

On the 21st instant, in Bay-street, Mrs. SARAH TYSON ROGERS, aged 76 years, mother of Mr. WILLIAM PILE ROGERS.

On Wednesday morning, at " *Kingston Cottage*," the residence of P. O'NEALE, Esq , after a long and painful illness, Mr. JAMES BASCOM, aged 31 years.

Figure 9 Barbados: death notices announced in *The Liberal*, Wednesday 30 August 1854 (CO 33/12, fo 117). Henry Grannum is the author's great-great-great-grandfather.

4.1.4 Further reading

General Register Office, *Abstract of Arrangements Respecting Registration*
Kemp, *International Vital Records*
Manross, *Fulham Papers in Lambeth Palace*

4.2 Censuses and other listings

The English government was interested in information about colonial populations long before it showed an interest in its own population. Before 1670 few returns were made, but with the creation of the Council for Foreign Plantations in 1670 regular reports from the colonies were sought. The information required was the numbers of men, women, children, servants, free people and slaves, the annual growth of the population, and the number in the militia. This information was needed so that the government could record not only the population growth of the new colonies, but also its economic wealth, and more importantly its military strength. Some colonial governors sent regular returns, others waited for specific requests.

The majority of censuses returned to London were in the form of head-counts of varying information. The most simple returns gave only the total population, the numbers of males and females and degrees of freedom. In more detailed censuses the population was broken down into sex, age group, marital status, degrees of freedom, colour or race. There are very few censuses giving names in the PRO and most of these only give the name of the head of the household with numbers of women, children, servants and slaves. These are found among the original correspondence of the individual colonies, merely as a list or maybe with printed demographic analysis. Statistical counts of the population occur in the *Blue Books of Statistics* and government gazettes for the individual colonies, and are occasionally printed in the British *Parliamentary Papers*.

White Families	Free People of Color	Numb.ʳ in each Family.	Number of Slaves
At George Town - formerly called the Hog-sties			**270**
John Drayton		6	23
Sarah Nixon		3	4
Abraham Bodden		6	5
Sterling Rivers		5	5
Rachel Rivers		8	17
William Jennett		3	
Geo. Bodden		7	4
Benj:ⁿ Bodden		6	
Will.ᵐ S. Prescott		5	2
Eliz: Conior		1	5
Mary Savery		6	5
John Bodden		8	8
John Edwᵈ Rivers		4	3
James Thompson		7	5
Cornelia Scott		5	1
Mary Wilson		1	
John S. Jackson		6	
	Chloe Parsons	1	2
	James Parsons	1	5
	W.ᵐ Parsons	3	6
	Lind Rivers	1	1
	George Barrow	1	3
At West-Bay			
John Bodden		6	2
Thomas Hyde		8	6
Jane Walker		1	9
William Rivers		5	2
Isabella Hoye		1	2

Figure 10   Cayman Islands: census of heads of households, 1802 (CO 137/108, fo 272).

I have identified many West Indian censuses in the PRO which give at least the name of the head of household (these are listed in **Chapters 10** and **11**). Details of pre-1776 American colonial censuses, with demographic analyses, are described in Wells' *Population of the British Colonies*. It is possible that other census returns containing names, especially any for the nineteenth and twentieth centuries, may be found in the islands' own archives. If returns which list inhabitants have been kept it is possible that these will be closed or subject to certain restrictions.

The slave registers in T 71 provide a census of slave owners and slaves for the period 1812 to 1834 (see **7.1**). Although the information on owners is limited to their name and parish, the information on the slaves is useful as the registers provide age, occupation and country of birth. The registers for the former Spanish and French colonies, such as St Lucia, St Vincent, Trinidad and Grenada, list the slaves in family groups, headed by the mother, and often record siblings if they are on the same estate. Unfortunately the registers for the older British colonies, such as Jamaica and Barbados, list the slaves only by sex and age.

The records of the PRO include many other types of population returns, for example petitions from prominent landowners, tax returns and electoral registers. The returns are in original correspondence and government gazettes series for the individual colonies; some are described in **Chapter 10**.

4.2.1 Further reading

Kuczynski, *Demographic Survey*
Wells, *Population of the British Colonies*

4.3 Wills and grants of administration

4.3.1 Local records

The governor was responsible for the probate of wills and grants of administration through the local courts. The types of record to be found include original wills and grants of administration, with copies entered into a wills or probate register or in the register of deeds, and inventories of goods. Wills usually give details of the testators' immediate family and their bequests, together with some information about the property, including slaves. Administrations are letters granting estate to the next of kin, or creditors, in cases where a will was not made. Letters of administration, however, give very little information except the name of the administrator or administratrix. Inventories are lists of the testator's estate detailing its value. Since they list the testator's property they may include lists of slaves.

Most West Indian wills were proved locally and should survive in the relevant archive, register office or even with the courts. Following a French invasion of St Christopher and Nevis in 1711, powers of attorney were granted for payment of compensation. Copies of these powers, 1712–1720, together with a number of wills, are in CO 243/4–5. Lists of wills proved and letters of administration sometimes occur in the government gazettes.

4.3.2 Prerogative Court of Canterbury

British subjects dying abroad or at sea with personal estate and property in England or Wales, and members of the navy and army, had their wills proved or administrations granted, in the Prerogative Court of Canterbury (PCC). Lists of West Indian wills proved in the PCC for the period 1628–1816 are in Oliver's *Caribbeana*, Volumes 2–5 (see **Bibliography**).

Until 1722 it was obligatory for every executor or administrator to return to the court's registry an inventory of the deceased's goods. After this date inventories were only called for as exhibits in the PCC court if the will was disputed. PROB 4, 1661–1720, is the largest collection of inventories, and there is a card index to the deceased as well as a topographical index. From 1722 some inventories are in PROB 31, exhibits, and PROB 37, causes. These records may also contain original and copy wills, and other papers, from courts outside the PCC.

The PCC also includes wills of West Indians and others with estate or family in the West Indies who died in Britain. These wills can provide useful information on their property, including slaves, and family in the West Indies.

The series of PCC records begin in 1383 for registered copy wills (PROB 11) and 1559 for administrations (PROB 6); both these series are available through the LDS (see **1.5**). Original wills 1484–1858 (PROB 10) currently require five working days' notice to produce. Registered copy wills were made by PCC clerks after probate and include details of the probate. Original wills tended to be copied until about 1700. Unregistered wills may only be found in PROB 10 rather than PROB 11.

There are chronological indexes, by initial letter of surname, to wills and administrations. The British Records Association has published alphabetical indexes to the wills 1383–1700 and administrations 1559–1660. The Friends of the Public Record Office has produced a microfiche index to wills and administrations 1700–1749. The Society of Genealogists has published indexes to wills 1750–1800 and they are currently working on administrations. The PRO will make digital copies of the copy wills available online for a fee through PRO-Online <www.pro.gov.uk/online/pro-online.htm>; the indexes to these wills are free. Indexes to Scottish wills and testaments 1500–1875 are available at <www.scottishdocuments.com>.

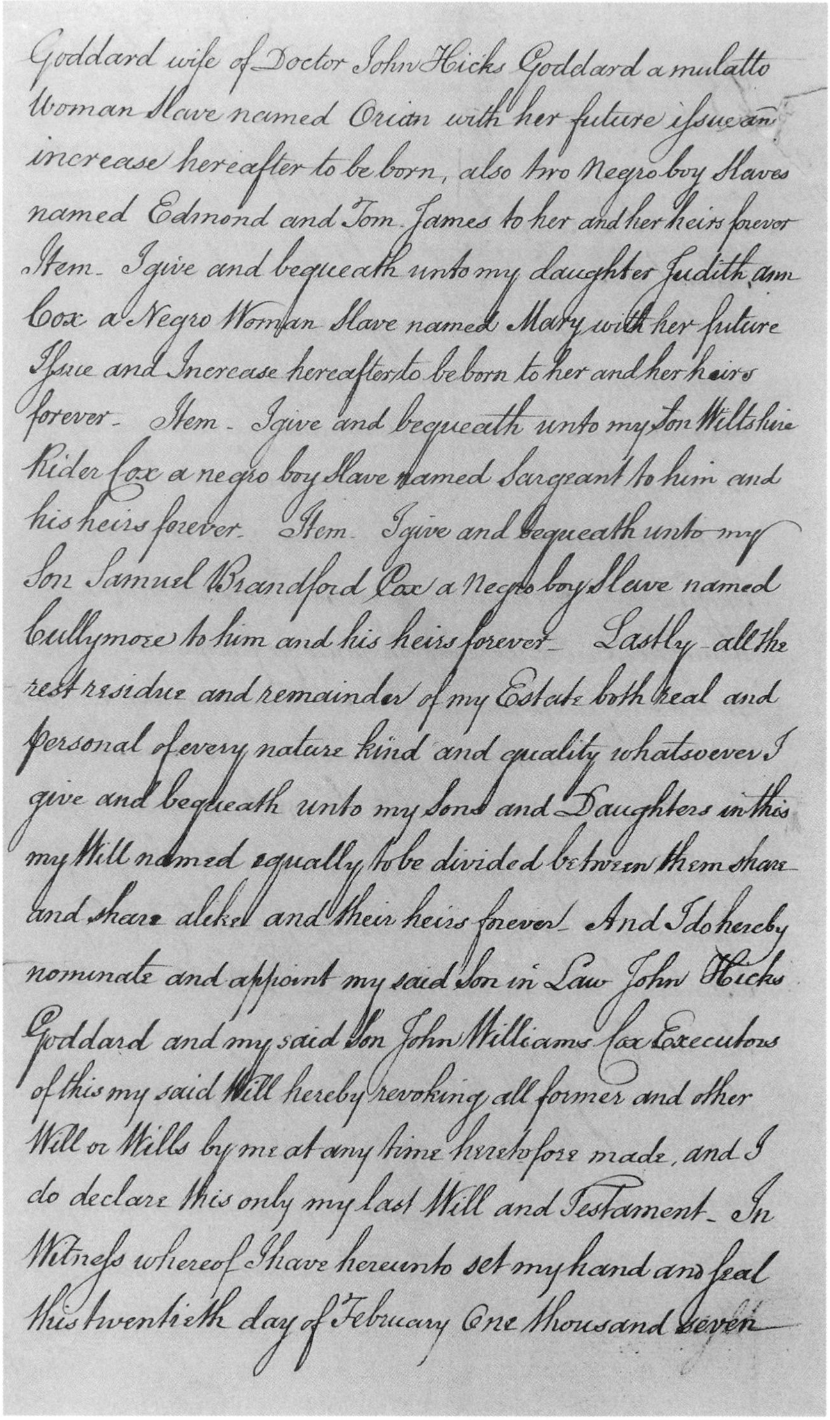

Goddard wife of Doctor John Hicks Goddard a mulatto
Woman Slave named Orian with her future issue an
increase hereafter to be born, also two Negro boy Slaves
named Edmond and Tom James to her and her heirs forever
Item – I give and bequeath unto my daughter Judith Ann
Cox a Negro Woman Slave named Mary with her future
Issue and Increase hereafter to be born to her and her heirs
forever – Item – I give and bequeath unto my Son Wiltshire
Rider Cox a negro boy Slave named Sargeant to him and
his heirs forever – Item – I give and bequeath unto my
Son Samuel Brandford Cox a Negro boy Slave named
Cullymore to him and his heirs forever – Lastly all the
rest residue and remainder of my Estate both real and
personal of every nature kind and quality whatsoever I
give and bequeath unto my Sons and Daughters in this
my Will named equally to be divided between them share
and share alike and their heirs forever. And I do hereby
nominate and appoint my said Son in Law John Hicks
Goddard and my said Son John Williams Cox Executors
of this my said Will hereby revoking all former and other
Will or Wills by me at any time heretofore made, and I
do declare this only my last Will and Testament – In
Witness whereof I have hereunto set my hand and seal
this twentieth day of February One thousand seven –

Figure 11   Barbados: will of Fearnot Cox dated 30 July 1784, showing slaves
being bequeathed to family members (PROB 37/897).

Before 1858 there were many other church courts where wills could be probated. People who died in the West Indies and had property in only one diocese in Britain or West Indians who died in Britain could also have their wills proved in one of the other courts; see Gibson's *Probate jurisdictions* for descriptions and locations of these church courts. The ecclesiastical courts in England and Wales were abolished under the 1857 Probate Act, with effect from 12 January 1858, and responsibility for probate passed to the Court of Probate, now the Principal Registry of the Family Division. Wills later than this date are held at the Principal Registry of the Family Division (see **Useful addresses**).

4.3.3 Further reading

PRO information leaflets

Bevan, *Tracing Your Ancestors*, Chapter 6

Coldham, *American Wills and Administrations: Canterbury*

Coldham, *American Wills Proved in London*

Cox, *Wills, Inventories and Death Duties*

Gibson, *Probate Jurisdictions*

K. Grannum, *Using Wills*

Oliver (ed.), *Caribbeana*. Volumes 2 to 5 contain lists of Prerogative Court of Canterbury (PCC) wills, 1628–1816, and some abstracts of early PCC wills for Nevis and St Kitts. Volumes 1 and 2 contain lists of Jamaican wills, and volumes 4 and 5 have lists of Barbadian wills. <www.candoo.com/olivers/caribbeana.html>

5 Land and property records

5.1 Land grants

In early colonial America the ownership of the land was vested in the Crown by right of discovery and settlement by its subjects. The Crown granted land to companies and to proprietors to organize settlement. During the Commonwealth, 1649 to 1660, most of the colonies reverted to the state, which granted land through its appointed governors.

During the eighteenth century many colonies of other European powers were occupied by and then ceded to Britain, among them Dominica, Grenada, Trinidad, Tobago, British Guiana, St Vincent and the French portion of St Christopher. The British authorities sought to encourage British settlement, and began to require returns to be made of lands granted, purchased or rented on many of these islands. Returns were also made of non-British proprietors.

Land granted directly by the Crown or Parliament can be found among patent (C 66) and close rolls (C 54). However, most land grants were recorded locally rather than in London, and these survive in the former colonies in deeds or patent registers. Some copies and abstracts of land grants were forwarded by the governor and can be found in the PRO among Colonial Office records (**Chapter 2**). Information on lands granted by the governor can be found in the original correspondence series and the entry books for each colony. Lands granted through local government, such as the legislative assemblies or councils, may be recorded in sessional papers.

From the mid nineteenth century the government gazettes are a rich source of information, and contain notices for sales of Crown land, auction notices for plantations, arrears of rent for government properties, land and house tax defaulters, land rolls, electoral lists, grants of land, grants of homesteads, transfer of land (sometimes known as transports), mortgages and applications for land claims.

5.1.1 Further reading

PRO information leaflets
Barck and Lefler, *Colonial America*

5.2 Maps and plans

The PRO holds numerous maps and plans relating to the West Indies, and the individual colonies. The most important collections are CO 700 1595–1909, CO 1047 1779–1947, and CO 1054 1897–1984 for the Colonial Office, and WO 78 1627–1953 for the War Office. Maps are also found in the Colonial Office records for each colony, especially among the original correspondence series. Many of these are described in *Maps and Plans in the Public Record Office: Volume 2 America and West Indies*. There is also a card catalogue and printed supplementary catalogues to maps and plans held by the PRO, but only a small percentage have been catalogued.

Maps of the islands can provide a lot of information about landowners. Plantations, which were often named after the owner, are usually listed and many have since become villages bearing the same name. Many maps were produced under subscription, and these include lists of the subscribers with their addresses. Some include the names of landowners, for example the plan of St George's, Grenada, surveyed by the Commissioners for the Sale and Disposal of His Majesty's Lands 1765 (CO 700 Grenada no 5) identifies each parcel of land and lists the proprietor. Many of the owners are included in the list of town lots granted by Governor Smith between 1762 and 1764 (CO 101/1, fos 245–246).

Collections of maps can also be found in local Caribbean archives and libraries and at the British Library (see **Useful addresses**).

The Directorate of Overseas Surveys, and its successor Ordnance Survey International, undertook aerial surveys of many of the islands from the 1930s, and these photographs have been used to create topographic maps of the islands. Maps and photographs, with some restrictions, are available from the Ordnance Survey (see **Useful addresses**). Please provide as much information as possible for identifying photographs, such as a sketch map of the area. Files on the surveys are in OD 6 in the PRO.

5.2.1 Further reading

PRO information leaflets
Penfold, *Maps and Plans: America and West Indies*

5.3 Plantation records

The PRO holds very few records of plantations because they are private papers. Surviving records can be found in a variety of places which reflect the movements of

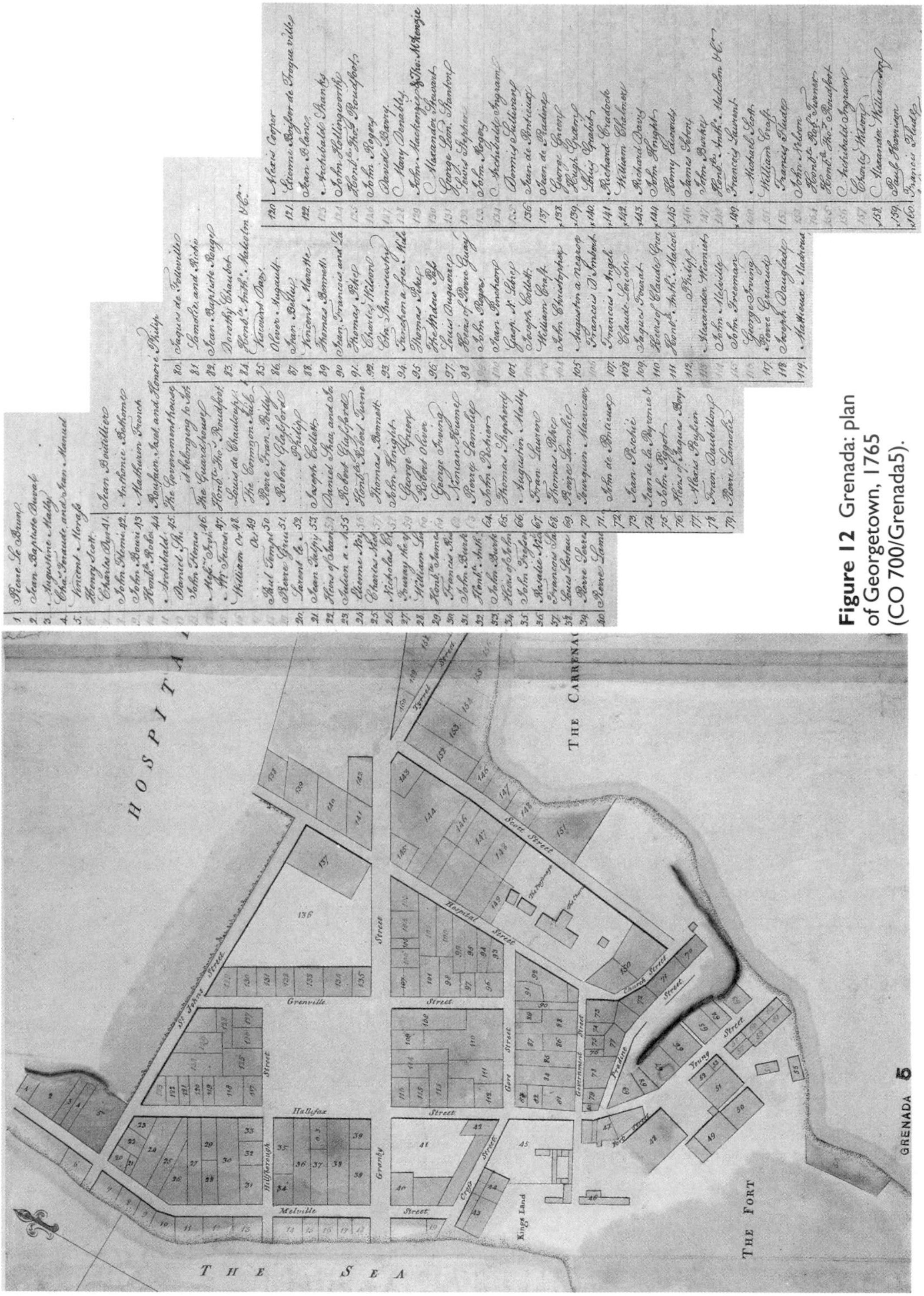

Figure 12 Grenada: plan of Georgetown, 1765 (CO 700/Grenada5).

the owner. For example if the owners were absentee landlords and lived in Britain, or eventually returned to Britain, these records may survive in a British local record office. The papers of families who remained in the colony may survive in that country's archive. It is also possible that the records may still remain with the family who owned, or managed, the estate.

The Royal Commission on Historical Manuscripts (see **Useful addresses**) may be able to advise on the whereabouts of surviving papers in Britain. Their National Register of Archives database can be searched at <www.hmc.gov.uk/nra/search_nra.htm>. You can also search the Access to Archives project (A2A) catalogues of English local authority archives <www.a2a.pro.gov.uk> and the Scottish Archives Network (SCAN) catalogues at <www.scan.org.uk>.

The few collections which the PRO holds relating to plantations occur because the estate or its owner was involved in litigation. The equity side of the courts of Chancery and Exchequer dealt with a large and varied range of disputes, such as inheritance, lands, debts, bankruptcy and marriage settlement. Papers, such as accounts, deeds, journals and correspondence, were provided as evidence in the Court of Chancery. Those that were not returned to the owner have survived as Chancery Masters Exhibits (C 103–C 114, and J 90) and Exchequer Exhibits (E 140, E 192, E 214 and E 219). Many of these records include lists of slaves and plantation accounts. The proceedings contain much information on the individuals, families and property involved in the suits, the records are in numerous C and E series and I suggest that you read the two guides by Henry Horwitz and the online catalogue for further information.

Other plantation records are found among the records of the West Indian Incumbered Estates Commission (CO 441, 1854–1893) and the West Indian Hurricane Relief Commission (PWLB 11, 1832–1881); many records predate the setting up of these commissions and some include schedules of slaves.

The West Indian Relief Commission was set up in 1832 following insurrections in Jamaica and hurricanes in Barbados, St Lucia, St Vincent, British Guiana and Trinidad, and was extended to Dominica following a hurricane in 1835. Money was made available to the colonial governments to relieve people affected and as loans to individual estate owners to rebuild their plantations. The loans were secured by the mortgage of the estates to the Crown. The records of the Commission (PWLB 11) contain records of about 120 estates in Jamaica, Barbados, St Lucia, St Vincent and Dominica and include mortgage indentures, schedules of slaves and evidence of ownership. No other records of the commission, such as correspondence and minute books appear to have survived. However, correspondence between the Treasury and the commission, colonial governments and individuals concerning the effects of the hurricanes and relief in general, including correspondence from other affected islands is in T 1/4395–4397 and in original correspondence series for the affected countries.

Names of Individuals	Motive for granting Relief	Estimated Amount of loss	Amo. of Relief Awarded
	Amount brought forward		18
Marie F. Louise	Mother of 12 Children the Youngest 6 Months Old	means of support destroyed	12
Lucie Alexandre	Extreme distress 4 Child	do.	5
Rose & Alexandre	2 Orphans 14 & 15 Years old	do.	6
Chenott	An Orphan 8 Years old	do.	4
Velpier Gerard	Extreme distress 80 Years old	do.	8
Salmen Rolland	Do. 80 Years Old	do.	4
Venus Galanagus	Do. 70 ditto	do.	4
Fanny Amoured	A Maniac 30 Years old	do.	5
Saint Amoured	an Imbecile 25 Do.	Do.	4
Pierre Gascon	Extreme distress	Do.	3
Fevrier Rolland	Do. 80 Years Old	Do.	4
Francoise Mathis	Do.	Do.	3
Prosper Roach	Do. no House	Do.	3
B. Camile	Do.	Do.	8
Veronique	Do. & 3 Children	Do.	3
Jean Carasco	Do. Wife & 2 Infants	Do.	3
Jeannette Eache	Do.	Do.	4
Rodrigue Seaman	3 Young Infants & an Aged Mother	Do.	10
Agathe	at times deranged in mind	Do.	4
Laguire Geoffy	Extreme distress (consumptive)	Do.	3
Vs. Lachnal	Do. 58 Years old	Do.	3
Marie Zavie	4 Infants to maintain 3 of them her Sister left destitute	Do.	12
Rosette Jarel	Extreme distress	Do.	5
Zabeth	Do. no home	Do.	3
Helen R. Dubois	Do. 4 Young Infants	Do.	8
Rolland (Pierre)	Do. & Sickly	Do.	3
Marie Apollon	Do. & 5 Children to support	Do.	8
	Carried forward	$	160

Figure 13   St Lucia: return of relief paid to persons in distress following the great hurricane of August 1831, *Laborie Quartier*, 16 January 1833 (T 1/4396, paper 6312/33).

The West Indian Incumbered Estates Commission was set up under the West India Incumbered Estates Act 1854 to investigate estates which had become overburdened by mortgages, and in some cases to sell them. The Commission existed until 1892 and sold 382 estates. Some estates were sold by agents locally on the islands but the majority (350) were sold in London. CO 441 contains the records of the Commission and the papers of 205 estates, the majority in Jamaica and Antigua. The records are arranged by date of sale, and contain transfer of mortgages, newspapers advertising sales, and various accounts and deeds, including plans.

Some correspondence and reports relating to both these commissions are published in the British *Parliamentary Papers*.

Other West Indian estate records may survive in the PRO but these will be difficult to find, for example, WO 9/48 includes accounts of John Moffat's Blenheim and Cranbrooke Plantations in Jamaica 1806–1807, and ADM 65/59 includes accounts and schedules of slaves of Golden Vale Plantation, Portland, Jamaica, c.1793–1811.

5.3.1 Further reading

PRO information leaflets
Bevan, *Tracing Your Ancestors*, Chapter 47
Horwitz, *Chancery Equity Records*
Horwitz, *Exchequer Equity Records*
Many sources of family, plantation and estate papers are listed in the various guides to sources for West Indian history in **Chapter 10**, for example:
Ingram, *Manuscript Sources: West Indies*
Walne, *Guide to Manuscript Sources*

6 Military and related records

From the first European settlements in the West Indies until the mid nineteenth century there was almost constant military conflict between the European powers in the West Indies, even when they were at peace in Europe. To protect her colonies from attack and internal unrest Britain had a permanent military presence. Every colony possessed local militia and troops of the regular British Army were also based on the islands. The Royal Navy patrolled the seas, moved troops, and protected convoys and the colonies from pirates and enemies. The merchant navy transported goods between Europe and the colonies, including slaves, and was a source of manpower for the Royal Navy. Many soldiers and sailors who served in the West Indies did not return to Britain: thousands died through tropical diseases and warfare, many deserted, and some remained in the colonies after discharge.

West Indians also served in all of the military services and in the merchant navy. However, with the exception of periods of war, Black and coloured West Indians, as well as other non-Europeans, were discouraged from joining the army and Royal Navy. Only 'British born men of British born parents of pure European descent' could be commissioned officers. During the First and Second World Wars the armed services reluctantly recruited Black and coloured servicemen and women and a few received temporary commissions, mainly in the Royal Air Force. Black and coloured West Indians also experienced prejudice in the merchant navy and were mostly restricted to ships which travelled to and from the West Indies.

There are many records among WO, CO, BT, MT (Ministry of Shipping and Transport) and LAB (Ministry of Labour) series discussing the issue of race and colour in the armed services and the merchant navy. Discrimination is also described in several articles and books listed in further reading for the army (6.1.4) and in general for the Second World War. For the latter see Sherwood, *Many Struggles: West Indian Workers and Service Personnel in Britain, 1939–1945*; Sherwood and Spafford, *Whose Freedom Were Africans, Caribbeans and Indians Defending in World War II?*; Bousquet and Douglas, *West Indian Women at War: British Racism in World War II*; and Murray, *Lest We Forget: The Experiences of World War II Westindian Ex-service Personnel* (see **Bibliography** for details).

The colour bar was officially lifted in 1948 but until 1968 the army had a quota of about 4,000 non-European recruits, although there were rarely more than 2,000 coloured recruits. I have not been to determine if the other services also had quotas for coloured recruits. See <www.mod.uk/2191.html> for information on colonial contribution to the armed services.

As the records of the services have been well described elsewhere (see **Bibliography**), I will simply highlight records which are pertinent to the West Indies and West Indians.

6.1 Army

The British Army was permanently stationed in the West Indies: each of the established imperial regiments (administered by the War Office) did a tour of duty there, and most colonies had barracks. The forces were made up predominantly of recruits from Britain, with a small number of other Europeans and some local men. Many foreign regiments on British pay also served in the West Indies, especially during the American War of Independence and the French Revolutionary and Napoleonic Wars. For example, the York Light Infantry Volunteers was raised from Dutch garrison battalions after the loss of the Dutch colonies of Berbice, Demerara and Essequibo in 1803; this corps was disbanded in 1817.

Most colonies also had a locally raised militia force administered by the colonial governments (see **6.1.3**). These were composed initially of European settlers but increasingly from the 1790s of Black and coloured slaves and freemen. Until the twentieth century West Indian regiments and militia regiments consisted of European officers and non-commissioned officers (NCOs), such as corporals and sergeants, and Black and coloured soldiers, although many Black and coloured soldiers were promoted to NCO ranks.

Records relating to military activities in the West Indies, recruitment, policy and West Indian local forces and imperial regiments are found in a wide variety of War Office (WO) and Colonial Office series. For the period before about 1900 it is best to start with PRO Lists and Indexes volume LIII, *An alphabetical guide to certain War Office and other military records*. Thereafter, the main series are WO 32, Registered files, 1845–1985; WO 106, Directorate of Military Intelligence and Operations, 1837–1962; CO 323, Colonies general: original correspondence, 1689–1951; CO 318, West Indies original correspondence, 1624–1951, relevant country original correspondence series; CO 820, Military original correspondence, 1927–1951; and CO 968, Defence departments original correspondence, 1941–1967.

6.1.1 Records of service

Officers

The starting point for information about officers is the *Army List*, which details the officer's regiment and the dates of his commission. The manuscript army lists, 1702–1752, are in WO 64. From 1754 they are published and copies are available at the PRO. Personal details of officers can be found among the Commander-in-Chief's memoranda in WO 31, 1793–1870, and in the widows' pension applications among the miscellaneous certificates in WO 42, 1755–1908. There is an incomplete run of officers' services in WO 25 for various periods between 1808 and 1872, and in WO 76 for various periods between 1829 and 1919; there is an incomplete card index of names for these returns.

Correspondence files of officers who served between 1914 and 1922 are held by the PRO in WO 339 (indexed by WO 338) and WO 374. The main series of files was destroyed by bombing in 1940: these are supplementary files but in some cases the supplementary file had been destroyed before 1940. Both WO 339 and WO 374 can be searched using the PRO catalogue by surname and initial. WO 338 includes references to officers who continued serving after March 1922, and these files have a 'P' reference and are held by the Ministry of Defence (see **Useful addresses**).

Other ranks (pre-1914)

The most detailed record of a soldier's service, for those who were discharged to pension between 1760 and 1913, is provided by the attestation and discharge papers in WO 97. These record the place of birth, age on enlistment, place of enlistment, a physical description, and the record of service. From 1883 details of next of kin, wife and children are given. WO 97 is arranged by date of discharge: 1756–1854 (soldiers have been listed in the PRO catalogue <catalogue.pro.gov.uk> and can be searched by first and last names and by regiment); 1855–1872, arranged alphabetically by surname under the regiment; 1873–1882, alphabetically by name under the type of corps (infantry, cavalry, artillery); and 1883–1913, alphabetically by surname and including not only those discharged to pension but also those discharged after limited engagements or by purchase. There are also two supplementary series of papers in WO 97 which had been misfiled; these are for discharges between 1843 and 1899, and between 1900 and 1913.

If the attestation and discharge papers do not survive, then details of a soldier's service can be obtained by searching the regimental musters and pay lists; you need to know the regiment or brigade for artillery regiments. The musters for infantry and cavalry 1740–1878 are in WO 12, artillery 1708–1878 are in WO 10, and engineers 1816–1878 in WO 11. From 1878 until 1898 they are all in WO 16; there are no musters or pay lists after 1898.

These volumes can be used to trace date of enlistment, movements, and date of discharge or death, of soldiers. On enlistment the pay books often give the age and place of birth. From 1868 details of marriages, with the numbers and ages of children, are shown. The regimental description books in WO 25 and depot description books in WO 67 give the physical description of soldiers on enlistment, which can include tattoos, markings and ritual scarring which may help identify ethnic origin for African born soldiers.

Until 1855 the artillery and engineers were the responsibility of the Board of Ordnance. Some additional musters and description books are in WO 54 and service records in WO 69.

If you do not know the regiment, but have information such as a date and a place where the person served then you may identify possible regiments by using the regimental returns in WO 17, WO 73 and WO 379. A useful guide to the stations of regiments for the period 1640 to the First World War is in Kitzmiller's *In Search of the 'Forlorn Hope'* (see **Bibliography**).

Soldiers who were discharged after completing an agreed term of service or as invalids were entitled to a pension. The Royal Hospital Chelsea administered pensions for the army and their records include those who were discharged and received pensions in the West Indies. The out-pension admission books are arranged chronologically by the date of the examination for pension and are in three series: pensions awarded for disability, WO 116, 1715–1913; pensions awarded for length of service, WO 117, 1823–1920; and WO 23, 1817–1903, for pensions awarded in the colonies and to Black pensioners. These admission books are arranged by date of pension board and by Chelsea pension number (which is usually recorded on the discharge papers in WO 97), and give a brief description, age, place of birth, particulars of service and reason for discharge.

In addition there are pension pay registers (WO 22, 1845–1880), arranged by colony, which give details of payment, and the date of death if it occurred within the period of the register. Sometimes the regiment is noted, which will aid research in the pay lists, and in the soldiers' documents. PIN 71 comprises selected war pensions award files for service before 1913; you can search this series by surname on the catalogue.

Other ranks (post-1913)

Records of service for soldiers who served in the First World War and were discharged before 1922 are held by the PRO in two series. WO 363 is the main series of service records but unfortunately the majority (about 70%) were destroyed by bombing in 1940. The records have been microfilmed and are arrange alphabetically by surname. I have been advised by the Ministry of Defence that the records of service for the

British West Indies Regiment (BWIR) have not survived. Indeed, I have not yet found any records for the BWIR in this series although it is possible to find ex-BWIR soldiers who served in other units.

The second series, WO 364, comprises discharge papers of soldiers discharged to pension during the war or who received medical discharges. For example, it is possible to find medical discharge papers for the Jamaican soldiers who suffered frostbite and other effects of the cold in Halifax, Nova Scotia, in 1916. This series is in two main alphabetical sequences and was compiled from records formerly held by the Ministry of Pensions and the Ministry of Health. There is also a 2% sample of pension papers, created by the Ministry of Pensions in PIN 26, which can be searched on the catalogue by surname.

The service records for soldiers who served in the British Army after 1922 are still held by the Ministry of Defence (see **Useful addresses**). They will give only brief details to the former soldier or to the official next of kin. Enquirers must apply in writing and there may be a fee for this service.

Most West Indians who joined the army during the First World War were enlisted in the British West Indies Regiment (see **6.1.3**). West Indians also enlisted in imperial regiments, but the War Office tried to prevent coloured West Indians enlisting in any corps except the BWIR; until the BWIR was established the War Office threatened to repatriate any who made their own way to the United Kingdom to enlist. In June 1918 the War Office informed the Colonial Office that it would allow coloured recruitment into the British Army (CO 323/781, War Office, 13 June 1918).

In addition to the BWIR, Bermuda raised two corps, the Bermuda Volunteer Rifles, a white unit, which was attached to the 1st battalion Royal Lincolnshire Regiment, and the Bermuda Garrison Artillery, which was a coloured unit. There were two other organized contingents, the Trinidad Merchants' and Planters' Contingent Committee, and the Barbados Citizens' Contingent Committee, which paid for white officers and soldiers to enlist in the UK. They included clerks in the colonial service, planters and merchants and public school men.

However, from discussions in Colonial Office papers it is clear that many, especially Trinidadians, were not of 'pure European descent'. These contingents joined many different imperial regiments; returns of men waiting to be repatriated in 1919 show that many had served in the 1/15 and 2/16 London Regiment, the Artists' Rifles, and the 2/6 Devonshire Regiment. Many, especially officers from Trinidad, were waiting to be repatriated from the Royal Air Force (see **6.4**). Lists of the Trinidad Merchants' and Barbados Citizens' contingents, with information such as name, rank, regiment, contingent, date of enlistment and remarks (such as gallantry awards, deaths or pensioned etc.) are found in CO 318/351, West India Contingent Committee, 2 April 1919 and CO 28/294, fos 457–460.

No. in Lincoln Regt.	No. in B.V.R. Corps.	Rank and Name.		Name and address of next of kin.	Relationship.
3	918	Pte.	Boorman F.J.	Mrs. Florence E. Dunston, Laffan St., Hamilton, Bermuda.	Mother.
4	862	Pte.	Bridges A.P.	Alfred Joseph Bridges, Somerset Bridge, Bermuda.	Father.
5	954	Pte.	Bruce Ed.	Dollie Louise Bruce, St. Georges, West Bermuda.	Wife.
6	810	Pte.	Burgess E.R.	Mrs. Ida Talem, Spanish Point, Bermuda.	Mother.
7	860	Pte.	Cannon C.R.	Elizb. Cannon, Hamilton, Bermuda.	Mother.
8	927	Pte.	Cannon J.R.	Elizb. Cannon, Hamilton, Bermuda.	Mother.
9	973	Pte.	Crone Jas.	John Crone, 136 Grosvenor Road, Belfast, Ireland.	Father.
17110	887	Pte.	Cooper J.C.	Joseph S. Cooper, Pembroke, Bermuda.	Father.
1	926	Pte.	Cooper A.L.	Orville Cooper, Somerset, Bermuda.	Father.
2	929	Pte.	Cuttenden C.H.	Edith Cuttenden, 109 Richmond Rd., Kingston-on-Thames.	Wife.
3	779	Pte.	Davies H.B.	Ernest Harrington Davies, Southampton W. Bermuda.	Father.
4	808	Pte.	Dickens A.E.G.	Edward Frank Dickens, Laffan St., Hamilton, Bermuda.	Father.
5	930	Pte.	Davison E.G.H.	Col. George Markham Davison, 11th Service Battn. Durham L.I.	Father.
6	711	Pte.	Doe A.E.	Henry Anstice Doe, Paget E. Bermuda.	Father.
7	82	Pte.	Farrell J.W.A.	Patrick Jos. Farrell, Spanish Point, Bermuda.	Brother.
8	888	Pte.	Farrell M.J.	Patrick Jos. Farrell, Spanish Point, Pembroke, Bermuda.	Brother.
9	968	Pte.	Foreman J.A.	Jas. Fredk. Foreman, Mangrove Bay, Somerset.	Father.
17120	984	Pte.	Hall B.E.	Maud Dellmer Davidson, Dellmer Cottage, Southampton E. Bermuda.	Mother.
1	863	Pte.	Herriott N.B.	Benjn. Jas. Herriott Paget E. Bermuda.	Father.
2	751	Pte.	Harris S.A.	Chas. Harris, New Road, Somerset, Bermuda.	Father.
3	886	Pte.	Heath F.E.	Wm. John Heath, Devonshire Bermuda.	Father.

Figure 14 Roll of the Bermuda Volunteer Rifle Corps, who were attached to the Lincolnshire Regiment (CO 318/336, War Office, 24 November 1915).

Many West Indians also joined the Canadian Overseas Expeditionary Force during the First World War and the records of service are held by the National Archives of Canada (see **Useful addresses**). Copies of records of service are available on their website at <www.archives.ca>.

6.1.2 Other records

In addition to records describing soldiers' services there are many other records which are useful for those with British army ancestors.

Regimental and army chaplains' registers of births (baptisms), marriages and deaths (burials), 1761 to date, are held by the Office of National Statistics (see **Useful addresses**). These returns include some original West Indian garrison and station registers: baptisms, marriages and burials for the St Lucia garrison, 1898–1905; deaths and burials for the Barbados Station (Windward and Leeward Islands Command) 1804–1906; and baptisms, births and marriages for the Trinidad and Martinique garrisons, 1812–1816.

Campaign medal rolls, WO 100, 1793–1913, are arranged by campaign and then by regiment. First World War medal rolls (British War Medal, 1914 Star, 1914–15 Star, Victory Medal and Silver War Badge) are in WO 329 (indexed by WO 372). Later medal rolls are with the Army Medal Office (see **Useful addresses**).

Casualty returns, 1809–1875 (but covering the period 1797–1910) in WO 25, refer to absences, desertions, discharges, wounded and dead. The information includes name, rank, place of birth, trade on enlistment, date, place and nature of casualty, debts or credits, and next of kin or legatee. Occasionally these records contain wills, inventories, correspondence and accounts.

WO 334, Army Medical Department: Returns and Reports, 1817–1892, includes annual death returns by country and by regiment, providing regiment, rank, name, disease, date of death and place of death; deaths of soldier's children are also recorded.

Information on soldiers who died in the First and Second World Wars can be obtained from the Commonwealth War Graves Commission (see **Useful addresses**). Their Debt of Honour register can be searched by surname from their website <www.cwgc.org> which provides brief details on the soldier such as date of death, place of burial or memorial and occasionally the names of parents or widows may be given.

Soldiers Died in the Great War, first published in 1921, is now available on CD-ROM. It gives place of birth, place of enlistment, cause of death, theatre of war where the soldier died, and date of death. Unfortunately, this compilation only includes deaths in UK army regiments; the British West Indies Regiment and West India Regiment are excluded. Medical records of the field medical centres (MH 106) contain admissions and discharges with brief details of the medical condition.

The Second World War army roll of honour WO 304, published on CD-ROM, contains the following: name, service number and date of death, together with coded information on rank, unit first served in, unit at time of death, place of birth, domicile and place of death.

War diaries for the First World War (WO 95) are arranged by theatre of war and then hierarchically by division, brigade etc. They describe, often very briefly, day-to-day activities of the unit. The amount of information varies significantly and they rarely name individuals apart from officers, although it is sometimes possible to find lists of soldiers, lists of wounded and killed, and citations for gallantry awards.

Second World War war diaries (WO 166 to WO 177) are also arranged by theatre of war and then hierarchically. The document descriptions are often abbreviated and to search the online catalogue you will need to try short forms and abbreviated forms of the regiment, for example 'Durham' or 'D.L.I.' or 'DLI' for the Durham Light Infantry. Activities in the Caribbean can be found in the relevant colonial original correspondence series for each colony and in CO 318, CO 323, CO 820 and CO 968.

6.1.3 West Indian regiments

West Indians served in all British regiments. However, except during periods of war the War Office resisted recruiting Black and coloured soldiers into the regular European regiments, although for much of the eighteenth and nineteenth centuries most regiments had Black musicians. Black West Indians were restricted primarily to joining the West India Regiments and the Corps of Military Labourers, and during the First World War the British West Indies Regiment.

West India Regiments

The West India regiments were raised in 1795 as a Black corps to complement the European regiments. The troops were predominantly Black with white officers and non-commissioned officers (NCOs), although some Blacks did rise to become NCOs. The origin of these regiments was the Carolina Black Corps. The Carolina Black Corps was formed from several loyalist corps of Black Dragoons, Pioneers and Artificers raised during the American Revolution. After the revolution the Carolina Black Corps formed various Black pioneer, garrison, and infantry corps serving in the West Indies. Supplementing these corps were locally raised Black pioneer and ranger corps. The West India regiments also bought slaves, first from existing slave owners but later directly from slave ships. It is estimated that from 1795 to 1807 the British army bought 7 per cent of all slaves sold in the British West Indies.

In 1807 the slave trade was abolished, and under the Mutiny Act all former military slaves were emancipated (freed) but remained in the army. The recruiters turned next to liberated Africans (see **3.5**) seized from illegal traders by customs officials and the Royal Navy, and established recruiting depots in ports such as Freetown, Sierra Leone and Havana. Other groups which enlisted included soldiers from the Bourbon Regiment from Mauritius, which was disbanded in 1816; Blacks from St Domingo, Martinique and Guadeloupe; Europeans, from Belgium and Germany; and American slaves who enlisted during the Anglo-American War of 1812.

Between 1795 and 1888 there were between 1 and 12 West India Regiments, which served in the West Indies, West Africa and, during the Anglo-American War of 1812, in the United States. By 1888 there was one regiment of two battalions; a third battalion was raised in 1897 and disbanded in 1904; and the second battalion was disbanded in 1920. The West India Regiment was disbanded in 1927, but it was re-formed for a short time between 1958 and 1961 during the short-lived Federation of the West Indies. On disbandment in 1961 the discharged soldiers formed the nucleus of the Jamaica Defence Force.

Corps of Military Labourers

Other locally raised corps were garrison companies and the Military Labourers, many of whom were also slaves and liberated Africans. The Corps of Military Labourers was formed on 25 August 1817 from supernumeraries from the 1st, 3rd and 6th West India regiments administered by local staff officers of the Quartermaster Generals Department for mainly garrison and general labouring duties. It was disbanded on 1 October 1888.

British West Indies Regiment

On the outbreak of hostilities in 1914 many West Indians left the colonies to enlist in the UK and were recruited into British regiments. However, the War Office became concerned with the numbers of Black and coloured West Indians in the army and tried to prevent them from enlisting, threatening to repatriate any who arrived. After much discussion between the Colonial Office and the War Office, and following intervention by King George V, agreement to raise a West Indian contingent was approved on 19 May 1915 and on 26 October 1915 the British West Indies Regiment was established.

I have been advised by the Ministry of Defence that no records of service have survived for soldiers of the BWIR. I have not yet managed to find any among the 'burnt' documents in WO 363, although records for those discharged to pension should be found in WO 364. These records may have been destroyed by bombing in 1940, but it is also possible that they were transferred to the colonial governments in the 1920s and 1930s.

Colonial governments accepted liability for paying separation allowances during the war and for pensions after the war. There is much correspondence in Ministry of Pensions (PIN series), Colonial Office and Treasury (T series) files concerning the paying of pensions in the colonies, including a cryptic message in CO 137/804/15 (Jamaica) dated 14 October 1935 which states that the 'work [payment of pensions] will be undertaken by the [Jamaican] Treasurer and the handing over of all of the records will be completed in the course of the next few days'; this correspondence is also found in Treasury and Ministry of Pensions files. Unfortunately, there is no mention of what these records were and it may be that only files of soldiers who were receiving pensions were passed to the Jamaican treasurer. It is also possible that the records were transferred to the local defence forces, especially when the West India Regiment was disbanded in 1927.

However, among the Colonial Office papers, especially CO 318 and the appropriate colonial original correspondence series, there are numerous lists of West Indian soldiers. Most of these are for the various contingents of the BWIR but also include the Bermuda Volunteer Rifle Corps, the Trinidad Merchants' and Planters' Contingent and the Barbados Citizens' Contingent. These records include: separation allowances, nominal rolls, embarkation returns, casualty lists, pensioners, and lists of those found unfit and returned.

For example, a list of 199 Jamaicans who were discharged in 1916, including 184 who were pensioned following the effects of the cold in Halifax on the *Verdula* in March 1916, is in CO 137/717, gov 30 Dec 1916. The information includes regimental number, date embarked, date returned to Jamaica, date discharged, date pension awarded.

These records are incomplete and unfortunately there are very few after 1916. The Colonial Office registers show that they were regularly received by the Colonial Office but were 'destroyed under statute' and no longer survive in Colonial Office files. Those for 1915 and 1916 may have been kept as examples of the types of records created and since the War Office would keep such documents as nominal rolls, casualty returns and personal records the Colonial Office decided not to keep them. Most rolls and casualty lists were routinely copied to the governors and it is possible that they may survive in the relevant archives.

The first contingent of the BWIR arrived at Seaford Camp, Sussex, on 5 September 1915 for training. Further contingents arrived at Seaford in 1915 and 1916 and in April 1916 left for Egypt. Later contingents sailed directly for Egypt. Some passenger lists for the contingents who arrived in Britain, which give name and age, are in BT 26; most however, only give the numbers of soldiers.

The few lists of names include: SS *Danube* with 120 of the 1st British Guiana contingent who disembarked at Plymouth on 5 September 1915 (BT 26/616, Sept, London pt 2);

New Regtl. No. Alltd.	Prev. Col. No.	Rank.	Name.	Christian Name.	Name of next-of-kin.	Particulars of next-of-kin.	Address of next-of-kin.
5086	2641	Pte.	Davis	James	Alberta Aquart	Sister	Bloomfield, Port Antonia, Jamaica.
5087	2474	Pte.	Diaz	Samuel	L. Diaz	Brother	Guala Guatemala, Central America.
5088	3230	Pte.	Diego	Lino	Juana Lodriquez	Mother	Stann Creek, Br. Honduras.
5089	2609	Pte.	Dixon	Alvern Ogilvie	A.H.McNab	Cousin	French Harbour, Puatton, Spanish Honduras.
5090	2601	Pte.	Domingo	Meshach Augustus	Emeline Domingo	Mother	1297 Freetown Rd., Belize, Br. Honduras.
5091	2359	Pte.	Domingo	Simeon	Emeline Domingo	Mother	1297 Freetown Rd., Belize, Br. Honduras.
5092	2449	Pte.	Duncan	Charles Daniel	James Duncan	Brother	Monkey River, Br. Honduras.
5093	2368	Pte.	Duran	Phillip	Jane Crawford	Mother	King St., Belize, Br. Honduras.
5094	2584	Pte.	Edwards	Faban George	Amelia, Henrietta Edwards.	Wife	Lataste St.Patricks, Grenada.
5095	2493	Pte.	Edwards	William	John Edwards	Nephew	Orange Walk, Belize, Br. Honduras.
5096	3220	Pte.	Ellis	Ernesto (Decease)	Mrs J.Ellis	Mother	Farmers Town, Stann Creek, Br. Honduras.
5097	2576	Pte.	Ellis	Richard	Amelia Greenfield	Grand-mother	Monkey River, Br. Honduras.
5098	2338	Pte.	Elmandarez	Emmanuel	Ann Walker	Mother	Rocky Rd., & Geo.St., Belize, Br. Honduras.
5099	578	Pte.	Elkington	Peter Louis	Jane Elkington	Mother	303 South St., Belize, Br. Honduras.

Figure 15 Roll of 5th battalion of the British West Indies Regiment comprising men mainly from British Honduras (Belize) (CO 318/340, War Office, 28 October 1916).

SS *Danube* with British Guiana (with 30 other ranks) and Barbados (29 other ranks) contingents and Trinidad Merchant Contingent (109 other ranks) who disembarked at Plymouth 1 November 1915 (BT 26/617, Nov, London pt 2); SS *Quillata* with 145 mainly Jamaican and Bahamian other ranks who disembarked at Plymouth 12 Jan 1915; and SS *Balantia* which arrived on 17 January 1916 with 3 of the 1st and 69 of the 2nd Trinidad contingents (BT 26/629, Jan, London pt 2).

Twelve battalions were raised and saw service in East Africa, Egypt, Palestine, Jordan, France and Italy, mainly as labourers in the ammunition dumps and gun emplacements, often under heavy fire. Towards the end of the war two battalions saw combat in Palestine and Jordan against the Turks. A total of 397 officers and 15,204 other ranks, representing all the Caribbean colonies, served in the BWIR, and of these 15,601 men, 10,280 (66%) were from Jamaica.

Caribbean Regiment

At the outbreak of the Second World War West Indians again tried to enlist in the British Army and again met with resistance. The War Office did not want to raise a West Indian regiment: West Indians who wanted to enlist had to arrange their passage to the UK and almost 10,000 West Indians enlisted individually in the British Army. In 1940 Churchill suggested re-forming the West India Regiment but the War Office only considered pioneer (labour) corps. After much deliberation the Caribbean Regiment was formed in April 1944 with just over 1,200 men, most of whom were volunteers from the local defence forces including Bermuda. The regiment was trained in Virginia and on 8 June 1944 became the first British regiment to celebrate the King's birthday in the US since the American Revolution. Without seeing any combat the regiment returned to the West Indies in 1946 and was disbanded.

The PRO does not hold service records for the Caribbean Regiment and it is unlikely that the Ministry of Defence holds them. As most members were recruited from local defence forces, I would suggest that any personal records would be with the relevant defence force.

6.1.4 Records of West Indian regiments

This list is not comprehensive and other records can be found by using the catalogue.

| T 1/664 | 1788 | List of Black pioneers belonging to the Royal Artillery victualled at Grenada |
| T 1/664 | 1788–9 | Musters of officers, soldiers, wives and children for the Black Dragoons, Black Artificers, Corps of Pioneers, Black Pioneers, |

		67th and 45th Regiments victualled at Grenada
T 1/4362 (pt 2)	1817	Return of pensioners discharged from disbanded West India regiments, garrison companies and invalids stationed in the Windward and Leeward Islands

Musters and pay lists

WO 12/10491	1781–1782	Barbados Rangers
WO 12/10785	1813–1819	Black and Bahamas Garrison Companies
WO 12/10917–10931	1837–1875	Military Labourers
WO 12/11040	1795	St Domingo Corps
WO 12/11064	1796	South American Rangers
WO 12/11233–11238	1805–1819	West India Rangers
WO 12/11239–11338	1795–1877	1st West India Regiment
WO 12/11339–11448	1795–1877	2nd West India Regiment
WO 12/11449–11508	1795–1870	3rd West India Regiment
WO 12/11509–11530	1797–1870	4th West India Regiment
WO 12/11531–11541	1797–1865	5th West India Regiment
WO 12/11542–11552	1796–1817	6th West India Regiment
WO 12/11553–11562	1795–1816	7th West India Regiment
WO 12/11563–11570	1798–1816	8th West India Regiment
WO 12/11571–11572	1799–1803	9th West India Regiment
WO 12/11573–11574	1799–1802	10th West India Regiment
WO 12/11575–11577	1799–1803	11th West India Regiment
WO 12/11578–11579	1799–1803	12th West India Regiment
WO 12/12039–12053	1803–1817	York Light Infantry Volunteers
WO 12/13289	1789–1791	Black Dragoons and others at Grenada
WO 16/2132–2152	1877–1888	1st battalion West India Regiment
WO 16/2153–2168	1877–1888	2nd battalion West India Regiment

Pension registers

WO 22/231–236	1845–1880	Black pensions
WO 22/248–257	1845–1875	Miscellaneous pensions in the colonies
WO 23/147–152	1817–1875	Pensions payable in the colonies
WO 23/153	1837–1840	Black and St Helena Corps pensioners
WO 23/154	c.1837	Black pensioners
WO 23/156–159	1839–79	Black pensioners
WO 23/160	1880–1903	Native and colonial pensioners
WO 43/108	1818	Lists of pensioners from the West India Regiments

Description books

WO 25/644–645	1810–1831	2nd West India Regiment
WO 25/646–651	1826–1870	3rd West India Regiment
WO 25/652–655	1804–1819	4th West India Regiment
WO 25/656	1811–1817	5th West India Regiment
WO 25/657–659	1797–1817	6th West India Regiment
WO 25/660–662	1801–1817	7th West India Regiment
WO 25/663–665	1804–1819	West India Rangers
WO 25/686–687	1803–1813	York Light Infantry

Casualty returns

These sometimes contain wills and copies of wills of deceased soldiers and inventories of their effects.

WO 25/2196–2197	1817–1819	Bahama Garrison Company
WO 25/2244–2245	1809–1819	West India Rangers
WO 25/2246–2262	1809–1831	1–8 West India Regiments
WO 25/2295	1812–1816	York Light Infantry Volunteers

Soldiers' documents

Surviving records of individual soldiers who were discharged before 1854 are searchable on the PRO catalogue.

WO 97/1154	1760–1854	West Indian Rangers
WO 97/1155–1162	1760–1854	West India Regiments
WO 97/1183	1760–1854	Corps of Military Labourers
WO 97/1712–1719	1855–1872	West India Regiments
WO 97/1720	1855–1872	Corps of Military Labourers
WO 97/2166–2170	1873–1882	West India Regiments
WO 97/2171	1873–1882	Corps of Military Labourers

First World War battalion war diaries

In addition to summarising activities of the battalions, these may contain nominal rolls and casualty returns.

WO 95/4427	1 Battalion British West Indies Regiment	1915 September–1916 November
WO 95/4433	1 Battalion British West Indies Regiment	1916 December–1917 May
WO 95/4410	1 Battalion British West Indies Regiment	1917 June–1918 March
WO 95/4732	1 Battalion British West Indies Regiment	1918 April–1919 April

WO 95/4427	2 Battalion British West Indies Regiment	1916 January–November
WO 95/4433	2 Battalion British West Indies Regiment	1916 December–1917 May
WO 95/4732	2 Battalion British West Indies Regiment	1917 June–1919 April
WO 95/4465	3 Battalion British West Indies Regiment	1916 March–July
WO 95/338	3 Battalion British West Indies Regiment	1916 September–1919 January
WO 95/409	4 Battalion British West Indies Regiment	1918 May–November
WO 95/4465	5 Battalion British West Indies Regiment	1916 July–1919 April
WO 95/495	6 Battalion British West Indies Regiment	1917 March–1919 April
WO 95/409	7 Battalion British West Indies Regiment	1917 June–December
WO 95/4262	7 Battalion British West India Regiment	1918 January–1919 January
WO 95/338	8 Battalion British West Indies Regiment	1917 July–December
WO 95/4262	8 Battalion British West India Regiment	1918 January–1919 January
WO 95/4186	British West Indies Base Depot	1917 March–1918 September
WO 95/5318	British West Indies Regiment	1916 July–November
WO 95/5370	British West Indies Regiment	1916 December–1918 February
WO 95/5318	British West Indies Regiment	1918 March–September
WO 95/4732	2 Battalion West India Regiment	1918 September–1919 June
WO 95/5318	2 Battalion West India Regiment	1918 March–August
WO 95/5370	2 Battalion West India Regiment	1917 July–1918 February
WO 95/5388	2 Battalion West India Regiment (Detachment)	1915 October–November
WO 95/397	Bermuda Contingent, Royal Garrison Artillery	1916 June–1917 May

First World War campaign medal rolls

1914 Star	1914–15 Star, Victory Medal, British War Medal and Silver War Badge. The indexes (WO 372) are on microfiche.
WO 329/2277	West India Regiment, British War and Victory medals, officers
WO 329/2299	Bermuda Volunteer Rifle Corps, British War and Victory medals, officers
WO 329/2303	British West Indies Regiment, British War and Victory medals, officers
WO 329/2325	West India Regiment and the British West Indies Regiment, British War and Victory medals
WO 329/2326	British West Indies Regiment, British War and Victory medals
WO 329/2327	British West Indies Regiment and Bermuda Contingent, Royal Garrison Artillery, British War and Victory medals
WO 329/2373	British West Indies Regiment, distribution lists, arranged by colony, and provides medal roll number, regimental number, rank, name, address and medals
WO 329/2933	West India Regiment, 1914–15 Star
WO 329/2953	West India Regiment, 1914–15 Star, officers

WO 329/2955   Bermuda Volunteer Rifle Corps, 1914–15 Star, officers
WO 329/3272   British West India Regiment, Territorial Efficiency Medal, officers

Second World War battalion war diaries

WO 169/16276	1 Caribbean Regiment	1944 October–December
WO 169/20038	1 Caribbean Regiment	1945 January–December
WO 169/20039	1 Caribbean Regiment holding battalion	1945 May–December
WO 170/1370	1 Caribbean Regiment	1944 June–September
WO 176/41	1 Caribbean Regiment	1944 March–May; 1945 December–1946 February
WO 204/1362	move of 1 Caribbean Regiment from USA to North Africa	1944 January–June

6.1.5 Militia

The militia were locally raised forces, formed to protect the colony itself. They were not expected to serve overseas. The PRO does not hold the records of West Indian militia. However, the government gazettes among the Colonial Office records often contain lists of militia, and notices of promotion and retirement. Useful material, such as military policy and activities, war diaries, lists of officers, and applications for commissions can be found in original correspondence series, CO 318, CO 820 and CO 968; CO 820/50/1 to CO 820/51/28 contain nominal rolls of European officers and men in colonial local forces, 1941–1942. Lists of officers and men of the various local defence and police forces awarded defence and war medals for the Second World War are in CO 820. Service records of West Indian militia may survive with the local defence forces or in the islands' archives.

6.1.6 Further reading

PRO information leaflets
Andrade, *Record of the Jews in Jamaica*. Includes list of the Jewish members of His Majesty's Forces from Jamaica, who served during the First World War 1914–18. Some were in the BWIR, while others served in British regiments. This list includes officers, non-commissioned officers and men, as well as casualties in all ranks.
Atkinson, 'Foreign Regiments in the British Army'
Bevan, *Tracing Your Ancestors*, Chapter 18
Buckley, *Slaves in Redcoats*
Cundall, *Jamaica's Part in the Great War*

Dyde, *The Empty Sleeve: Story of the West India Regiments*
Ellis, 'George Rose: Exemplary Soldier'
Fowler and Spencer, *Army Records for Family Historians*
Healy, 'Colour, Climate, and Combat: The Caribbean Regiment'
Holmes, *The Bahamas during the Great War*
Howe, *West Indians and World War I*
Imperial War Museum, *Tracing your Family History: Army*
Ingham, *Defence not Defiance: The Bermuda Volunteer Rifle Corps*
Joseph, 'The British West Indies Regiment 1914–1918'
Kieran, *Lawless Caymanas: Slavery, Freedom and the West India Regiment*
Kitzmiller, *In search of the 'Forlorn Hope'*
Public Record Office Lists and Indexes, vol. LIII, *Alphabetical Guide to War Office*
Roper, *Records of the War Office*
Spencer, *Army Service Records of the First World War*
Thomas, *Records of the Militia*
Watson, *Carib Regiment of World War II*
Watts and Watts, *My Ancestor was in the British Army*
<www.regiments.org> – brief histories of British and Commonwealth regiments, by T. F. Mills
<website.lineone.net/~bwir/> – histories of the regiments of the British West Indies, by F. Goodwill
<freepages.genealogy.rootsweb.com/~portwestind/research/archives/service_in_great_war. htm> a list of people of Portuguese descent who left Trinidad to serve in the First World War, translated from Charles Reis's, *Brief History of the Associação Portuguesa Primeiro de Dezembro* (Port-of-Spain, 1926)
<www.bermuda-online.org/regiment.htm> history of the Bermuda Regiment
<www.jdfmil.org> official website of the Jamaica Defence Force
<www.ttdf.mil.tt> official website of the Trinidad and Tobago Defence Force

6.2 Royal Navy

The Royal Navy patrolled the islands, protecting them against invasions, pirates and privateers. It also protected merchant shipping between the colonies, and escorted convoys between Africa and the West Indies, and between the islands and Britain.

6.2.1 Records of service

Officers

The starting point for tracing an officer's service is by Syrett and DiNardo (see **Bibliography**), and the published *Navy List* from 1782. Service registers were started during the nineteenth century, but few begin before the 1840s. The most important registers are ADM 196, which begin in 1840, although returns can be retrospective to the 1770s, and run to the 1930s; there are indexes in ADM 196 but these are incomplete. Other returns and surveys of officers' services between 1817 and 1846 are in ADM 6, ADM 9, ADM 10, and ADM 11. Lieutenants' and engineers' passing certificates, 1691–1902 (ADM 6, ADM 107 and ADM 13) summarize an officer's career and training; they sometimes contain supporting papers such as certificates of baptism or birth.

The PRO does not hold service records for executive officers (cadets, midshipmen, lieutenants, captains and admirals etc) whose service began after May 1917 or for warrant officers whose service began after 1931. These records are held by the Ministry of Defence (see **Useful addresses**).

Other ranks

The PRO holds two series of registers for ratings: ADM 139, 1853–1872, and ADM 188, 1872–1923, with service to 1928. In addition to ships served on, these records give the date and place of birth, and physical description. Certificates of service of warrant officers and ratings who applied for superannuation or admission to Greenwich Hospital are in ADM 29, 1802–1894.

Before 1853 if there are no records in ADM 29, then you must refer to the ships' musters and pay lists, ADM 36–ADM 39, ADM 41, ADM 115 and ADM 117. A muster should provide a man's age and place of birth from 1764, and from about 1800 description books (which give age, height, complexion, scars and tattoos) may be included. These records cover the period 1667 to 1878 and are arranged by ship. The ship must be known, although if the place where the sailor was serving is known it may be possible to identify the ships attached to the particular station; you can then search the musters of each ship on that station.

The records for ratings who joined after 1923 or whose service continued after 1928 are still held by the Ministry of Defence (see **Useful addresses**), which will supply information to the sailor or to the next of kin (for a fee).

6.2.2 Other records

The primary source for naval operational records and correspondence relating to individuals is ADM 1, which contains correspondence from naval officers, other government departments and individuals on naval activities and individuals. Case papers are in ADM 116, ADM 137 (for the First World War) and ADM 199 (for the Second World War). Ships' logs, ADM 51, ADM 52 and ADM 53, detail ships' movements and activities.

Casualty returns can be found in a variety of sources: ADM 104 contains registers of deaths, 1854–1956. Seamen's wills, 1786–1882, are in ADM 48 (indexed by ADM 142). Seamen's effects, ADM 44, 1800–1860 (indexed by ADM 141), contains claims by executors or next of kin for the back pay of ratings who died in service and can include wills, birth and marriage certificates and other supporting evidence. Wills for officers and warrant officers are in ADM 45. ADM 242, War Graves Rolls, contains information on Royal Navy and Royal Marines officers and men who died during the First World War. The information is: full name, rank, service number, ship's name, date and place of birth, cause of death, where buried and next of kin. Brief information on Naval service personnel who died in the First and Second World Wars can be obtained from the Commonwealth War Graves Commission <www.cwgc.org>.

Registers of Naval births, deaths and marriages, from 1881 are held by the Office of National Statistics (see **Useful addresses**), marriages held on board Royal Naval ships, 1842–1889, are in RG 33/156, some naval registers of baptisms, marriages and burials are in ADM 6, and the Chaplain of the Fleet's registers of baptisms, confirmations, marriages and burials, 1845–1995, are in ADM 338.

Medal rolls, ADM 171, are arranged by campaign or service medal. Early rolls are arranged by ship, for the First World War arranged by naval service (RNR, RNVR, RN) in alphabetical order and give the service number. Later rolls are held by the Royal Navy Medal Office (see **Useful addresses**).

6.2.3 Royal Naval Reserve

The Royal Naval Reserve (RNR) was raised in 1860 from officers and men of the merchant navy (see **6.5**) who could be called upon for service in the Royal Navy in times of emergency. Records of service of officers who served before the First World War and of honorary officers between 1862 and 1960 are in ADM 240. A selection of records of ratings who served between 1860 and 1913 are in BT 164. Indexes to service numbers from 1860 to 1922 are in BT 377. BT 377 also holds service details of ratings who served during the First World War. Medal rolls are in ADM 171.

6.2.4 Royal Naval Volunteer Reserve

The Royal Naval Volunteer Reserve (RNVR) was formed in 1903 and was composed of volunteers, except merchant seamen who went into the Royal Naval Reserve. Records of service for officers, 1914–1922, and ratings, 1903–1918, are in ADM 337. Ratings' service records are arranged by division and then by service number, which can be found in the medal rolls in ADM 171. Most RNVR divisional records have not survived although there is a selection in ADM 900/75–86. Later records of service are with the Ministry of Defence (see **Useful addresses**).

In December 1939 the Trinidad Royal Naval Volunteer Reserve was formed to carry out patrols and to distribute supplies to the West Indies. The Trinidad RNVR comprised men from most of the British Caribbean countries and lists of those awarded the War Medal, 1939–1945, are in CO 820/63/1 to CO 820/63/3.

6.2.5 Naval dockyards

Most of the islands possessed naval dockyards for the maintenance, refitting and victualling of Royal Naval ships. Musters and pay lists for the larger yards are in the Yard Pay Books, ADM 42. Those for the minor yards and establishments are in ADM 32, ADM 36 and ADM 37. The main series of yard musters and lists survive into the mid nineteenth century. The only later surviving records are the pensions registers in ADM 23, 1830–1926, and the naval establishment: artificers' and labourers' civil pensions, PMG 25, 1836–1928. There are pay lists, musters and pension registers for many West Indian islands including: Antigua, for the period 1743–1835; Barbados, 1806–1816; Bermuda, 1795–1857; Cape Nicholas, Haiti, 1798; Jamaica, 1735–1835; and Martinique, 1775–1815.

The Bermudas were important as a naval and military station, and in 1810 work was begun on the naval station on Ireland Island, using convict labour. Between 1824 and 1863 some 9,000 convicts were sent from Britain, but it never became a penal settlement and they were able to return to Britain on the completion of their sentence. Quarterly returns of prisoners on the Bermuda hulks in Ireland Island are in HO 8 and provide the following information: number, name, age, offence, where and when convicted, sentence, health, behaviour and remarks. The PRO holds baptisms, 1826–1946, and burials, 1826–1848, for the naval base at Ireland Island in ADM 6/434–436. Later baptisms for Ireland Island, 1947–1957, are in ADM 338/11.

6.2.6 Further reading

PRO information leaflets
Bevan, *Tracing Your Ancestors*, Chapter 19
Crewe, *Yellow Jack and the Worm*
Imperial War Museum, *Tracing Your Family History: Navy*
Pappalardo, *Tracing Your Naval Ancestors*
Rodger, *Naval Records for Genealogists*
Stranack, *The Andrew and the Onions*
Syrett and DiNardo, *Commissioned Sea Officers*

6.3 Royal Marines

The Royal Marines were the Royal Navy's soldiers, and records for them survive among the records of the Royal Navy (see **6.2**).

6.3.1 Records of service

Officers

The sources for tracing Royal Marine officers are the same as those for tracing Royal Navy officers (**6.2.1**). From 1782 the published *Navy List* gives all commissioned Royal Marine officers by substantive rank and seniority, and the ships they were attached to. The *Army List* from 1740 also contains details of Royal Marine officers. The main series of service records is ADM 196, 1770s to 1920s. An index to the service records of all Royal Marine officers commissioned between 1793 and 1970 is in ADM 313/110.

Other ranks

The basic arrangement of records of other ranks' service is according to Division (Portsmouth, Chatham, Woolwich, Plymouth, Royal Marine Artillery or Deal). There are three main series for records of service: description books, 1755–1940 (ADM 158); attestation forms, 1790–1925 (ADM 157); and records of service from 1842 (ADM 159). These registers are closed for 75 years. Indexes to these records are in ADM 313, and there is an incomplete card index of names to ADM 157 in the Research Enquiries Room. The effective and subsistence lists, 1688–1837 (ADM 96) list Royal Marines by company. If a marine is known to have served on board a particular ship then the ships' musters and pay lists in ADM 36–ADM 39, ADM 115 and ADM 117 (1667–1878) may contain some information; there are no musters after 1878.

For information on officers and men who enlisted less than 75 years ago, enquiries should be made to the Royal Marines Drafting and Record Office (see **Useful addresses**) who will supply information to the Royal Marine or to the next of kin (for a fee).

6.3.2 Other records

Operational records for the Royal Marines are included with the Royal Navy (see **6.2.2.**) Medal rolls are in ADM 171. Before the First World War they are arranged by campaign and then by ship. For the First World War they are arranged alphabetically and give the division and service number, which will help obtain service records. Later rolls are with the Naval Medal Office (see **Useful addresses**).

6.3.3 Colonial Marines

This corps was established during the Anglo-American War of 1812. The British forces offered to free any American slaves who joined them. Many enlisted in the West India regiments and the Royal Navy, but some eight hundred formed the 3rd, or Colonial, battalion of the Royal Marines. Black refugees who did not enlist were discharged in Bermuda and then moved to Nova Scotia; a few went to Trinidad.

The Colonial Marines were formed in May 1814, but most of the records do not begin until September 1814. There appear to be no attestation papers for these marines in ADM 157. The only lists of these marines are in the ships' musters (ADM 37), and in the effective and subsistence lists (ADM 96). For example, the musters for HMS Albion in ADM 37/5005 and 5006 and HMS Severn, ADM 37/5430, list Colonial Marines and Black American refugees for April 1814 to March 1815. ADM 96/366 includes the lists for the Colonial Marines for 1816. The corps was disbanded in August 1816 in Bermuda and the marines were settled in the military townships in Trinidad.

6.3.4 Further reading

PRO information leaflets
Bevan, *Tracing Your Ancestors*, Chapter 20
Rodger, *Naval Records for Genealogists*
Thomas, *Records of the Royal Marines*
Weiss, *The Merikens: Free Black American Settlers*
Weiss, 'The corps of Colonial Marines 1814–16'

6.4 Royal Air Force

The Royal Air Force (RAF) was formed on 1 April 1918 with the amalgamation of the Army's Royal Flying Corps (RFC) and Royal Naval Air Service (RNAS). Officers and men of these services were transferred to the RAF and joined by later recruits. Many West Indians served in the RAF and saw service in the First and Second World Wars. For example, many officers and soldiers of Trinidad Merchants' and Planters' Contingent and the Barbados Citizens' Contingent were repatriated from the RAF after the First World War. Lists of these contingents with information, such as name, rank, regiment, contingent, date of enlistment and remarks (eg gallantry awards, deaths, or pensioned etc), are found in CO 318/351 (West India Contingent Committee, 2 April 1919) and CO 28/294, fos 457–460.

Many thousands of West Indians joined the RAF during the Second World War. Most were ground crew but about 1,000 served as aircrew. Policy regarding recruitment in the West Indies is in CO 820. AIR 2/6876 contains two lists of West Indian RAF personnel:

1. A list of 298 British West Indians (including 50 officers) who attested in Canada for training as aircrew in about 1944. Information includes: number, name, colony, date attested, disposal (rank and date embarked for UK), colour (white or coloured), officer's personal number, rank, decorations, date appointed to commission and details of casualties.

2. Nominal roll of 340 coloured candidates (including 47 officers) of October 1944. This roll includes candidates from other colonies. It contains: colony, name, trade, date of attestation, notes such as awards and casualties.

6.4.1 Records of service

Officers

The career of RAF officers can be traced in the *Air Force List* and in the *Confidential Air Force List*, 1939–1954 in AIR 10. It is possible to identify to which squadrons officers were attached from the Air Force List between March 1920 and April 1939 and the confidential lists. AIR 76 contains records of service for officers in the RAF and RFC who were discharged before 1920. Service records of officers formerly in the RNAS for the period 1914 to March 1918 are in ADM 273.

Service records for those who joined after 1920 are still held by the Ministry of Defence. Ex-servicemen and next-of-kin may obtain details by writing to Ministry of Defence at RAF Innsworth (see **Useful addresses**); there may be a fee.

Other ranks

If an airman died or was discharged before the formation of the RAF on 1 April 1918 records of service will be under the army for RFC (see **6.1.1**) or Royal Navy for RNAS (see **6.2.1**) as appropriate. Service records for RFC and RNAS airmen who joined the RAF are in AIR 79, indexed by AIR 78; service information for RNAS airmen before 1 April 1918 is in ADM 188.

Service records of men whose service number is greater than 329001 or who served in the Second World War are with the Ministry of Defence (see **Useful addresses**); there may be a fee.

Number	Name	Colony	Date Attested	Disposal	Colour	Service No.	Rank	Decoration	Date	Status
605401	Daley L.H.	Trinidad	17.10.42.	A.W.C.L. 26.1.43.	N.T.	N/T				
605470	Short V.B.	"	28.7.42.	P/O Pilot U.K. 26.1.43.		136419	F/L	D.F.C. 24.11.44	4.12.43	Missing Edward killed 24.12.44
605470D	Ironsice V.H.M.	"	28.7.42.	Sgt. Pilot U.K. 5.1.43.		N/T				s.Erioweng Farrand 8.5.43.
605472	Ironsice T.M.	"	28.7.42	P/O. Pilot U.K. 31.5.44.		136417	F/L	– N/T	4.12.43	
605473	Proverbs I.G.	"	28.7.42.	Sgt. Pilot U.K. 51.43.		N/T				
605474	King H.A.	"	28.7.42.	Sgt. Pilot U.K. 9.3.43.		N/T				Missing (F6) 14.4.44
605475	Maingot K.P.	"	28.7.42.	Sgt. Pilot U.K. 28.3.43.		N/T				
605476	Pollard O.R.H	"	28.7.42.	Sgt. Pilot U.K. 5.1.43.		142428	P/O	–	25.2.44	Missing (F8) 1.7.44.
605477	Schenlt E.	"	28.7.42	P/O. PilotU.K. 23.11.44.		136411	F/L	– N/T	4.12.43	–
605478	Swan J.O.	"	28.7.42.	Sgt. Air Bomber U.K. 9.3.43.		54494	F/O(a)	–	26.4.44	Killed (F8) 29.4.43
605479	Deane D.S.	"	28.7.42.	Sgt. Pilot U.K. 5.7.43.	NT	N/T				
605480	Bain D.A.	"	28.7.42.	P/O. Pilot U.K. 24.11.44.		109015	P/O	–	20.10.44	
605481	Look Yan W.M.	"	28.7.42.	F/O PilotU.K. 26.1.43.		136422	F/O	– N/T	4.12.42	Killed (F8) 14.1.44.
605482	Graham O.W.	"	28.7.42	P/O. A/B. U.K. 9.3.43.		151341	F/O	!	19.3.43	
605483	Harris T.M.	"	28.7.42.	P/O. Pilot U.K. 5.1.43.		136418	F/L	!	4.12.42	P.O.W. 28.2.44
605484	Ross D.F.C.	B.W.I.	18.8.42.	P/O. Pilot A/3 S.F.T.S.		55238	F/O	!	3.9.43	
605485	Blair J.J.	Jamaica	28.10.42.	P/O. Nav. U.K. 15.2.44.	O.	55659	P/O	–	28.1.44	–
605486	Henry V.H.	"	28.10.42.	Dis.KR.652(22) 16.8.44.	C.	N/T				
605487	Cooper V.H.	"	28.10.42.	P/O. Nav. U.K. 15.2.44.	O.	154924	P/O	–	23.12.43	–
605488	Bacquie F.C.	"	28.10.42.	F/O. Pilot U.K. 1.1.44.	O.	153751	F/O	–	10.10.43	–
605490	Rodney A.S.	"	28.10.42.	Sgt. Nav. U.K. 11.7.44.	M.	N/T				
605491	Fouyat T.O.C.	"	28.10.42.	Killed -.12.43.	O.	N/T				Killed 7.12.43
605492	Brown R.D.	"	28.10.42.	P/O. W/AG. of AT Group 2.3.44	M.	154102	F/O	–	1.11.43	
605493	Campbell O.	"	28.10.42.	Dis.KR.652(23) 24.6.44.	M.	N/T				
605494	Hall J.M.	"	28.10.42.	Sgt. A/G. U.K. 4.4.44.	W.	N/T				
605495	Smith M.	"	28.10.42.	Sgt. A/G. U.K. 4.5.43.	O.	N/T				P.O.W. 22.1.44.
605496	Bartlett V.H.	"	28.10.42.	Sgt. A/G. U.K. 4.5.43.	O.	N/T				Death. Pres. 29.4.43.

Figure 16　Roll of West Indian RAF recruits who trained in Canada (AIR 2/6876).

6.4.2 Other records

Operational records

The majority of records relating to operations during the First World War are in AIR 1. This series includes squadron war diaries, recommendations for gallantry awards and details of officers' careers. Later operational records are in the Operations Record Books (ORBs): AIR 24 commands, AIR 25 groups, AIR 26 wings, AIR 27 squadrons, AIR 28 stations, and AIR 29 miscellaneous units. ORBs record daily events of the squadron and usually list flying personnel in each plane with the times they left and returned; casualties during operations are usually listed. ORBs sometimes include nominal rolls, lists of officers, and details of promotions, transfers and awards.

The PRO does not hold campaign medals rolls for the RAF, but medal rolls for the RFC are in WO 329 and RNAS in ADM 171. Other rolls are at RAF Innsworth (see **Useful addresses**).

Flying casualties are listed in the Operations Record Books. Deaths of RAF personnel, 1939–48, are held by the Office of National Statistics (see **Useful addresses**), who also hold registers of births, marriages and deaths, from 1920, of RAF personnel serving overseas.

6.4.3 Further reading

PRO information leaflets
Bevan, *Tracing Your Ancestors*, Chapter 21
Fowler, Elliot, Nesbit and Goulter, *RAF Records in the PRO*
Spencer, *Air Force Records for Family Historians*

6.5 Merchant navy

6.5.1 Records of service

Officers

Until 1845 there was no system of registering merchant navy officers. In 1845 a system of voluntary examinations of competency for those intending to become masters or mates of foreign-going ships was introduced. Masters and mates passing the voluntary examination between 1845 and 1850 should be found in BT 143.

In 1850 certificates of competency for foreign-going ships were made compulsory and gradually extended to other categories. These certificates were obtained either by long service (service) or by examination (competency). The certificates were entered into registers in numerical order. The details entered were name, place and date of birth, register ticket number, rank examined for or served in, and date and place of issue of ticket. Additional information can include names of ships sailed in, deaths, injuries and retirement. For the period 1845 to 1921 the indexes are in BT 127 and the registers to which they relate are BT 122 to BT 126, and BT 128. These registers are continued in BT 317, 1917–1968, and BT 352, 1910–1969.

Seamen

Registration of seamen was started in 1835 and continued until 1857. The registers and indexes are in BT 112 to BT 120. The details given include name, date and place of birth, date and capacity (rank) of first going to sea, capacity since, Royal Navy ships served on, and home address.

In 1913 registration was re-introduced, with the *Fourth Register*, 1913–1941, continuing from the *Third Register*, which ended in 1857. Unfortunately cards for 1913 to 1920 of the two main series (CR 1 and CR 2) were destroyed in 1969. Four series have been transferred on microfiche to the PRO; the original cards are now in the Southampton Archive Service (see **Useful addresses**). The four series are: BT 350 (CR 10), 1918–1921, an alphabetical series which gives date and place of birth, rating, discharge number, description, photograph, and list of ships served on by official number, and the date signed on. BT 348 (CR 1), 1921–1941, alphabetical, includes date and place of birth, discharge number, rating and description. BT 349 (CR 2), arranged numerically by discharge number, contains a list of ships on which the seaman served, usually by the ship's official number, and dates of signing on; some cards have photographs. The fourth series, BT 364, comprises a mixed selection of CR 1, CR 2 and CR 10 cards, extracted from the other series; it is arranged numerically by discharge number.

In 1942 the *Fifth Register*, the Central Register of Seamen, was started and continued until 1972. CR 1 and CR 2 cards of seamen who were serving in 1941 were removed from the *Fourth Register* and added to the *Fifth Register*. There are two series: BT 382 (CRS 10) Docket Books, 1941–1972, arranged alphabetically within a number of subseries. The information includes date and place of birth, discharge number, rating, qualifications, list of ships with date and place of engagement and discharge. BT 372 (CRS 3) Seamen's Pouches, c.1913–1972: when seamen were discharged some or all of their documents were placed in the pouches. The pouches are arranged by discharge number and the catalogue lists all pouches, with discharge number, surname, initials, and date and place of birth, and you can search for seamen on the catalogue by using their surname.

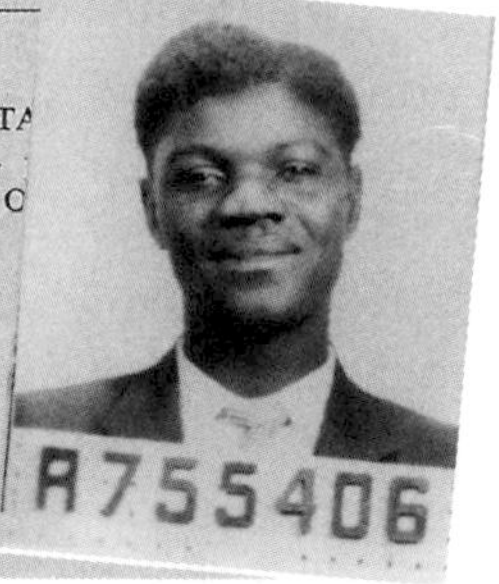

Figure 17   Seamen's papers for Edward Valentine Browne, born in Montserrat, discharge number R755406 (BT 372/2403). A list of the ships he served on is in BT 382/2136.

6.5.2 Other records

For officers and seamen who served before the start of registrations or whose record of service is incomplete or absent, you will need to use the musters, the agreements and crew lists. These lists contain brief details of the voyage and the crew, including the previous ship they served on. The agreements and crew lists include the town or county or country of birth. The musters run from 1747 to 1835, but only those for Shields, Dartmouth, Liverpool and Plymouth survive before 1800. Agreement and crew lists were started in 1835. All surviving musters and agreements before 1861 are in BT 98. Before 1854 these are arranged by the port of registration of the ship but later ones are arranged by the ship's official number, which can be found in *Lloyds Register of Shipping* and the *Mercantile Navy List*.

Most crew lists later than 1860 are in BT 99, but the PRO holds only a 10 per cent sample for the periods 1861–1938 and 1951–1989. Most of the remainder between 1863 and 1972 are in the Maritime History Archive (see **Useful addresses**). They will do a search for a fee if the name of the ship and the years of service are known. The National Maritime Museum holds the remaining 90% of crew lists for 1861, 1862 and all years ending in 5, except 1945. All agreements and crew lists for the period 1939–1950 are being transferred to the PRO and most will be in BT 380 and BT 381. With the exception of the 10% sample at the PRO and those for 1975 and 1985 at the National Maritime Museum, all other crew lists between 1973 and 1989 have been destroyed.

Records of the deaths of seamen are in BT 153–BT 157 1851–1890, and BT 334 1891–1972. For those who died in the First and Second World Wars you should check the Rolls of Honour in BT 339 and the Commonwealth War Graves Commission <www.cwgc.org> (see **Useful addresses**).

6.5.3 Further reading

PRO information leaflets
Bevan, *Tracing Your Ancestors*, Chapter 25
Imperial War Museum, *Tracing your Family History: Merchant Navy*
Smith, Watts and Watts, *Records of Merchant Shipping and Seamen*
Watts and Watts, *My Ancestor Was a Merchant Seaman*

7 Slaves

Chapter 1 gave basic guidance in discovering whether any of your ancestors were slaves and how to trace them (**1.3**). This chapter looks at taking this research further to try and place slave ancestors in their social and historical context.

Most records of slaves, including their births and deaths, are to be found amongst the personal papers of their owners. For the most part records relating to slaves in the PRO only occur when the slave or owner came to the attention of the Crown or the colonial authorities. Many of the sources for slaves have already been discussed under records of the Colonial Office (**Chapter 2**), slave trade (**3.5**), American Loyalists (**3.8**), births, marriages and deaths (**4.1**), wills (**4.3**), and plantation records (**5.3**).

The most important records for slaves in the Public Record Office are those of the Colonial Office, the slave registry and the Slave Compensation Commission. Colonial Office records relating to slaves are numerous and include reports of slave rebellions, reports of protectors of slaves, inhabitants of workhouses, slaves being given their freedom (manumission), numbers of slaves being imported and registration of slaves. Many of these returns are published in British Parliamentary Papers. Colonial newspapers contain notices of runaways, which name the slave and often give a brief physical description, as well as notices for slave auctions.

7.1 Slave Registry and the Slave Compensation Commission (T 71)

These records are the most important and comprehensive for slave research in the British West Indies for the period 1812 to 1834.

The slave trade from Africa to British colonies was made illegal from 1807, but the trade between the islands did not become illegal until 1811. On 26 March 1812 an Order in Council set up a registry of slaves in Trinidad as a means to monitor legally held slaves (PC 2/192). On 24 September 1814 an Order in Council extended the registry to St Lucia and Mauritius (PC 2/196). Between December 1816 and May 1817 the other colonies passed acts to set up their own registries. These were submitted to the Privy Council and approved on 9 January 1818 (PC 2/200).

A Colonial Office circular of 6 February 1818 (CO 854/1, fos 58–61) was sent to West Indian governors with instructions for the registrars of slaves. The instructions described how a register was to be maintained: each volume was to have an index to owners and plantations at the front, and on completion of each register the registrar was to compile, in a separate book, an index to slaves. I do not know if this later instruction was routinely carried out or even if it was practical in such colonies as Barbados and Jamaica, where few slaves had last names, since the index would contain pages of Williams or Marys. The PRO holds some indexes to slaves for St Lucia and Trinidad (in T 71), but in these cases most slaves had last names.

7.1.1 Slave Registry

The Slave Registration Act 1819 established a central registry of slaves in London, under the Commissioners of the Treasury. Under this act no slaves could be bought, sold or inherited if they had not first been entered in the appropriate island register. A Colonial Office circular of 1 May 1821 (CO 854/1, fo 94) instructed governors to forward duplicates of the slave registers and associated indexes to the London central registry. The records of the central registry are in T 71 and the original registers may survive in the relevant country archive or register offices.

The records of the central registry continue until 1834 when slavery was abolished. The registers are arranged by colony, then usually by parish, and many are arranged alphabetically by the name of the owner or estate. Many have separate volumes of indexes which should be looked at first, but most contain internal indexes to owners or estates and a few contain indexes to slaves.

The registers contain much information on the slaves and their owners. For slaves they give at least name, age, colour and country of origin. They record increases and decreases on the last registration period, including births and deaths, purchases, sales, inheritances and manumissions. For the owner they can be used to show deaths, marriages and details of family members. Slaves were bequeathed, inherited, and often given 'in right of marriage' when the wife's slaves became the property of her husband on marriage, and the wife is often named. Slaves of minors were registered by their guardians.

The information given in the registers differs between colonies. After the first registration most colonies only note increases and decreases in their numbers of slaves, although a few, such as St Lucia and Bermuda, list all slaves. Most registers list slaves by sex and age, but some, for example St Lucia and Trinidad, are arranged by family and record other family members such as brothers, sisters and cousins if on the same return. Mothers are occasionally noted in the returns, but fathers are rarely recorded.

7.1.2 Slave Compensation Commission

Slavery was abolished in 1834, under the Abolition of Slavery Act 1833, and a sum of £20 million was provided to compensate slave owners. The records of the Slave Compensation Commission are in T 71 and contain information which was used to compensate slave owners on the abolition of slavery. The Commission was terminated in 1842, but one of the commissioners was appointed to adjudicate on outstanding claims. The National Debt Office dealt with payment of claims, and the records are in NDO 4, West Indies Slave Compensation. Other compensation returns are in AO 14/37–48.

The records of the slave compensation commissioners are arranged by colony and include the following returns:

1. Valuers' returns: bound volumes of printed forms used for calculating compensation for slaves on 1 August 1834. The categories of slaves used for calculation were praedial (agricultural slaves), non-praedial (domestic slaves), children under the age of six, and the aged, diseased or otherwise non-effective. They may give the name of the estate.

2. Registers of claims: these are in claim number order, and show whether there was a claim or counter-claim. A claim was if the slave owners claimed for compensation; a counter-claim occurred if there was a dispute on the estate and other parties also claimed for compensation.

3. Indexes to claims: arranged by the initial letter of the surname, they give the surname, first names, the estate, the parish, and claim number.

4. Original claims and certificates: bound volumes in claim number order, with a copy certificate of claim and the original claim, these are signed and may include further details omitted from the registers, for example children born to slaves after the final registration.

5. Counter-claims: loose papers with evidence used in counter-claims, they may include much family material.

6. Adjudication in contested claims: ledgers in claim number order, with the name of the counter-claim, date of deeds, subject of counter-claim, name of claimant and remarks.

7. Certificates and awards: copy certificates issued by the compensation commissioners.

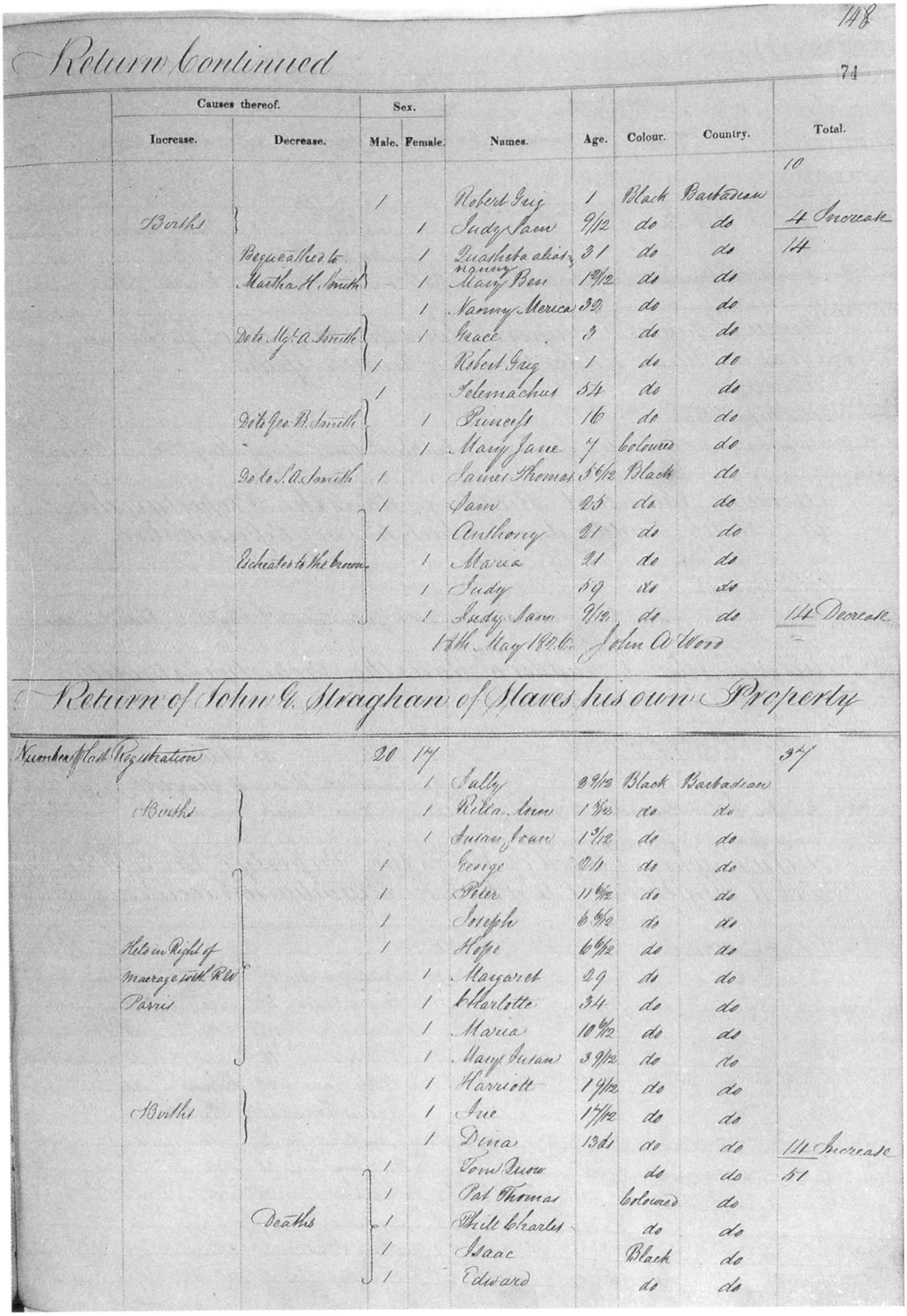

148

Return Continued

74

Causes thereof. Increase.	Decrease.	Sex. Male.	Female.	Names.	Age.	Colour.	Country.	Total.
								10
Births		1		Robert Grig	1	Black	Barbadian	
			1	Judy Sam	9/12	do	do	4 Increase
	Bequeathed to Martha H Smith		1	Quasheba alias Nanny	31	do	do	14
			1	Mary Ben	19/12	do	do	
			1	Nanny Merica	32	do	do	
	Do to Mgt A Smith		1	Grace	3	do	do	
		1		Robert Grig	1	do	do	
		1		Telemachus	54	do	do	
	Do to Geo B Smith		1	Princess	16	do	do	
			1	Mary Jane	7	Coloured	do	
	Do to S A Smith	1		James Thomas	56/12	Black	do	
	Escheated to the Crown	1		Sam	25	do	do	
		1		Anthony	21	do	do	
			1	Maria	21	do	do	
			1	Judy	59	do	do	
			1	Judy Sam	9/12	do	do	14 Decrease

14th May 1826. John A Wood

Return of John G. Straghan of Slaves his own Property

Increase.	Decrease.	Male.	Female.	Names.	Age.	Colour.	Country.	Total.
Number of last Registration		20	17					37
Births			1	Sally	28/12	Black	Barbadian	
			1	Rilla Ann	1 8/12	do	do	
			1	Susan Jean	1 7/12	do	do	
Held in Right of Marriage with R W Parris		1		George	24	do	do	
		1		Peter	11 6/12	do	do	
		1		Joseph	8 6/12	do	do	
		1		Hope	6 6/12	do	do	
			1	Margaret	29	do	do	
			1	Charlotte	34	do	do	
			1	Maria	10 6/12	do	do	
			1	Mary Susan	3 9/12	do	do	
			1	Harriott	1 9/12	do	do	
Births			1	Sue	1 7/12	do	do	
			1	Dina	13 ds	do	do	14 Increase
	Deaths	1		Tom Quow		do	do	51
		1		Pat Thomas		Coloured	do	
		1		Phill Charles		do	do	
		1		Isaac		Black	do	
		1		Edward		do	do	

Figure 18 Barbados: slave register, 1826 (T 71/537, p. 148). Return of James H Smith, who had died since the last return in 1823, showing slaves bequeathed. Return of John Grant Straghan who had married since the last return in 1823. His marriage to Rebecca Williams Parris, 24 April 1826, can be found on <www.familysearch.com>.

8. Parliamentary returns of awards: these were presented to Parliament and contain the amount paid. The volumes consist of two lists: List A, uncontested claims; and List B, litigated claims. List A gives the date of award, claim number, party to whom payment was awarded, number of slaves, and the sum payable. List B contains the same information as List A but does not include the number of slaves. The returns are in claim number order. These are published in the British *Parliamentary Papers*, session 1837–38 (215) volume XLVIII.331 (mfm 41.338–392).

9. Exhibits: sales of slaves 1823–1830, which were used by the commissioners to assess the values of slaves. They recorded returns of sales of slaves and are filed according to the type of sale, for example: of slaves alone, sales of slaves with land and buildings of estates, and sales through judicial process of the court of chancery, or through the marshal's office.

NDO 4, West Indies Slave Compensation, 1835 to 1842, contains payment books which show the sum awarded, the date of the Treasury warrant, and include the signatures of the claimants' representatives. There are also miscellaneous accounts, correspondence, and some death and marriage certificates.

7.2 Other records

7.2.1 Colonial Office returns

From the 1820s the Colonial Office requested various returns and reports relating to slaves and slavery. The first circular requesting this information, dated 3 July 1821 (CO 854/1, fos 95–96) asked for the following returns:

- Number of slaves imported and exported under licence since 1 January 1808, noting the year, number and sex of slaves imported/exported, and the place from which they were exported/imported.

- Return of manumissions (grants of freedom) since 1 January 1808.

- Return of marriages legally solemnized between slaves, as well as free Black and coloured people, since 1 January 1808.

- List of people committed to gaols or workhouses as runaways but who had declared themselves free since 1 January 1808, and account of how disposed.

- Return of slaves escheated (reverted in absence of owners) to the Crown since 1 January 1808.

- Return of population in each year since 1812 with numbers of births and deaths, distinguishing between white, free Black or coloured, or slave, by sex and age.

- Returns of all slaves taken or sold for debt from 1 January 1818.

There were several further circulars until 1830 to bring the information up to date. Some governors answered these circulars literally and provided nominal returns; others provided statistical information. The returns to the circular of 11 April 1826, including some lists of manumissions for 1821–1825, were published in the British *Parliamentary Papers*, session 1826–27 (128), vol XXII.43 (mfm 29.171–172). Examples of nominal returns mostly for 1821–1825 include: Jamaica, CO 137/162; St Vincent, CO 260/42; St Lucia, CO 253/17 (1818–1823) and CO 253/29 (1825–1830); Antigua, CO 7/14; Grenada, CO 101/66; and Barbados, CO 28/97.

7.2.2 Reports of protectors of slaves

The protectors of slaves were established to look into the welfare of slaves; later they became protectors of apprentices, during the period of apprenticeship c.1834–8, and protectors of immigrants or protectors of labourers, to oversee the welfare of East Indian immigrants. The reports include: punishments, criminal cases, births, deaths, marriages, free baptisms and manumissions. The PRO holds reports of protectors of slaves for the following:

1. Berbice, 1826–1834, CO 116/143–153
2. Demerara and Essequibo, 1826–1834, CO 116/156–163
3. St Lucia, 1826–1834, CO 258/5–15
4. Trinidad, 1824–1834, CO 300/19–33

Several of the reports were published in the British *Parliamentary Papers*: session 1829 (335) vol XXV.255 (mfm 31.153–155) and session 1830–31 (262) vol XV.1 (mfm 33.87–95).

I do not know whether all colonies had protectors of slaves but any surviving reports should be in the country's archive.

7.2.3 Manumissions (grants of freedom)

There were three main ways that slaves could be freed:

1. By deed. These were entered into the deeds register or into a separate manumissions register. Rights and fees for grants of manumission were dependent on local legislation.

Date of each Manumission	Names of Slaves Manumitted	Sex	Age	Price in lawful hand for Slaves Redemption	At whose expense Effected	Amount of Tax or Fine	Fees paid at the Register Office
1823							
January 29	Lucee	Female			Maria Grivous Rutherford		1.. 16..
" 30	Rose Elizabeth	Female			Eliz. Herraro		1.. 16..
" 30	Catherine	Female			Gabriel Rose		1.. 16..
February 1	Rose James	Female		110..	James Yard		1.. 16..
" 10	Nancy	Female			Andrew Marshall		1.. 16..
"	Maria Rose	Female	19 Years		Randall Righton		1.. 16..
"	Josephine	Female	17 Years		Ditto		1.. 16..
"	Maria Emilia	Female	40 Years		Ditto		1.. 16..
"	Fabian	Female	5 Years		Ditto		1.. 16..
"	Selerina	Female	6 Years		Ditto		1.. 16..
"	Augusta	Female	10 Years		Ditto		1.. 16..
"	Elisa	Female	35 Years		Ditto		1.. 16..
"	Jean Joseph	Male	13 Years		Ditto		1.. 16..
"	Maria Antoinette	Female	21 Years		Ditto		1.. 16..
"	Mont Rose	Male	15 Years		Ditto		1.. 16..
"	Maria Roselia	Female	27 Years		Ditto		1.. 16..
"	Kitetti	Female	28 Years		Ditto		1.. 16..
"	Angette	Female	30 Years		Ditto		1.. 16..
"	Joseph Henry	Male	13 Years		Ditto		1.. 16..
"	Maria Luca	Female	30 Years		Ditto		1.. 16..
" 19	Mary	Female		50..	Richard Curtis		1.. 16..
" 20	Sally Purcell	Female		100..	Charles Smith		1.. 16..
"	Walter Benjamin	Male		82.10..	Exor of Samuel Potts		2.. 2..
" 22	William Southwell	Male					
" 27	Joanna	Female					
"	Tracey McGillivray	Female					
"	Edward Lee	Male		300..	Samuel Ackle		3.. 12..
"	Georgeanna Lee	Female					
"	John Edwards	Male					
"	Joseph Jack	Male					
March 5	Alexandrine	Female	38 Years		Randall Righton		1.. 16..
"	Paul (alias Chotman)	Male	15 Years		Ditto		1.. 16..
" 7	Selina	Female	4 Years		Jacquo Homan		1.. 16..

Figure 19 Antigua: list of slaves manumitted, January to March 1823 (CO 7/14).

2. By act of the assembly or court. These were often granted for special services to the colony, such as provision of information leading to the suppression of slave revolts or the capture of rebels. These grants will be found in the appropriate acts or sessional papers; they should also be registered in the deeds registry. Some court records may be found in the PRO in original correspondence series, but most are to be found locally. Acts of the council or court could also validate or deny freedom and were also used by freedmen and women to confer certain rights. CO 139, Jamaican acts contain many references to slaves being manumitted and petitions from free people for entitlement to the same rights and privileges as English subjects, with certain restrictions. Edward Crawford has summarised Jamaican acts relating to individual slaves and free people between 1760 and 1810 at <www.rootsweb.com/~jamwg/actass1.htm>

3. By will. This did not guarantee freedom as conditions for freedom were often attached, such as reaching a certain age or on the death of the owner's widow. Also, since slaves were property, heirs could challenge requests for freedom.

The PRO does not hold deeds registers or comprehensive lists of those manumitted. The slave registers in T 71 will show those manumitted in the decreases column since these were a reduction to the slave population. Colonial Office circulars between 1821 and 1830 asked for information on manumission: some governors provided returns with names, while others were statistical. These are held in the relevant country's original correspondence series. Manumissions granted by the assembly may be found in the colonial acts or sessional papers. The final series of records in the PRO which make reference to manumissions are the reports of protectors of slaves (**7.2.2**). Locally, deeds registers may be in the archive or the register office.

7.2.4 Acts on the status, condition and treatment of slaves

Although these do not name individual slaves they can be used to identify the types of documents created and the officials who had some responsibility for the welfare or conduct of slaves and free people. For example a Jamaican act of 1787 (CO 137/87, fos 86–109) states that justices were to examine mutilated slaves, freed slaves and Indians (Amerindians) without tickets of freedom. Keepers of gaols or workhouses were to advertise names and other details of runaways in their custody in the gazette and chronicles. The clerk of the peace was to attend the trials of slaves and record proceedings. Tickets granted to slaves to work away from their owners or plantations were to be signed by the clerk of the vestry and to be entered into a vestry book for that purpose. Free Black and coloured people and Indians were to attend the vestry and give an account of how they had obtained their freedom which was to be entered into a vestry book. Therefore, for Jamaica it may be worth checking parish vestry minutes and records, newspapers and justices of the peace records for further information.

Further reading

See **1.3** for books on African-American genealogy.
Beckles and Shepherd (eds), *Caribbean Slave Society*
Burnard, 'Slave naming patterns'
Burroughs, *Black Roots*
Craton, 'Changing patterns'
Eltis, 'The traffic in slaves'
Gutman, *Black Family in Slavery and Freedom*
Handler, 'Slave manumissions'
Handler and Jacoby, 'Slave names and naming in Barbados'
Higman, *Slave Population and Economy in Jamaica*
Higman, *Slave Populations of the British Caribbean*
Patterson, *Sociology of Slavery*
Rose, *Black Genesis*

8 The colonial civil servant

The Personnel Division of the Colonial Office was established on 1 October 1930. Before that the Secretary of State had entire control of the appointments to all but the most subordinate official posts, which were appointed by the governor. Posts were under his 'patronage' and were dealt with in his private office by his private secretaries.

There were three classes of post, based on salary. Class 3 positions were the most subordinate and were appointed entirely by the governor. For class 2 posts the governor would make a provisional appointment which was reported to the Secretary of State for confirmation but seldom refused. The governor could recommend class 1 officers, but on the understanding that the Secretary of State had the final decision. From 1930 there was a gradual unification of the various colonial posts, such as administration, forestry, agriculture, medicine and railways, and the selection of candidates under the control of the Secretary of State was not just by grade, but also by post.

From 1900 there were the rudiments of a centrally managed service. When senior posts in the colonies became vacant, officials of the Colonial Office would review the records and qualifications of officers already in the service and make recommendations to the Secretary of State for filling vacancies by promotion or transfer. Promotion to higher posts was frequently made by transfer from one colony to another. Requests by officers already serving were considered before any posts were filled by outside recruitment, and promotion was based on official qualifications, experience and merit. The Secretary of State recruited and nominated candidates from outside to fill vacancies but could also offer a post in one territory to an officer already serving in another.

The records of the Patronage Department, 1867–1919, are in CO 429. The registers (CO 430) relate to both the department's original correspondence and original correspondence of individual colonies. Letters applying for specific appointments were recorded in the colonial registers. In 1930 the Personnel Division was established, comprising an Appointments Department, dealing with recruitment and training, and a Colonial Service Department, concerned with promotions and transfers, conditions of employment and pensions. The records of the Personnel Division, 1932–1952, are in CO 850 with the registers in CO 919. Those of the Appointments Department, together with some earlier correspondence from 1920 to 1952, are in CO 877 with the registers in CO 918.

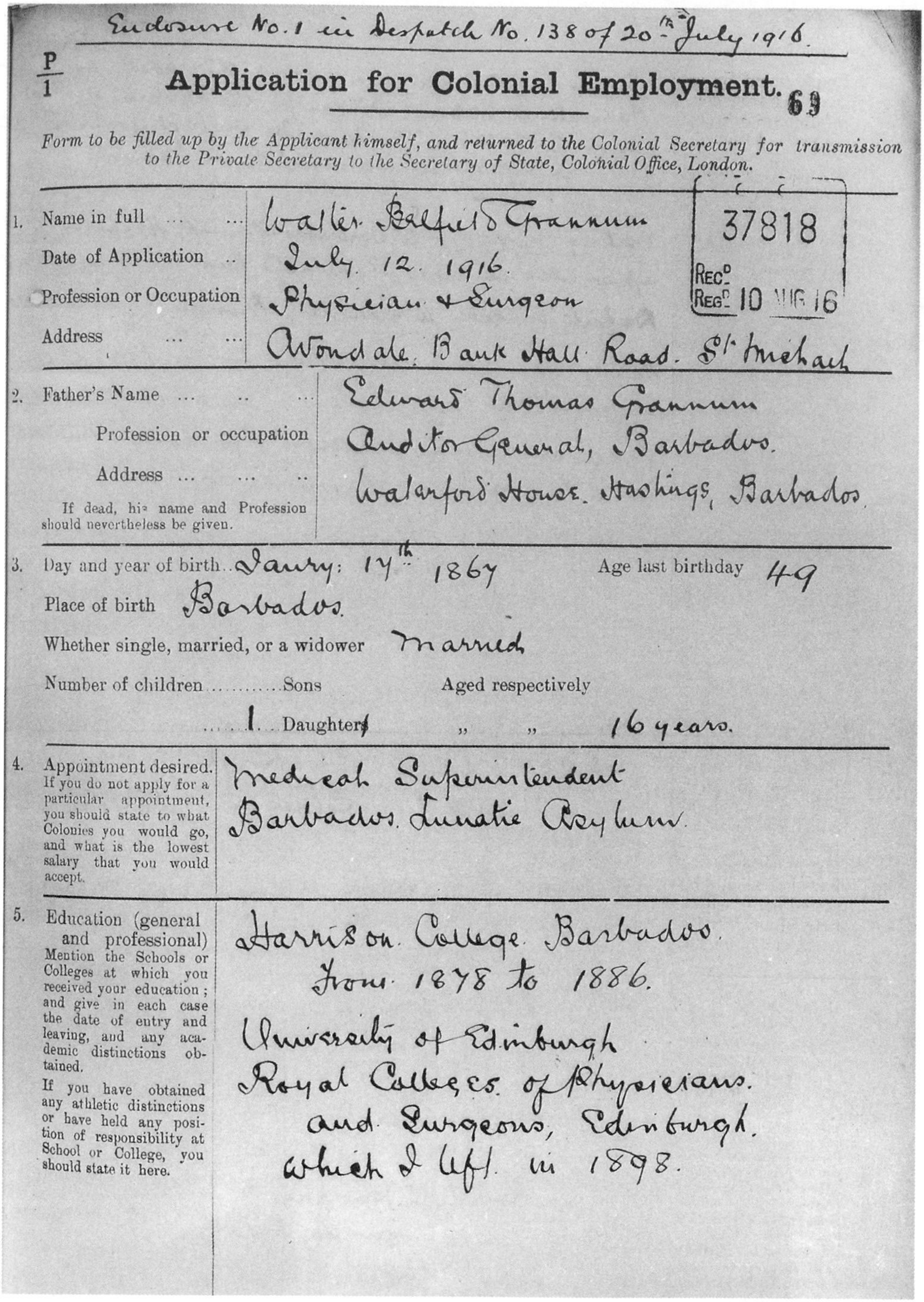

Enclosure No. 1 in Despatch No. 138 of 20th July 1916.

P/1

Application for Colonial Employment. 69

Form to be filled up by the Applicant himself, and returned to the Colonial Secretary for transmission to the Private Secretary to the Secretary of State, Colonial Office, London.

37818

RECD REGD 10 AUG 16

1. Name in full ... Walter Belfield Grannum
   Date of Application .. July. 12. 1916.
   Profession or Occupation Physician & Surgeon
   Address ... ... Avondale, Bank Hall Road. St Michael

2. Father's Name ... Edward Thomas Grannum
   Profession or occupation Auditor General, Barbados.
   Address ... Waterford House. Hastings, Barbados.
   If dead, his name and Profession should nevertheless be given.

3. Day and year of birth.. Jany: 17th 1867 Age last birthday 49
   Place of birth Barbados.
   Whether single, married, or a widower married
   Number of children ....Sons Aged respectively
   ....1...Daughter " " 16 years.

4. Appointment desired. If you do not apply for a particular appointment, you should state to what Colonies you would go, and what is the lowest salary that you would accept.
   Medical Superintendent Barbados Lunatic Asylum.

5. Education (general and professional) Mention the Schools or Colleges at which you received your education; and give in each case the date of entry and leaving, and any academic distinctions obtained. If you have obtained any athletic distinctions or have held any position of responsibility at School or College, you should state it here.
   Harrison College Barbados. from 1878 to 1886.
   University of Edinburgh
   Royal Colleges of Physicians and Surgeons, Edinburgh. which I left in 1898.

Figure 20 Application form of Walter Belfield Grannum for the post of Medical Superintendent, Barbados Lunatic Asylum, 1916 (CO 28/289, fo 69). He is the brother of the author's great-grandfather.

In 1945 the division was renamed the Colonial Service Division, and was changed again to the Overseas Service Division in 1954. The records of the Colonial Services Division and Overseas Service Division, 1948–1966, are in CO 1017. These are continued in OD 16, Department of Technical Co-operation and successors: Personnel Services: Registered Files, 1947–1972, and by FCO 79, Diplomatic Service Administration Office and Foreign and Commonwealth Office: Personnel Departments: Registered Files, 1966–1971, and FCO 77, Diplomatic Service Administration Office and Foreign and Commonwealth Office: Establishment and Organisation Department: Registered Files, 1966–1971.

The starting point for tracing a colonial civil servant's career is the *Blue Books* (2.6.1) of each colony. These list all public employees and provide such information as position, date of appointment, by whom appointed (or under what authority, for example, by letters patent) and annual salary. *Blue Books* also list government pensioners.

The annual *Colonial Office List*, 1862–1966, briefly describes the history and economy of each colony, and lists government employees with their salary. At the back of each volume there are potted biographies of senior colonial officials. The PRO does not hold applications or personal records for a civil servant appointed by the local government department; any records that survive will be in the relevant country. However, other useful information may be found in later (or earlier) *Blue Books* and in the government gazettes.

If he or she was appointed by the governor or the Colonial Office it is possible that information will be found in the PRO. Commissions for the most senior colonial officers, such as governor, chief justice, chief auditor, naval officer, and councillors were recorded in the Privy Council registers (PC 2 and PC 5), letters patent (C 66), and in the Colonial entry books (CO 324). The appointment was also announced in the *London Gazette* (ZJ 1) and in colonial gazettes. Colonial appointments by the Secretary of State 1819–1835 are in CO 323.

The original correspondence series for the relevant country and the several personnel and patronage department series contain appointments by the Secretary of State and governors' recommendations of appointment, promotion and transfer. They also include individuals' letters to the Secretary of State asking for appointment. Other records to be found include application forms, medical reports, and applications for leave, half pay, retirement and pension. Government gazettes give notification of appointment, promotion and transfer of officials, retirement, and leave of absence and resumption of duty.

Private papers of former colonial civil servants may survive in local and academic archives in the UK and elsewhere, for example in the countries where they had previously served. Check with the Historical Manuscripts Commission (see **Useful**

M 64

CIVIL ESTABLISHMENT.

OFFICE.	NAME.	Date of Appointment.	By whom Appointed, and under what Instrument.	Annual Salary. £ s. d.	From what Fund the Salary is paid.
JUDICIAL.					
Chief Justice...	Sir D. P. Chalmers	Jan. 22, 1879	By Letters Patent under Mandamus	2,500 0 0	
Puisne Judge	N. Atkinson	June 8, 1885	Royal Warrant	1,500 0 0	
Puisne Judge	W. A. M. Sheriff	May 5, 1887	Ditto	1,500 0 0	
Attorney General	J. W. Carrington, D.C.L., C.M.G. Q.C.	Dec. 12, 1888	Ditto	1,500 0 0	
Clerk to do.	C. Chawner	Feb. 19, 1886	Governor	215 0 0	
Solicitor General	Alfred Kingdon, Q.C.	Jan. 29, 1887	Royal Warrant	400 0 0	
Crown Solicitor	Vacant (a)			400 0 0	
REGISTRAR'S OFFICE.					
Registrar	E. H. G. Dalton	May 16, 1876	Governor	833 6 8	Fee Fund.
Accountant	J. Veecock	April 1, 1888	Secretary of State.	500 0 0	
1st Sworn Clerk and Notary Public.	W. O'Meara (b)	Oct. 1, 1882	Governor	500 0 0	
2nd ditto	M. P. Olton (c)	Oct. 1, 1882	Ditto	400 0 0	
3rd ditto	E. A. V. Abraham (d)	Nov. 1, 1882	Ditto	400 0 0	
4th ditto	J. A. Richardson (d)	Aug. 23, 1887	Ditto	400 0 0	
1st Assistant Sworn Clerk	J. A. King (e)	Aug 23, 1887	Ditto	350 0 0	
2nd ditto	J. Walls (f)	Feb. 1, 1890	Ditto	300 0 0	

REMARKS.

(a) Mr. F. Abraham acted throughout the year.
(b) Mr. O'Meara acted as Provost Marshal throughout the year.
(c) Mr. Olton acted as 1st Sworn Clerk from 1st Jan. to 16th July.
(d) Mr. Abraham and Mr. Richardson acted respectively as 2nd and 3rd Sworn Clerks from 1st Jan. to 16th July, and as 1st and 3rd from 17th July to the end of the year.
(e) Mr. King acted as 4th Sworn Clerk from 1st Jan. to 16th July and as 3rd from 17th July to 9th December.
(f) Succeeded Mr. Booch Booch Reece, who died 9th January. Salary £200 to £250.

M 65

CIVIL ESTABLISHMENT.

Amount of Fees, &c. during Fines, &c. during the Year 1890.	Whether a house for his personal Residence; or any Allowance for such be allowed.	Whether the Office is held in connection with any other office. If so, the amount of pay and allowance of such office.	Absent from the Colony during the year 1890.	Whether the Principal enjoy any, and what other Advantage or Profit, not required to be stated in the preceding Column.	Date of First Appointment under the Colonial Government.
		Judge in Vice-Admiralty Court.			Aug., 1869
			17th July to 29th Octr.		Nov. 25, 1874
			31st July to end of the year. (a)		1872
Patent Fees, £15 12. 6.					Decr., 1878
					Feb. 19, 1886
			17th July to 12th November. (b)	Private Practice. £200 per annum, as Counsel to Revenue Departments, in Revenue Cases. (b)	Jany., 1881
		Registrar of Vice-Admiralty Court. (Fees). Registrar General of Births and Deaths, £100.	17th July to end of year.	Commissioner of Affidavits, Fees.	1860
					Decr., 1860
				Commissioner of Affidavits, Fees.	1868
				Ditto	Jany., 1866
				Ditto	Jany., 1872
				Commissioner of Affidavits, Fees.	Decr., 1878
			10th to 31st Decr.		Jany., 1878
			1st to 31st Jany.		Feb., 1880

REMARKS.

(a) Mr. H. Kirke acted as Puisne Judge from 29th Oct. to end of year.
(b) Mr. C. S. Dawson acted as Solicitor General.

Figure 21   Guyana: *Blue Book of Statistics*, 1890, staff in the judicial department (CO 116/259, pp. M64–5).

addresses) or search their National Register of Archives <www.hmc.gov.uk> for surviving papers in the UK. Rhodes House Library (see **Useful addresses**) holds papers and interviews of former colonial officials collected from the 1960s under the Oxford Colonial Records Project.

Further reading

Bertram, *Colonial Service*
Colonial Office List
Fiddes, *Dominions*
Jeffries, *Colonial Empire*
Jeffries, *Whitehall and the Colonial Service*
Kirk-Greene, *Biographical Dictionary*
Kirk-Greene, *British Imperial Administrators*

9 Migration from the West Indies

West Indians are a migratory people. Many early settlers saw the islands as somewhere to make money and then retire to the UK. During the seventeenth and eighteenth centuries newly acquired islands were settled by people from other islands, for example settlers from St Christopher migrated to Nevis and the other Leeward Islands and Barbadians were among the first British settlers in Jamaica. West Indians have also migrated to other British and foreign countries in the West Indies, Central and South America and to the United States and Canada. Much of the migration within the Caribbean and to Latin and South America was seasonal to work on estates, whereas migration to Canada, the USA and further afield was often more permanent.

The records of these immigrants are to found among the usual sources used to find local ancestors such as wills, censuses, church records and civil registration returns. Until the British colonies and dominions such as Canada became independent, British West Indians as British subjects did not need to naturalize but in foreign countries they may have done so. The Foreign Office looked after British interests in foreign countries and some information regarding British West Indians can be found amongst FO series (see **9.2.1**).

9.1 Migration to the United Kingdom

Since the settling of the British West Indies, West Indians have returned or emigrated to Britain. Many planters and merchants sent their children to school in England and may themselves have retired to Britain, bringing their servants, including slaves, with them. West Indian merchant seamen, soldiers and sailors were often discharged in the UK and decided to remain, and many arrived as businessmen and students. Most settled in the major ports and major towns of London, Cardiff, Hull, South Shields, Liverpool, Edinburgh, and Glasgow. However, it was not until this century, and more especially after the Second World War, that large numbers of West Indians arrived in Britain.

Until 1962 there were few restrictions to British West Indian immigration: they were British subjects and did not need to naturalize when they emigrated to Britain to have full rights as a British citizen. To find information on West Indian ancestors in the United Kingdom you need to use the same sources as for the native population.

Country of origin is rarely mentioned except in the census, although wills may mention family members or property in the West Indies. There are many books and websites devoted to tracing families in Britain and some are listed in **Chapter 1.**

There are very few records of West Indian immigrants. With the exception of passenger lists in BT 26, 1878–1960, the British government did not register West Indians entering these shores. Passenger lists contain the names of people arriving in British ports from outside Europe and are arranged by the year and month of arrival, the port of arrival and the name of ship. The information given includes name, age, occupation and address in the United Kingdom.

It is important to note that these passenger lists are only for ships landing in Britain. Information received by the Ministry of Labour from the Colonial Office relating to West Indians arriving in 1955 (LAB 8/1902) shows that many arrived by train to London Victoria, via Calais and Dover, after disembarking from their ships at Continental ports such as Marseilles, Genoa and Vigo. The PRO does not hold these passenger lists, although they may survive in the country of arrival. There are no records of passengers who travelled by aeroplane.

West Indian communities and individuals can be found in the decennial censuses for Scotland and for England and Wales 1841–1901. Irish returns are less complete: none survive for 1861–91; the returns are incomplete for 1821–51; they are complete for 1901 and 1911. Census returns are arranged by address and there are few surname indexes. Censuses name members of a household with their relationship to the head of household, their age, sex, marital status, occupation and where born. Most family history societies have produced indexes to the 1851 census and many for other census years. Scots Origins <www.origins.com> has indexes and images for the 1881, 1891 and 1901 Scottish censuses. The 1901 census for England and Wales can be seen at <www.census.pro.gov.uk>, and the PRO has a project to digitize and index other censuses. The Church of Jesus Christ of Latter-day Saints (LDS) has produced a transcription of the 1881 census for Scotland, England and Wales on CD-ROM. All of these indexes can be searched by surname but the LDS and PRO indexes also allow you to search by place of birth.

Other examples include the records of the Committee for the Relief of Poor Blacks 1786–1787, whose aim was to set up a free colony in Africa for freed slaves. In return for relief poor Blacks (many of whom were runaway servants and slaves or discharged seamen and soldiers) signed up to be sent to Sierra Leone. The proceedings and other papers of the Committee, including lists of those receiving relief and the intending settlers are among papers in T 1/631–638 and 641–647.

In 1919 there were a number of racial riots in the major seaports, especially Liverpool, Cardiff, Hull, Glasgow and South Shields. Many Black and coloured seamen were

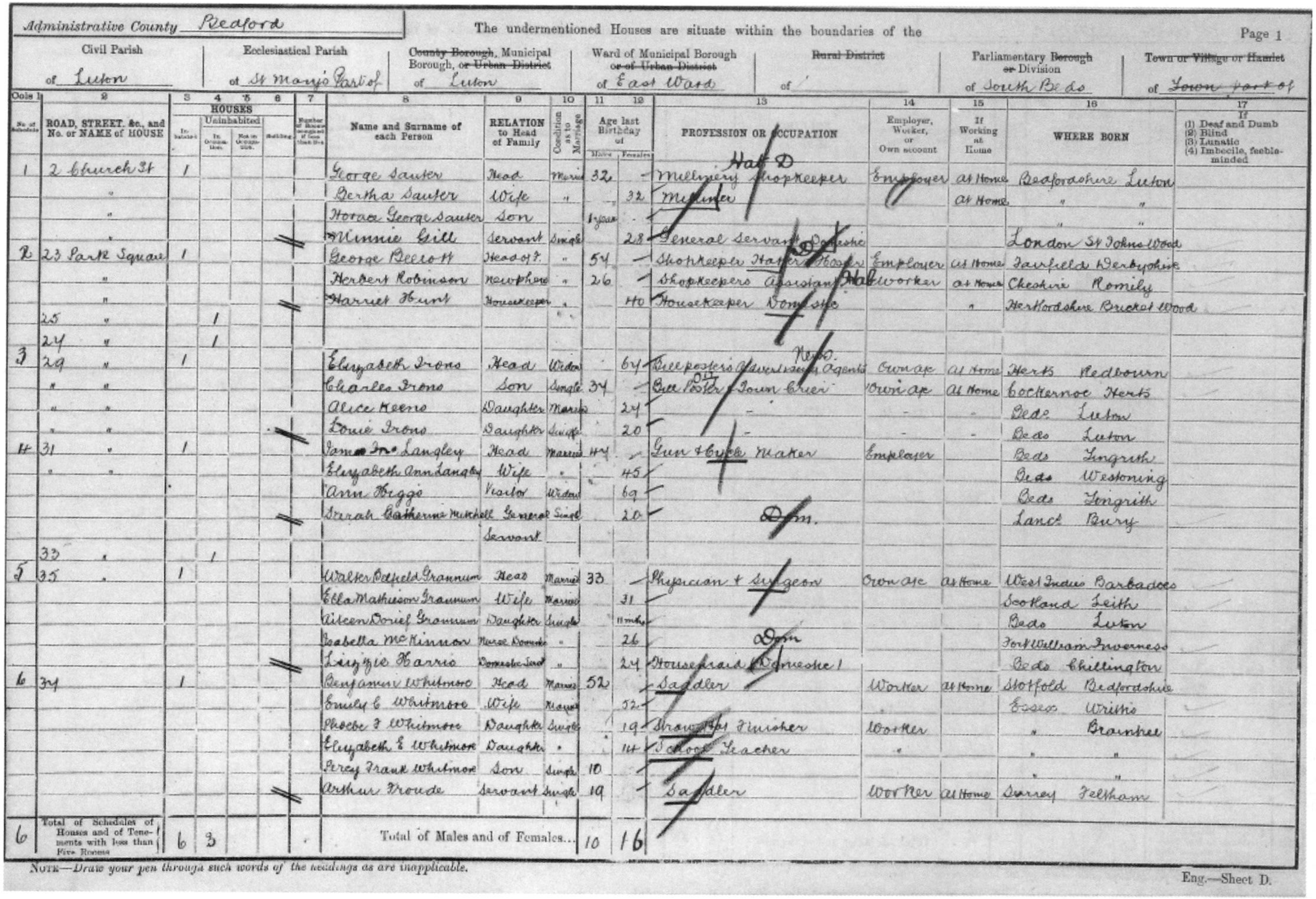

Administrative County Bedford

The undermentioned Houses are situate within the boundaries of the

Page 1

Civil Parish of Luton | Ecclesiastical Parish of St Mary's Part of | County Borough, Municipal Borough, or Urban District of Luton | Ward of Municipal Borough or of Urban District of East Ward | Rural District of | Parliamentary Borough or Division of South Beds | Town or Village or Hamlet of Town part of

1 No. of Schedule	2 Road, Street, &c., and No. or Name of House	3 Inhabited	4 Uninhabited: In Occupation	5 Uninhabited: Not in Occupation	6 Building	7 Number of Rooms occupied if less than five	8 Name and Surname of each Person	9 Relation to Head of Family	10 Condition as to Marriage	11 Age last Birthday: Males	12 Age last Birthday: Females	13 Profession or Occupation	14 Employer, Worker, or Own account	15 If Working at Home	16 Where Born	17 (1) Deaf and Dumb (2) Blind (3) Lunatic (4) Imbecile, feeble-minded
1	2 Church St	1					George Sauter	Head	Married	32		Millinery Shopkeeper	Employer	At Home	Bedfordshire Luton	
	"						Bertha Sauter	Wife	"		32	Milliner		At Home	" "	
	"						Horace George Sauter	Son		1 year					" "	
							Minnie Gill	Servant	Single		28	General Servant Domestic			London St Johns Wood	
2	23 Park Square	1					George Beecroft	Head of F.	"	54		Shopkeeper Hatter Hosier	Employer	At Home	Fairfield Derbyshire	
	"						Herbert Robinson	Nephew	"	26		Shopkeepers Assistant	worker	At Home	Cheshire Romily	
	"						Harriet Hunt	Housekeeper	"		40	Housekeeper Domestic		"	Hertfordshire Bricket Wood	
	25 "		1													
	24 "		1													
3	29 "	1					Elizabeth Irons	Head	Widow		64	Billposter's Advertising Agents	Own ac	At Home	Herts Redbourn	
	" "						Charles Irons	Son	Single	34		Bill Poster Town Crier	Own ac	At Home	Cockernoe Herts	
	" "						Alice Keens	Daughter	Married		24	–	–	–	Beds Luton	
	" "						Louie Irons	Daughter	Single		20		–	–	Beds Luton	
4	31 "	1					James Ino Langley	Head	Married	44		Gun & Cycle Maker	Employer		Beds Lingrith	
	" "						Elizabeth Ann Langley	Wife	"		45				Beds Westoning	
							Ann Biggs	Visitor	Widow		69				Beds Lingrith	
							Sarah Catherine Mitchell	General Servant	Single		20	Dom.			Lanc Bury	
	33 "		1													
5	35 "	1					Walter Belfield Grannum	Head	Married	33		Physician & Surgeon	Own ac	At Home	West Indies Barbados	
							Ella Matheson Grannum	Wife	Married		31				Scotland Leith	
							Aileen Dorief Grannum	Daughter	Single		11 mths				Beds Luton	
							Isabella McKinnon	Nurse Domestic	"		26				Fort William Inverness	
							Lizzie Harris	Domestic Servant	"		24	Housemaid Domestic			Beds Chillington	
6	34	1					Benjamin Whitmore	Head	Married	52		Saddler	Worker	At Home	Stotfold Bedfordshire	
							Emily E Whitmore	Wife	Married		52				Essex Writtle	
							Phoebe F Whitmore	Daughter	Single		19	Straw Hat Finisher	Worker		" Braintree	
							Elizabeth E Whitmore	Daughter	"		14	School Teacher	"		" "	
							Percy Frank Whitmore	Son	Single	10					" "	
							Arthur Froude	Servant	Single	19		Saddler	Worker	At Home	Surrey Feltham	
6	Total of Schedules of Houses and of Tenements with less than Five Rooms	6	3				Total of Males and of Females			10	16					

Note—Draw your pen through such words of the headings as are inapplicable.

Eng.—Sheet D.

Figure 22 1901 census for the family of Walter Belfield Grannum born in Barbados (RG 13/1517, fo 52). He served as Parochial Medical Officer for Luton between 1900 and 1902.

offered free passage back to West Africa and the West Indies but few took this up. CO 318/351 contains a list of 83 repatriated seamen on SS *Santille*, and HO 45/11017/377969 contains the names of 285 coloured West Africans and West Indians in Liverpool, of whom 59 were repatriated. Other reports and correspondence about the riots can be found in CO 318/349, CO 318/352, CO 323/814, and CO 323/848.

Following the 1919 and other racial riots the government tried to restrict coloured seamen from settling in the UK. The Special Restriction (Coloured Alien Seamen) Order 1925 allowed coloured British seamen discharged in the UK who could not prove their nationality to be treated as aliens who would have to register with the local police force. The PRO does not hold these aliens' registers but they may survive in local archive services.

On the outbreak of the Second World War many West Indians were recruited for war service in the United Kingdom, and many stayed after the war. Twelve hundred British Hondurans were recruited to fell timber in Scotland, and about 500 remained. Ten thousand West Indians, in particular Jamaicans, were recruited as ground crew in the Royal Air Force, and about 2000 remained. Many who served in the merchant navy also remained. After the war many of those who served in the RAF used their gratuities to pay for passages back to Britain (see **Chapter 6** for records of service personal and merchant seamen).

However, it was from 1948 with the arrival of the *Empire Windrush* on 21 June 1948 (the passenger list is in BT 26/1237) that significant numbers of West Indians migrated to the UK. During the 1960s British Rail, London Transport, hospital boards and the British Hotels and Restaurants Association recruited many West Indians. These schemes appear to have been conducted in the West Indies and there are few records in the PRO.

A Home Office report of 1963 summarises migration into the UK between 1840 and 1962 and uses figures from the censuses of people born in the Caribbean to show the growth of West Indian immigration (HO 344/76):

1891	8689	
1901	8680	
1911	9189	
1921	9054	
1931	8595	(there was no census in 1941)
1951	15301	
1961	171800	(Walvin, *Passage to Britain*)

The 1962 Commonwealth Immigrants Act restricted free migration to the UK from colonies and the Commonwealth except for students, visitors and dependants. People

IN-COMING PASSENGERS   P.M.2B. Second Schedule

Name of Ship S/S " ANTILLES "
Owner or Agent G. RASWELL CO Ltd
Date of Arrival 8th May 1955
Whence Arrived

NAMES AND DESCRIPTIONS OF **BRITISH COMMONWEALTH AND IRISH REPUBLICAN** PASSENGERS LANDED AT THE PORT OF

Names of passengers (Surname first)	Class of Travel	Port of Embarkation	Sex	Date of Birth (Adults 12 years and over)	Children between 1 and 12 years	Infants under 1 year	Married or Single	Address in the United Kingdom	Occupation	Country of which a citizen	Country of last permanent residence	Country of intended future permanent residence
HOPE Lyndon	3rd	TRINIDAD 183	M	53			M	Hotel LONDON	Agr.Instruct.	British	Brit.Guiana	Brit.Guiana
JOHNSON Wilfford	"	" 184	M	29			M	30 Bibblesdale SW 16 LONDON	Electrician 50	-"-	-"-	-"-
JOHNSON Eustache	"	" 185	M	31			S	St Evarns Rd W 10 LONDON	Labourer	-"-	-"-	England
JOSEPH Susanna	"	" 186	F	27			M	37 Collingham Pl.SW5 LONDON	Housewife 92	-"-	Grenada	-"-
KIARBAL M.R.	"	" 187	M	25			S	Hotel LONDON	Goldsmith	-"-	Brit.Guiana	-"-
KARM Mohammed	"	" 188	M	52			M	6 Roger St WC1 LONDON	Ophthalmic 64	-"-	-"-	-"-
LAVIA Albert	"	" 189	M	24			S	Hotel LONDON	Mechanic	-"-	-"-	Brit.Guiana
LARDY Dora	"	" 190	F	46			M	53 Oldfield Rd W LONDON	Housewife 91	-"-	Trinidad	England
FREMAUD Jamma	"	" 191	M	21			S	Bedford Pk W4 LONDON	Clerk	-"-	Brit.Guiana	-"-
OSBORNE Ashton	"	" 192	M	28			S	Holmwood Ave Stadfield Rd Stockwell SW4 LONDON	Stenographer 22	-"-	Trinidad	-"-
OTWAY Jensen	"	" 193	M	22			S	Degradine 5C Carlton Rd Tufnell Pk N7 LONDON	Teacher	-"-	Grenada	-"-
QUAIL Ignatius	"	" 194	M	29			S	Tufnell Pk N10 LONDON 191 Junction Road	Musician 27	-"-	Brit.Guiana	Brit.Guiana
RAMCCAR ra	"	" 195	F	29			S	48 Frances Rd BIRMINGHAM	Housewife	-"-	-"-	-"-
MCMILLY Adrian	"	" 196	M	26			M	16 Kilburn Pk NW2 LONDON	95	-"-	Trinidad	England
ROMAD John W.	"	" 197	M	25			S	44 Edbrook Rd W9 LONDON	Civil Servant	-"-	Brit.Guiana	Brit.Guiana
SALAMET audra	"	" 198	F		9		S	40 Bromham Gdn Earlscourt LONDON SW5	none	-"-	Trinidad	England
SOLARZANO Mary J.	"	" 199	F	47			M	same address	Dressmaker	-"-	-"-	-"-
SMITH Adalbert	"	" 200	M	45			S	149 Nth Church Rd Palington LONDON N1	Civil Servant 20	-"-	-"-	Trinidad
SMITH Audrey	"	" 201	F	55			S	27 Grandly LONDON	Proprietress	-"-	-"-	-"-
THOMSON Merla	"	" 202	F	26			M	Oldfield Rd NW10 WILLESTEN	Housewife 92	-"-	-"-	England
TAITT George	"	" 203	M		9		S	Hotel LONDON	Schoolboy	-"-	Brit.Guiana	Brit.Guiana
THOMAS Victoria	"	" 204	F	45			S	90 Brittania Walk N1 LONDON	Seamstress 31	-"-	Trinidad	England
WHITEMAN John	"	" 205	M	23			S	46 Palace Rd Tulse Hill LONDON	Student	-"-	Trinidad	-"-
ALLEYNE Venis	"	BARBADOS 206	M	22			S	30 Sutherland Pl.LONDON W2	Mason 40	-"-	Barbados	-"-
BISHOP Doris	"	" 207	F	33			M	46 Hogreth Rd Earlscourt LONDON	Seamstress	-"-	-"-	-"-
BISHOP Kathleen	"	" 208	F		5		S	same address	none	-"-	-"-	-"-
GOTING Ursula	"	" 209	F	45			S	5W Cromwell Rd Earlscourt LONDON	Housewife	-"-	-"-	-"-
REID Miriam	"	" 210	F	33			S	13 Edith Rd W 1R LONDON	Teacher 01	-"-	-"-	-"-
CHANDRES Catherine	"	P.A PITRE 211	F	23			S	Hotel LONDON	-"-	-"-	Antigua	-"-
JOSEPH Noami	"	" 212	F	25			S	Hotel LONDON	Nurse 06	-"-	-"-	-"-
EVANS Norma Ann	1st	BARBADOS 213	F	20			M	53 London Rd STANMORE Mid.	Housewife	-"-	Caracas	-"-

* If in the British Isles state whether England, Scotland, Wales, Northern Ireland or the Republic of Ireland.
† Use abbreviations, e.g. Holiday, Leave, Tourism, Family, etc., V ; Business Trip, B.V ; Diplomatic, D ; In transit through U.K. ; I.T.

Figure 23   Passenger list for SS *Antilles*, arrived Plymouth, 8 May 1955 (BT 26/1332).

BRITISH NATIONALITY ACT 1948

CONFIRMATION OF REGISTRATION AS A

CITIZEN OF THE UNITED KINGDOM AND COLONIES

174547

Jamaica

This certificate confirms that the person named below, being a British subject or Commonwealth citizen or a citizen of the Republic of Ireland, has been registered as a citizen of the United Kingdom and Colonies under section 6 (1) of the British Nationality Act 1948 as amended by section 12 (2) of the Commonwealth Immigrants Act 1962.

NOTES (1) This certificate is valid only if it bears the embossed stamp of the Home Office.

(2) The personal details are those supplied by the person himself and this document does not certify their accuracy. They are, however, important for the purpose of identification and *any unauthorised alterations may render this certificate invalid.*

Full name	EVA JULIET BOROUGH

Name at birth if different from above

Full address	11, BRAESIDE. PUTNOE, BEDFORD. BEDS.	Usual signature of applicant	*E M Borough.*

Place and country of birth KINGSTON, JAMAICA. W.I.

Date of birth 12th SEPTEMBER, 1908.

Whether single; married; a widower, a widow; divorced (State which) SINGLE.

Details of applicant's father, and of applicant's wife or husband

	Full name	Place of birth	Country of birth	Date of birth	If dead, date of death
Applicant's Father	KENNETH EUGENE BOROUGH.	KINGSTON	JAMAICA W.I.	25th SEPT. 1871	12th AUG 1959.
Applicant's Wife or husband					

Issued by **K. CULLUM**

Date – 2 SEP 1971

by direction of the Secretary of State

HOME OFFICE, LONDON.

Ref. No. B. 24 0174

Figure 24 Certificate of registration for Eva Juliet Borough, born Jamaica, certificate number R1/174547, issued 2 September 1971 (HO 334/1817).

who did not have a passport issued in the UK or were not registered as Citizens of the UK and Colonies had to obtain labour vouchers from the Ministry of Labour in order to be granted entry. There were three categories of vouchers: 'A' for those with a definite offer of a job, 'B' for those who held certain professional qualifications or skills, and 'C' was a general category of vouchers issued in order of application, with priority given to those with war service. A selection of vouchers issued to Commonwealth subjects, including rejected, returned or unused vouchers, are in LAB 42, 1962–1972, and continue, together with foreign applications, in LAB 48, 1973–1975. The 1962 Act also allowed, for the first time, for Commonwealth subjects to be deported, for example HO 372/29 1962–1963 contains recommendations for deportation, and HO 344/73 1962–1963 contains cases of deportation.

Some provisions and restrictions of the 1962 Commonwealth Immigrants Act were amended under the 1968 Commonwealth Immigrants Act which gave right of entry to people with a parent or grandparent who had been born in the UK. This act effectively excluded most Black and coloured West Indians since they were unlikely to fulfil this condition. This was developed further under the 1971 Nationality Act, which reduced the status of Commonwealth citizens to that of aliens unless at least one parent or grandparent was a citizen of the UK and colonies through birth, naturalization or registration. Correspondence between governors and the Colonial Office on the subject of citizenship status for newly independent West Indian countries seems to imply that only legitimate children had right of citizenship since this right was through the father. Information leaflets on the 1981 Nationality Act and immigration can be obtained from the Home Office, Immigration and Nationality Directorate (see **Useful addresses**) and online at <www.homeoffice.gov.uk> and <194.203.40.90>

Under the 1948 Nationality Act, people from the self-governing Commonwealth, for example Canada and India, could register as Citizens of the UK and Colonies. This was extended under the 1962 Commonwealth Immigrants Act to include the colonies. Applications for registration as Citizens of the UK and Colonies 1948–87 are in HO 334. The information includes: name, name at birth if different, address, date and place of birth, marital status, father's name and date and place of birth, and whether he was still alive. Certificates from 1980 are briefer and include only name, name at birth if different, address, and place and date of birth. The PRO does not hold indexes to these registrations; to obtain the registration number please write to the Home Office, Immigration and Nationality Directorate (see **Useful addresses**).

Many papers reflecting the concerns of Parliament and government departments about immigration in general and coloured immigration in particular are to be found among the records of the Cabinet Office, the Home Office, the Colonial Office, the Commonwealth Relations Office, the Foreign and Commonwealth Office, and the Ministry of Labour. The most useful series which describe Commonwealth migration, employment conditions, racial discrimination, and the 1962 and later immigration and nationality acts are listed below. There are also the original correspondence series for the individual countries.

AST 7	Unemployment Assistance Board and successors: Administration of Assistance Schemes, Registered Files	1910–1972
CO 318	West Indies General Correspondence	1624–1951
CO 876	Welfare Department, later Students Department: Registered Files	1942–1952
CO 1006	Colonial Office: Working Party on The Employment in The United Kingdom of Surplus Colonial Labour: Minutes and Papers	1948
CO 1026	Legal Department: Registered Files	1951–1967
CO 1028	Students Department, later Students Branch: Registered Files	1952–1962
CO 1032	General Department	1950–1968
CO 1031	West Indian Department	1951–1967
CO 1042	West Indies Development and Welfare Organisation: Registered Files	1938–1958
DO 175	Commonwealth Relations Office and Commonwealth Office: General Department and successors: Registered Files, Migration	1954–1967
DO 200	Commonwealth Relations Office and Commonwealth Office: West Indies Department and Atlantic Department: Registered Files, Commonwealth West Indies	1961–1967
FCO 50	Commonwealth Office and Foreign and Commonwealth Office: Migration and Visa Department and predecessor: Registered Files	1967–1971
FCO 63	Commonwealth Office and Foreign and Commonwealth Office: North American and Caribbean Department and Caribbean Department: Registered Files	1968–1977
HO 213	Aliens Department: General (GEN) Files and Aliens' Naturalization and Nationality (ALN and NTY Symbol Series) Files	1914–1984
HO 230	National Advisory Committee for Commonwealth Immigrants: Minutes and Papers	1963–1965
HO 231	National Committee for Commonwealth Immigrants: Minutes and Papers	1964–1968
HO 376	Home Office: Racial Disadvantage (RDI Symbol Series) Files	1963–1981
HO 344	Home Office: Commonwealth Immigration (BSI and CWI Symbol Series) Files	1949–1979
HO 352	Home Office: Aliens, General Matters	1928–1975

	(ALG Symbol Series) Files	
HO 355	Home Office: Immigration Branch: AIB and IBR	1922–1973
	(Symbol Series) Files	
HO 394	Home Office: Immigration (IMG Symbol Series) Files	1960–1975
LAB 8	Ministry of Labour and successors: Employment Policy,	1907–1979
	Registered Files (EM series and other series)	
LAB 26	Ministry of Labour and National Service and successors:	1940–1956
	Welfare Department	

Many UK archives services are identifying material for the study of Black, including Caribbean, history in their localities, and some information can be found via the Access to Archives database at <www.a2a.pro.gov.uk>. The CASBAH (Caribbean Studies and Black and Asian History) Project is identifying and mapping national research resources for Caribbean studies and the history of Black and Asian people in Britain, and the results of this project will be made available at <www.casbah.as.uk>. The PRO will be hosting two online exhibitions relating to Caribbean immigration: *Moving Here*, and *Black and Asian Peoples in Britain, 1550–1850*.

9.1.1 Further reading

PRO information leaflets
Bevan, *Tracing Your Ancestors*, Chapter 12
Byron, *Post-war Migration*
Carberry and Thompson, *A West Indian in England*. Draft copies are in CO 875/59/1
Diamond and Clarke, 'Demographic patterns'
File and Power, *Black Settlers*
Foner, *Jamaica Farewell*
Francis, *With Hope in Their Eyes*
Fryer, *Politics of Windrush*
Fryer, *Staying Power*
Hoskins, *Black People*
Kershaw and Pearsall, *Immigrants and Aliens*
Layton-Henry, *Politics of Immigration*
Martin, *Incomparable World*. Novel of 1790s London
Panayi, *Racial Violence*
C. Phillips, *The Final Passage*. Novel about 1950s migration
M. Phillips and T. Phillips, *Windrush*
Selvon, *The Lonely Londoners*. Novel of West Indians in 1950s London
Sewell, *Keep on Moving*
Shyllon, *Black People in Britain*
David Steel, *No Entry*
Walvin, *Black and White*

Walvin, *Passage to Britain*
Western, *Passage to England*
<www.bbc.co.uk/history/community/multicultural/> articles on multicultural Britain
<www.channel4.com/blackhistorymap/> a gateway to websites about Black and Asian
   history across the UK

9.2 West Indian migration outside the United Kingdom

West Indians have not only migrated to Britain but to other British colonies and
Commonwealth countries as well a to foreign countries, especially in the Caribbean
and throughout the Americas. Before the nineteenth century merchants and
adventurers moved with their servants and slaves to new British colonies, for
example people from St Christopher moved to Nevis and the other Leeward Islands
as they became British during the seventeenth and eighteenth centuries and
Barbadians settled in South Carolina and Jamaica in the seventeenth century.

From 1834, with the abolition of slavery, there were much larger movements of people
who migrated for land and work to Trinidad and British Guiana, especially from the
more populated countries such as Barbados and Jamaica. British West Indians also left
their countries to work in non-British countries in the Caribbean and in Central and
South America, such as Costa Rica, Nicaragua, Cuba, the Netherlands Antilles, the
Dominican Republic, and especially Panama. In the 1850s many West Indians, mainly
from Barbados and Jamaica, worked on the trans-isthmian railway in Panama;
between 1880 and 1914 more than 100,000 left to work on the Panama Canal.
However, the United States and Canada saw the greater number of West Indian
migrants, who arrived for education, work and to buy land.

Information relating to immigration, recruitment schemes, deportations, welfare,
relief, distressed British subjects, West Indian relations, overseas births, marriages and
deaths of British subjects, criminal activities, and working conditions is to be found
among the records of the Colonial Office, Dominions Office, Commonwealth
Relations Office, Commonwealth Office and Foreign Office (before 1967), and the
Foreign and Commonwealth Office (from 1967). The International Labour Division
and Overseas Department of the Ministry of Labour, 1923–1979 (LAB 13) contains
reports from labour attachés on recruitment schemes and employment conditions.
The Labour Gazette contains advertisements and articles about overseas work, and
the PRO holds copies between 1893 and 1952 in ZPER 45. However, most surviving
records relating to individual immigrants will be found in the country of settlement.

The records of the Colonial Office are described in **Chapter 2** and information can be
found in the original correspondence series for the countries of departure and
settlement. Information is also found in the records of the West Indian department

5. Ann Lynch,Born at St Almo Hill,Black River District,
    about 60 years ago. Father was Thomas Lynch and
    mother,Johanna Chambers,same address;christened
    at St Mary's Church;came to Panama about forty
    years ago.
    Mental diagnosis: Psychosis associated with arterio
    sclerosis. Is feeble and requires Hospital treat-
    ment.

6. Catherine Tucker: Born in Bellfield District
    St Mary's,christened about 1860 at the Baptist
    Church,Annotto Bay by Rev.Byron. Married Ebenezer
    Watts,at the Baptist Church,same place,in 1893.
    Sisters,Eugenia Campbell,Marcella Palmer,albertha
    and Beatrice Tucker who were living at Annotto
    Bay. Came to Panama in April,1907. Police permit
    was signed by Inspector Dunham,Sutton St. Station,
    Kingston.
    Diagnosis: Dementia precox - demented,requires
    Hospital treatment.

7. Alice Martin: Born about April,1895' at Port
    Antonio (Fayne Road District);father,Samuel
    Niemeyer Martin,Fellowship P.O.,Port Antonio;
    mother,Eliza Knowland,christened at Baptist
    Church,Port Antonio;worked for Mrs Millie
    Abram and Mrs Euginia Scott,Sentry Hill,Port
    Antonio. Arrived at Bocas del Toro in April
    1912. Her husband,Bert.Wright is domiciled at
    Bocas del Toro.
    Diagnosis: constitutional inferiority-may be
    tried outside the Asylum with proper care.

8. Henrietta Roden: (Alias Henrietta O'Neal),born
    December 1880 at Port Royal Mountain,Dallas
    Castle,Queen's Hill;father,Robert O'Neal;mother
    Letitia O'Neal;christened at the Wesleyan Church
    in Stupport district,St Andrews;marriedMay
    10,1894 to Alexander Roden at the Registrars
    Office,Kingston;worked for Sargent Kildier at
    Foster Lane and Barry St.. Arrived in Colon
    7th July,1906. Permit was signed by sar geant
    Kildier of Sutton St.Station.
    Diagnosis: Dementia precox - has lucid intervals.
    Is pugnacious at times;may be tried outside the
    Asylum in quiet surroundings.

Figure 25 Panama: list of British West Indians in the Lunatic Asylum, Canal Zone, Panama, 1918
(CO 318/346, Foreign Office, 25 April 1918).

(CO 318 and CO 1031), the General department (CO 323 and CO 1032) and the West Indies Development and Welfare Organisation files (CO 1042).

The Dominions Office and Commonwealth Relations Office contain information relating to the self-governing Commonwealth countries such as Canada, Newfoundland, Australia and New Zealand, and West Indian counties which became independent before 1967. The most important series are:

DO 35	Original Correspondence	1926–1971
DO 175	General Department and successors: Registered Files, Migration (MIG Series)	1954–1967
DO 200	West Indies Department and Atlantic Department: Registered Files, Commonwealth West Indies (WID Series)	1961–1967

For separate country series, please see the catalogue (under DO) and Anne Thurston's *Records of the Colonial Office* (see **Bibliography**).

9.2.1 Records of the Foreign Office

Records relating to West Indian migration and settlement in non-British countries can be found in Foreign Office (FO) series. There are three types of archives: general correspondence, embassy and consular archives, and consular archives.

General correspondence

These papers were created and accumulated in the Foreign Office and are composed of original correspondence and reports from British officials abroad, and drafts of outgoing correspondence. Until 1906 these are arranged by country (FO 1 to FO 84). From 1906 Foreign Office general correspondence is filed in subject series. The most important series is FO 371, Foreign Office political departments. Other series include FO 369, consular departments, which contains references to the protection and welfare of British subjects abroad such as the disposal of estates and wills, and FO 372, treaty departments, which includes papers on naturalization, extradition and passports.

These records can be accessed by a series of indexes and registers. Before 1906 you need to use FO 605 and FO 566. There is a card index for the period 1906 to 1919, and a printed index (FO 409) for the periods 1920 to 1953, and 1959; later indexes are with the Foreign and Commonwealth Office. Kraus International Publications has published the indexes for the period 1920 to 1951 in 131 volumes (1969–82). With the exception of FO 605, which was compiled by the Foreign Office from the records, these indexes have been compiled from the Foreign Office's registers of incoming correspondence and not all records described in them have survived.

Embassy and consular archives

These papers were created by the British embassies. They contain original correspondence received from the Foreign Office, local correspondence from other embassies and consulates, and with the government of the relevant foreign state. These records include wills, naturalizations, passport registers, and papers of the disposal of estates. For example, FO 986 embassy and consular archives for Panama City includes many records on the estates of British West Indians, many of who are named in the catalogue.

Consular archives

These are mainly registers held by the consul, such as registers of births, marriages and deaths of British subjects under the Consular Marriages Act 1848 (see **9.2.3**), and passport registers.

The Foreign and Commonwealth Offices merged in October 1967 and the records of the Foreign and Commonwealth Office are in FCO series. These are arranged by broad geographical regions and subject series. For example, most records relating to West Indian migration are in FCO 50, Migration and Visa Department and predecessor: Registered Files, 1967–1971.

Before 1782 the records of foreign affairs are in State Papers Foreign (SP) series.

9.2.2 Immigration records

Until the First World War most people did not need passports to emigrate or immigrate, although from the 1880s West Indians needed passports or national identity cards to enter Venezuela. Passport applications or registers may survive in the relevant archive or may still be with the issuing department. However, some registers of passports issued by British embassies and consuls survive in Foreign Office consular archives series.

The PRO does not hold passenger lists for ships which did not land in the UK. Outward passenger lists may survive in the emigrant's country and inward passenger lists may survive in the country of settlement. For example, passenger lists to the USA from 1820 are held by the National Archives and Records Administration (address in **Chapter 13**). Between 1892 and 1924 some 22 million passengers and ships' crews came through Ellis Island and the Port of New York, the index to the passenger lists with images of most lists is available online at <www.ellisislandrecords.org>. Passenger lists to Canada between 1865 and 1935 are held by the National Archives of Canada (see **Useful addresses**).

9.2.3 Registers of births, marriages and deaths

A Foreign Office circular to embassies and consuls dated 1 May 1816 (FO 83/116, fo 16) instructed them to 'keep an authentic and complete record of marriages celebrated in His Majesties residences and Foreign Courts' The returns, which also included births and deaths, were to be sent to the London Registry of the Bishop of London. This registry, know as 'International Memoranda' has been transferred to the Guildhall Library (see **Useful addresses**).

From 1849, under the Consular Marriages Act 1849, consular staff were to register marriages of British subjects in two duplicate registers. One register was sent to the General Register Office (GRO) and is held by the Office for National Statistics (see **Useful addresses**). If nationality is recorded the GRO forwards copies to the appropriate register office in Scotland and Northern Ireland; but the GRO has advised me that they do not forward West Indian registrations to the appropriate register officers. The second register was sometimes sent to the Foreign Office and many have been transferred to the PRO in embassy, legation and consular archive series.

In November 1849 the Foreign Office issued instructions to the consuls to register births and deaths; this instruction was extended to legations in 1859. The legations and consuls were to keep one register for recording births and deaths and to submit annually certified copies of entries to the GRO. When complete the register was forwarded to the Foreign Office and may have been transferred to the PRO.

The PRO also holds miscellaneous non-statutory foreign returns of births, marriages and deaths for 1627 to 1969 in RG 32–RG 35; these are indexed in RG 43. These registers were originally held by the GRO and comprise correspondence relating to events, certificates issued by foreign governments and churches, copies of entries in registers kept by British embassies, incumbents of English churches and chaplains, and documents sent by individuals for safe keeping.

Lists of the countries covered by the International Memoranda, Foreign Office registers and non-statutory registers are in the Guildhall Libary's *The British Overseas* (see **Bibliography**) and records in the PRO are covered in section 4.15 of *Tracing Your Ancestors*.

9.2.4 Further reading

PRO information leaflets
Anderson, *Caribbean Immigrants*
Atherton, 'Never complain, never explain'
Bevan, *Tracing Your Ancestors*, Chapters 4 and 13

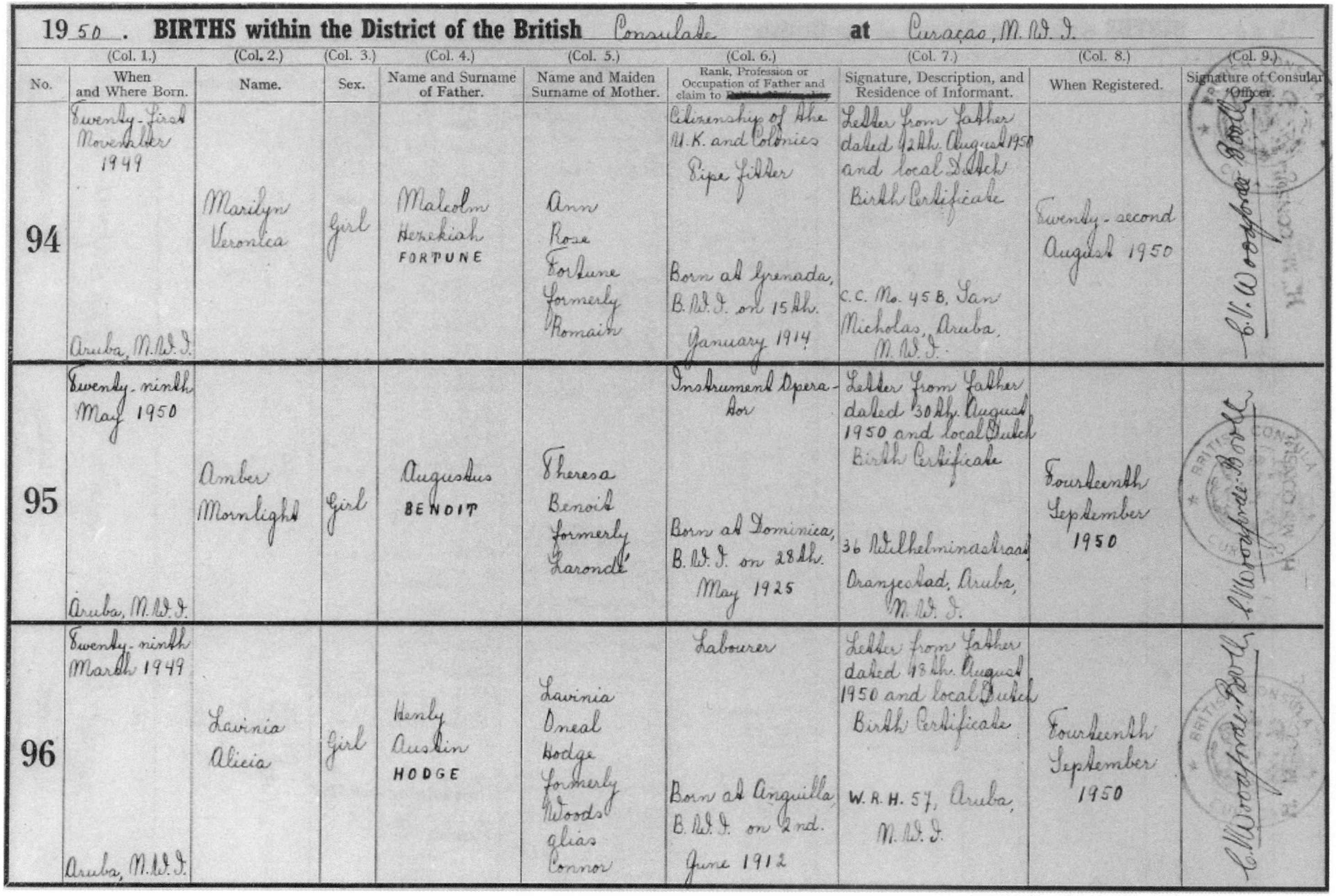

1950 . BIRTHS within the District of the British Consulate at Curaçao, N.W.I.

No.	(Col. 1.) When and Where Born.	(Col. 2.) Name.	(Col. 3.) Sex.	(Col. 4.) Name and Surname of Father.	(Col. 5.) Name and Maiden Surname of Mother.	(Col. 6.) Rank, Profession or Occupation of Father and claim to [illegible]	(Col. 7.) Signature, Description, and Residence of Informant.	(Col. 8.) When Registered.	(Col. 9.) Signature of Consular Officer.
94	Twenty-first November 1949 Aruba, N.W.I.	Marilyn Veronica	Girl	Malcolm Hezekiah FORTUNE	Ann Rose Fortune formerly Romain	Citizenship of the U.K. and Colonies Pipe fitter Born at Grenada, B.W.I. on 15th. January 1914	Letter from father dated 12th. August 1950 and local Dutch Birth Certificate C.C. No. 45 B, San Nicholas, Aruba, N.W.I.	Twenty-second August 1950	[illegible]
95	Twenty-ninth May 1950 Aruba, N.W.I.	Amber Mornlight	Girl	Augustus BENOIT	Theresa Benoit formerly Laronde	Instrument Operator Born at Dominica, B.W.I. on 28th. May 1925	Letter from father dated 30th. August 1950 and local Dutch Birth Certificate 36 Wilhelminastraat Oranjestad, Aruba, N.W.I.	Fourteenth September 1950	[illegible]
96	Twenty-ninth March 1949 Aruba, N.W.I.	Lavinia Alicia	Girl	Henly Austin HODGE	Lavinia Oneal Hodge formerly Woods alias Connor	Labourer Born at Anguilla, B.W.I. on 2nd. June 1912	Letter from father dated 13th. August 1950 and local Dutch Birth Certificate W.R.H. 57, Aruba, N.W.I.	Fourteenth September 1950	[illegible]

Figure 26 Curacao: return of births registered at the British Consul, 1950 (FO 907/5, p. 32).

Chamberlain, *Narratives of Exile and Return*. About Barbadian migration

Chamberlain (ed.), *Caribbean Migration*

Filby and Meyer, *Passenger and Immigration Lists*. Lists more than 3,681,000 immigrants who came to the New World

Foner, *Islands in the City*

Foner, *New Immigrants*

Gmelch, *Double Passage*

Harney, *Nationalism and Identity*. About Trinidadian migrants

Kershaw, *Emigrants and Expats*

Roper, *Records of the Foreign Office*

Vickerman, *Crosscurrents: West Indian Immigrants*

Waters, *West Indian Immigrant Dreams*

Watkins-Owen, *Blood Relations*

<worldgenweb.org> gateway to worldwide genealogical and historical resources

<www.rootsweb.com/~websites/> registry of genealogical website

<istg.rootsweb.com> Immigrant Ships Transcribers Guild online passenger lists project

<academic.brooklyn.cuny.edu/library/records_survey/> Brooklyn College, Caribbean community pages

10 British West Indies resources

This chapter describes the primary series at the Public Record Office for the study of the West Indies and West Indians. Until 1967 most of the records are in the records of the Colonial Office and you will need to refer to **Chapter 2** for descriptions of the different series. As countries became independent, diplomatic relations with Britain and matters of British nationality and citizenship, were handled by the Commonwealth Office (DO series). After 1967 records are in Foreign and Commonwealth Office series (FCO series, see **9.2.1**).

Many of the countries were captured and ceded to Britain during the eighteenth and nineteenth centuries: records relating to earlier administrations may survive in the archives of the relevant European power. However, some records, especially those relating to military activities and occupation during the period before the countries became colonies, are in the records of the War Office (WO series). The primary means of reference into these series is through *Public Record Office Lists and Indexes, Volume LIII* (see **Bibliography**).

Under each country I have included references to baptisms, marriages and burials, nominal censuses (which name at least the head of household), land grants, and miscellaneous lists of inhabitants found in Colonial Office records. These records are not comprehensive but are intended to give an idea of the range and value of records available to researchers in the PRO. I have also included the more useful records of the London slave registry and the Slave Compensation Commission (see **7.1**) for West Indian family historians. The lists of references are incomplete and other miscellaneous returns and papers, commissioners' hearing notes and assistant commissioners' proceedings, which may contain useful information, are also found in T 71.

I have also provided addresses of country archive and register offices and other useful addresses, published guides to locally held archives and further reading. Unfortunately, there are very few modern published guides to West Indian archives and many of the records described in the guides were not at the time located in the archive or register office. It is possible that many of these records may have since been transferred to these repositories and it is also likely that other genealogical records have come to light. Unfortunately it is also possible that some no longer survive. Many records have been microfilmed by the Church of Jesus Christ of Latter-day Saints (see **1.5**) and can be ordered through their Family History Centres. I have included some general books on the history of the West Indies and individual countries. Many other books can be found through online public and university library catalogues, and bookshops.

10.1 British West Indies, general

10.1.1 Colonies general

Colonial Papers	1574–1757	CO 1
Original Correspondence	1689–1952	CO 323
	1950–1960	CO 1032
Registers of Correspondence	1852–1952	CO 378
Registers of Out-letters	1871–1925	CO 379

10.1.2 Registry

General Registers	1623–1849	CO 326
Indexes to correspondence	1795–1874	CO 714
Daily Registers	1849–1929	CO 382

10.1.3 West Indies

Original Correspondence	1624–1951	CO 318
	1948–1966	CO 1031
Entry Books	1699–1872	CO 319
Registers of Correspondence	1849–1951	CO 375
Miscellanea	1820–1840	CO 320
Registers of Out-letters	1872–1926	CO 509

There are other series relating to the West Indies.

10.1.4 Colonial Office

West Indies: United States Bases: Original Correspondence	1941–1951	CO 971
West Indies: United States Bases: Registers of Correspondence	1940–1951	CO 972
West India Royal Commission	1938–1939	CO 950
West Indies Development and Welfare Organisation: Registered Files	1938–1958	CO 1042

10.1.5 Commonwealth Relations Office and Commonwealth Office

Nationality and Consular Department and predecessors: Registered Files, Commonwealth Nationality (NAT Series)	1952–1967	DO 176
West Indies Department and Atlantic Department: Registered Files, Commonwealth West Indies (WID Series)	1961–1967	DO 200

10.1.6 Foreign and Commonwealth Office

American and Latin American Departments: Registered Files (A and AL Series)	1967–1972	FCO 7
Atlantic Department: Registered Files (G Series)	1966–1968	FCO 23
West Indian Department 'A' and Associated States Department: Registered Files, Antigua, Dominica, Grenada, St Kitts-Nevis-Anguilla, St Lucia and St Vincent (WA Series)	1967–1968	FCO 43
West Indian Department 'B' and Foreign and Commonwealth Office, West Indian Department: Registered Files, Smaller Commonwealth West Indian Territories (WB and HW Series)	1967–1971	FCO 44
Hong Kong and West Indian Department 'C' and Hong Kong Department: Registered Files, Hong Kong and British Honduras (HW and HK Series)	1967–1972	FCO 40
North American and Caribbean Department and Caribbean Department: Registered Files (AN Series)	1968–1977	FCO 63

10.1.7 Further reading

Camp, 'Some West Indian sources in England'
Caribbean Historical and Genealogical Journal
Dunn, *Sugar and Slaves*
Dyde, *Caribbean Companion*
Edwards, *History of the British West Indies*
Fermor, *Travellers' Tree*
Greenwood, Hamber and Dyde, *Caribbean Certificate History Books 1, 2 and 3*
Gropp, *Guide to Libraries*
Ingram, *Manuscripts Relating to Commonwealth*
Ingram, *Manuscript Sources*
Lawrence-Archer, *Monumental Inscriptions*

Lucas, *Historical Geography of the British Colonies*

Oliver, *Monumental Inscriptions of the British West Indies*

Oliver (ed.), *Caribbeana* <www.candoo.com/olivers/caribbeana.html>

Royal Commission on Public Records, 'Official records in the West Indies', pp. 115-120

Titford, 'Settlers of the Old Empire: West Indies manuscript sources'

Tyson, *Guide to Manuscript Sources*

Walne, *Guide to Manuscript Sources*

<lcweb2.loc.gov/hlas/> Library of Congress online handbook of Latin American studies

<www.candoo.com/genresources/> Jim Lynch's Caribbean genealogical resources

<www.cyndislist.com/hispanic.htm> Cyndi Howell's gateway to Caribbean and Hispanic genealogical resources

<home.ptd.net/~nikki/caribbean.htm> Nikki Roth-Skiles' gateway to Caribbean historical and genealogical resources

<www.rootsweb.com/~caribgw/indexe.html> Caribbean Genealogical Web Project

<www.rootsweb.com/~nrthamgw/> North American Genealogical Web Project, includes pages for Central American countries

<www.rootsweb.com/~sthamgw/> South American Genealogical Web Project

</www.hist.unt.edu/09w-blk4.htm> University of North Texas, Caribbean Studies

<home.netcom.com/~hhenke> Virtual Institute of Caribbean Studies

10.2 Anguilla

Anguilla was first settled by the British in 1650 and was attached administratively to St Christopher. Between 1671 and 1816 Anguilla formed part of the Leeward Islands federation. When the federation broke up in 1816 Anguilla formed a separate government with Nevis, St Christopher and the Virgin Islands. In 1833 they were reunited under one governor in chief and in 1871 the Leeward Islands federation was reconstituted. In 1882 Anguilla joined with St Christopher and Nevis to form a single presidency. The Leeward Islands was finally dissolved in 1956 and St Christopher-Nevis-Anguilla became a separate colony with the capital in St Christopher, which between 1958 and 1962 formed part of the Federation of the West Indies. In 1971 Britain assumed administrative responsibility for Anguilla and in 1980 Anguilla was formally separated from St Christopher and Nevis. Anguilla is a British Dependent Territory.

10.2.1 Colonial Office series

See also under Leeward Islands (**10.16**) and St Christopher (**10.19**). After 1951 see West Indies general (**10.1**)

Original Correspondence	1702–1872	CO 239
Acts	1672–1972	CO 240

Sessional Papers	1704–1960	CO 241
Government Gazettes	1879–1989	CO 242
Miscellanea	1704–1887	CO 243

10.2.2 Nominal censuses

1716	CO 152/11, no 56 (iii). Printed in *Caribbeana*, vol. 3, p. 255
1717	CO 152/12, no 67 (iv)

10.2.3 Slave registers and records of the Slave Compensation Commission

Slave registers, 1827–1834	T 71/261–263
Valuers' returns	T 71/743
Register of claims	T 71/879
Claims and certificates, original	T 71/1033

Other records of the registry or commission may be found under St Christopher (**10.19**).

10.2.4 Archives and other useful addresses

Anguilla was part of St Christopher until 1980 and it is probable that most records relating to Anguilla will be in St Christopher (**10.19**). Series which relate solely to Anguilla may have been transferred to Anguilla.

National Archives, Government Headquarters, Church St, Box 186, Basseterre, St Kitts, tel: (869) 465–2521

Registrar General, PO Box 236, Basseterre, St Kitts, tel: (869) 465-5251

Anguilla Library Service, The Valley, Anguilla, BWI, tel: (264) 497-2441

Registrar of Births, Deaths and Marriages, Judicial Department, The Valley, Anguilla, BWI, tel: (264) 497-2377

Anguilla National Trust, P.O. Box 1234, The Valley, Anguilla, BWI <web.ai/ant/index.html>

Anguilla Archaeological and Historical Society, PO Box 252, The Valley, Anguilla

10.2.5 Guides to the archives

Baker, *A Guide to Records in the Leeward Islands*.

Records for Anguilla are listed under St Christopher. In 1982 a fire destroyed many of the records which were housed in the Court House, Basseterre, St Christopher; these may be the records described by Baker as being in the archives room, Basseterre.

10.2.6 Further reading

Jones, *Annals of Anguilla*
Titford, 'Settlers of the Old Empire: Anguilla'
Westlake, *Under an English Heaven*

10.3 Antigua and Barbuda

Christopher Columbus named the island after the church, Santa Maria de la Antigua in Seville, in 1493. The Spanish attempted to settle the island in 1520 but found it too dry. In 1629 the French also attempted to settle the island, and also failed. Antigua was eventually colonized by the British from St Christopher under Sir Thomas Warner in 1632. It was captured by the French in 1666 but returned to Britain under the Treaty of Breda in 1667. Between 1671 and 1816 it formed part of the Leeward Islands federation and was its centre of government. The federation broke up in 1816 and Antigua formed a separate government with Montserrat until 1871 when the Leeward Islands federation was reformed. The Leeward Islands federation was finally dissolved in 1956 and Antigua became a separate colony which between 1958 and 1962 formed part of the Federation of the West Indies. Antigua became independent on 1 November 1981.

10.3.1 Colonial Office series

See also Leeward Islands (**10.16**). After 1951 see West Indies general (**10.1**).

Original Correspondence	1702–1872	CO 7
	1689–1951	CO 152
Registers of Correspondence	1850–1951	CO 354
Entry Books	1816–1872	CO 393
Acts	1668–1967	CO 8
Sessional Papers	1704–1966	CO 9
Government Gazettes	1872–1965	CO 156
	1967–1989	CO 1049
Miscellanea	1666–1887	CO 10
	1683–1945	CO 157
Registers of Out-letters	1872–1926	CO 507

10.3.2 Colonial Office returns of baptisms etc

1726–1727	CO 152/16	Baptisms and burials: St Peter (fos 213–214)
1733–1734	CO 152/21	Baptisms and burials: St Paul (fos 123–124, 127–128), and St Mary (fos 125–126)
1739–1745	CO 152/25	Burials and marriages: St John, 1745 (fos 100–102); baptisms and burials: St George, 1739–1745 (fos 107–110); St Paul's, Falmouth, 1742–1745 (fos 111–112)

10.3.3 Nominal censuses

1677/8	CO 1/42, fos 229–241	Indicates whether English, Irish, Scottish, French or Dutch. Printed in Oliver, *History of Antigua* (1894) vol 1, p. lviii
1753	CO 152/27, fos 271–303	Printed in Oliver, *History of Antigua*, vol 1, p. cix

10.3.4 Miscellaneous

1701–1707	CO 152/6, no 64 (iii)	Sundry account of the Royal Africa Company for slaves imported into Antigua, giving name of purchaser with the numbers of men, women, boy and girl slaves and the cost
1821–1825	CO 7/14	Various slave returns including manumissions

10.3.5 Slave registers and records of the Slave Compensation Commission

Slave Registers	1817, 1821, 1824, 1828 and 1832, T 71/244–250
Valuers' returns	T 71/735–738
Register of claims	T 71/877
Index to claims	T 71/923
Claims and certificates, original	T 71/1027–1029
Counter claims	T 71/1219–1223
Certificates for compensation and lists of awards	T 71/1333–1334
Amended awards	T 71/1382
Parliamentary returns of awards	T 71/1403

10.3.6 Archives and other useful addresses

The National Archives, Rappaport Centre, Victoria Park, St John's Antigua, West Indies, tel: (268) 462-3946, e-mail: archives@candw.ag

The Registrar General's Office, High Court, High Street, St John's Antigua, West Indies, tel: (268) 462-3929

Museum of Antigua and Barbuda, Long Street, Box 103, St John's, Antigua and Barbuda, West Indies <www.antiguaobserver.com/antigua/hmuseum.html>

Antigua and Barbuda Public Library, PO Box 146, St John's, Antigua and Barbuda, West Indies, e-mail: antigualibrary@cmatt.zzn.com

Chris Codrington, Historical Antigua and Barbuda <www.rootsweb.com/~atgwgw/>

10.3.7 Guides to the archives

Baker, *Guide to Records in the Leeward Islands.* Note that the Antiguan and Leeward Islands records in the care of the PRO were returned to Antigua in 1990 and are now held in the National Archives.

Fires and earthquakes have destroyed many historic records. On 2 April 1841 the Customs House was destroyed by fire, on 19 August 1950 a fire in the federal building destroyed records relating to Antigua and the Leeward Islands federation, an earthquake destroyed the public library in 1974, and in 1999 the records held at the prison were destroyed by fire.

10.3.8 Further reading

Dyde, *Antigua and Barbuda*
Dyde, *History of Antigua*
Kincaid, *A Small Place*
Lannigan, *Antigua and the Antiguans*
Oliver, *History of Antigua*
Titford, 'Settlers of the old Empire: Antigua'

10.4 Bahamas

British settlements were established on New Providence from 1629 and on Eleuthera from 1646. The Spaniards attacked New Providence on several occasions between 1680 and 1684, and in 1703 a combined force of French and Spanish destroyed the settlement. After this the Bahamas were popular with pirates of all nations until Captain Woodes Rogers finally removed them in 1718. Between 1670 and 1717 the Bahamas were governed by the lords proprietors of Carolina who encouraged colonization, including a large number of German palatines. During the American Revolution the Bahamas were taken by Americans and again by the Spanish in 1781 and were retaken by the British in 1783. After the American Revolution, Loyalists fleeing from Georgia and the Carolinas increased the population. On 10 July 1973 the Bahamas achieved independence.

The Turks and Caicos Islands are part of the Bahamas chain of islands and were annexed to the Bahamas in 1799, but were separated in 1848 to become a dependency of Jamaica.

10.4.1 Colonial Office series

After 1951 see under West Indies general (**10.1**).

Original Correspondence	1696–1951	CO 23
	1696–1714	CO 5/1257–1301
Registers of Correspondence	1850–1951	CO 333
Entry Books	1717–1872	CO 24
Acts	1729–1973	CO 25
Sessional Papers	1721–1965	CO 26
Government Gazettes	1894–1989	CO 564
Miscellanea	1721–1941	CO 27
Registers of Out-letters	1872–1926	CO 508

10.4.2 Nominal censuses

1731	CO 23/3, fos 4–10
1734	CO 23/3, fos 129–132

10.4.3 Land records

1734	CO 23/3, fos 180–181	An account of taxes on plots of land in the Town of Nassau
1847	CO 23/125	Return of land grants, 1841–1846

10.4.4 Miscellaneous

1784	CO 23/25, fo 131	Return of 52 loyalist households who arrived in the Bahamas Islands
1833–1834	CO 23/91, fos 228–236	Returns of people in the workhouse on 29

June 1833 and 29 March 1834. Details
include: name, when committed, by whom
and for what offence

10.4.5 Slave registers and records of the Slave Compensation Commission

Slave registers, 1822, 1825, 1828, 1831, 1834	T 71/456–460
Valuers' returns	T 71/772–778
Register of claims	T 71/890
Index to claims	T 71/936
Claims and certificates, original	T 71/1063
Counter claims	T 71/1262
Certificates for compensation and lists of awards	T 71/1350
Amended awards	T 71/1393
Parliamentary returns of awards	T 71/1414

10.4.6 Archives and other useful addresses

Department of Archives, PO Box SS-6341, Nassau, Bahamas <www.bahamasnationalarchives.
  bs>, tel: (242) 393-2175, e-mail: archives@batelnet.bs
Registrar General's Office, PO Box N532, Nassau, Bahamas, tel: (242) 322-3316
Bahamas Historical Society P.O. Box SS-6833, Nassau, BahamasBahamas genealogical web project <www.rootsweb.com/~bhswgw/>

10.4.7 Guides to the archives

Public Record Office, *Supplement to the Guide to the Bahamas*
Saunders and Carson, *Guide to the Records of the Bahamas*

10.4.8 Further reading

British Museum, *List of Documents Relating to the Bahama Islands*
Cash, Gordon and Saunders, *Sources for Bahamian History*
Craton, *History of the Bahamas*
Craton and Saunders, *Islanders in the Stream*
Georgia State University bibliography of Bahamian genealogy <www.gsu.edu/~libpjr/
  bahgen.htm>
Johnson and Hallett (eds), *Early Colonists*

Malcolm, *Historical Documents*
Whittleton, 'Family history in the Bahamas'

10.5 Barbados

Discovered by the Spaniards in 1519 but never settled. The British annexed the island in 1625 and settled in 1627. Many criminals and rebels were transported to Barbados including rebels from Monmouth's Rebellion of 1685, and the Jacobite rebellions of 1715 and 1745. Many people left Barbados to settle other West Indian and American colonies. For example between 1643 and 1667 12,000 left Barbados to fight or to settle in Jamaica, Tobago, Trinidad and other islands, Surinam, Carolina, Virginia and New England. Barbados was a member of the Windward Islands group between 1833 and 1885 and the Federation of the West Indies between 1958 and 1962. Barbados became independent on 30 November 1966.

10.5.1 Colonial Office series

Between 1833 and 1885 see also Windward Islands (**10.25**), and after 1951 see under West Indies general (**10.1**).

Original Correspondence	1689–1951	CO 28
	1874–1885	CO 321
Registers of Correspondence	1850–1885	CO 376
	1886–1948	CO 565
Entry Books	1627–1872	CO 29
Acts	1643–1966	CO 30
Sessional Papers	1660–1965	CO 31
Government Gazettes	1867–1975	CO 32
Miscellanea	1678–1947	CO 33
Registers of Out-letters	1872–1926	CO 501

10.5.2 Colonial Office returns of baptisms etc

1715–1716	CO 28/15	Baptisms and burials: Christ Church (fos 95–97), St George (fo 102), St John (fo 103), St Andrew (fo 105), St Joseph (fos 107–109), and St Peter (fos 110–114). Printed in Hotten, *Original Lists of People of Quality*

10.5.3 Nominal censuses

1679/80	CO 1/44, no 47 i–xxii	Printed in Hotten's *Original Lists* and Brandow's *Omitted Chapters from Hotten*
1715	CO 28/16, no 2	Some of the parishes list all white inhabitants with their ages. The parishes of St Michael, Christ Church and St George are printed in the *Journal of the Barbados Museum and Historical Society*, vol. IV, p. 72

10.5.4. Miscellaneous

1729	CO 28/21, fos 104–109, 165–209	Returns of the Negro Tax, 2/6 levy (some duplication is found in T 1/275, fos 22–44, CO 28/40, fos 37–60, and CO 28/45, fos 107–114)
1832–1835	T 1/4395 (papers 19604/31 and 6198/33) and T 1/4396 (paper 20486/36)	Barbados claims following the hurricane of 11 August 1831 money distributed under the West Indies loans act. Date, name of claimant, parish, return of loss, value and money paid
1821–1825	CO 28/97	Various slave returns including manumissions and a return of paupers and pensioners
1951	CO 32/124	Electoral register

10.5.5 Slave registers and records of the Slave Compensation Commission

Slave registers, 1817, 1820, 1823, 1826, 1829, 1832, 1834	T 71/520–565
Valuers' returns	T 71/790–803
Register of claims	T 71/895–900
Index to claims	T 71/940
Claims and certificates, original	T 71/1083–1108
Counter claims	T 71/1280–1287
Certificates for compensation and lists of awards	T 71/1356–1359
Amended awards	T 71/1397
Parliamentary returns of awards	T 71/1418

10.5.6 Archives and other useful addresses

Department of Archives, Lazaretto Building, Black Rock, St Michael, Barbados, tel: (246) 425-1380, e-mail: bda@caribsurf.com

Registration Department, Supreme Court of Barbados, Law Courts, Coleridge St, Bridgetown, Barbados, tel: (246) 426-3461

Barbados Museum and Historical Society, St Ann's Garrison, St Michael, Barbados <www.barbmuse.org.bb>

National Library Service, Public Services Division, Coleridge Street, Bridgetown 2, Barbados

Barbados National Trust, Wildey House, Wildey, St Michael, Barbados

Bajan Genealogical Web Project <www.rootsweb.com/~brbwgw/>

10.5.7 Guides to the archives

Chandler, *Guide to Sources in Barbados*
Handler, *Guide to Source Materials for Barbados*
Handler, *Supplement to a Guide to Source Material*
Many of the Barbados archives were microfilmed for the University of West Indies.

10.5.8 Further reading

Beckles, *History of Barbados*
Brandow, *Genealogies of Barbados Families*
Handler, 'Slave Manumissions'
Handler, Hughes and Wiltshire, *Freedmen of Barbados*
Handler and Jacoby, 'Slave names and naming in Barbados'
Handler, Lange and Riordan, *Plantation Slavery in Barbados*
Hoyos, *Barbados: A History*
Kent, *Barbados and America*
Oliver (ed.), *Monumental Inscriptions in Barbados*
Salazar, *Love Child: Genealogist's Guide* <www.candoo.com/projects/lovechild.html>
Sanders, *Barbados Records: Baptisms*
Sanders, *Barbados Records: Marriages*
Sanders, *Barbados Records: Wills and Administrations*
Shilstone, *Monumental Inscriptions*
Stanford, 'Genealogical sources in Barbados'

10.6 Bay Islands

These islands off the coast of Central America were occupied by Britain in 1839 and became a colony under the governorship of Jamaica in 1852. The islands were ceded to the Republic of Honduras in 1859.

10.6.1 Colonial Office series

See also under Jamaica (**10.15**) and Belize (**10.7**); after 1859 see under Honduras (**11.6**).

Original Correspondence	1852–1861	CO 34
Registers of correspondence	1852–1854	CO 351
	1854–1861	CO 348
Acts	1852–1859	CO 35
Miscellanea	1855–1859	CO 36

10.7 Belize (formerly British Honduras)

British settlement was first established on the islands off the Mosquito Coast in 1630, and on Honduras in 1638 by adventurers from Jamaica, who logged mahogany and logwood. Although not a British colony at this time British Honduras was nominally under the superintendence of Jamaica. The Treaty of Paris in 1763 allowed British settlers to continue logging while Spain retained sovereignty. Spain continued to assert sovereignty but did not manage to evict the British settlers and in 1862 British Honduras became a colony under the governorship of Jamaica. In 1884 the colony was separated from Jamaica. Belize became independent on 21 September 1918.

10.7.1 Colonial Office series

See also under Spain (**11.9**) and Jamaica (**10.15**) until 1884. From 1951 see under West Indies general (**10.1**)

Original Correspondence	1744–1951	CO 123
Registers of Correspondence	1855–1951	CO 348
Entry Books	1630–1872	CO 124
Acts	1855–1977	CO 125
Sessional Papers	1848–1965	CO 126
Government Gazettes	1861–1975	CO 127
Miscellanea	1807–1943	CO 128
Registers of Out-letters	1872–1926	CO 503

10.7.2 Land grants

c.1748–1774   WO 55/1815   Names of people who have grants of land in George Town (near Cala Font) Honduras.

10.7.3 Slave registers and records of the Slave Compensation Commission

Slave registers, 1834	T 71/251–252
Valuers' returns	T 71/739
Register of claims	T 71/878
Index to claims	T 71/924
Claims and certificates, original	T 71/1030
Counter claims	T 71/1223
Certificates for compensation and lists of awards	T 71/1335
Amended awards	T 71/1383
Parliamentary returns of awards	T 71/1404

10.7.4 Archives and other useful addresses

Belize Archives Department, 26/28 Unity Boulevard, Belmopan, Belize <www.belize.gov.bz/archives_dept/belize.htm>, tel: (501) 8-22247, e-mail: archives@btl.net

Registrar General, Supreme Court, Belize City, Belize, tel: (501) 2-77377

National Library Service, Bliss Institute, PO Box 287, Belize City, Belize

Belize Genealogical Web Project <www.rootsweb.com/~blzwgw/>

10.7.5 Guides to the archives

Burdon, *Archives of British Honduras*

Gropp, *Guide to Libraries*

The Spanish attacked British Honduras in 1754 and destroyed every building. In 1918 a fire destroyed the colonial secretary's office and other public buildings and many records were lost following a hurricane and subsequent tidal wave in 1931.

10.7.6 Further reading

Bolland, *Formation of a Colonial Society: Belize*

Dobson, *History of Belize*

Grant, *Making of Modern Belize*

Humphries, *Diplomatic History of British Honduras*

10.8 Bermuda

Bermuda, although not in the Caribbean, was considered part of the West Indies by the Colonial Office and its predecessors for administrative convenience. Discovered in 1515 by Juan Bermudes, a Spanish mariner. The Spanish did not settle on the islands which were uninhabited until 1609 when Admiral Sir George Somers was shipwrecked on one of the reefs. Bermuda also became known as the Somer or Summer Islands. British settlements were established in Bermuda from 1612. Bermuda is a British Dependent Territory.

10.8.1 Colonial Office series

Original Correspondence	1689–1951	CO 37
Registers of Correspondence	1850–1951	CO 334
Entry Books	1615–1872	CO 38
Acts	1690–1989	CO 39
Sessional Papers	1687–1965	CO 40
Government Gazettes	1902–1965	CO 647
Miscellanea	1715–1950	CO 41
Registers of Out-letters	1872–1925	CO 499

10.8.2 Returns of baptisms and burials

1826–1946	ADM 6/434–436	Baptisms and burials, naval base, Ireland Island. ADM 6/435 includes confirmations, 1849–1900
1903–1918	ADM 6/439	Baptisms, Boaz Garrison
1946–1957	ADM 338/11	Baptisms, Ireland Island

10.8.3 Slave registers and records of the Slave Compensation Commission

Slave registers, 1821, 1827, 1830, 1833–34	T 71/452–455
Valuers' returns	T 71/767–771
Register of claims	T 71/889
Index to claims	T 71/935
Claims and certificates, original	T 71/1059–1062
Counter claims	T 71/1262
Certificates for compensation and lists of awards	T 71/1349
Amended awards	T 71/1392
Parliamentary returns of awards	T 71/1413

10.8.4 Archives and other useful addresses

Bermuda National Archives, Government Administration Building, 30 Parliament St, Hamilton HM 12, Bermuda, tel: (441) 295-5151

Registry General, Ministry of Labor and Home Affairs, Government Administration Building, 30 Parliament St., Hamilton, 5–24, Bermuda, tel: (441) 297-7709

Bermuda Historical Society, c/o Bermuda Library, Par-la-ville Park, Hamilton, Bermuda

Bermuda Library, 13 Queen Street, Par-la-Ville, Hamilton HM 11, Bermuda

The Bermuda National Trust, PO Box HM 61, Hamilton HM AX, Bermuda <www.bnt.bm/index2.html>

Institute of North American & Atlantic Colonial History (INAACH) in Bermuda <www.bermuda-online.org/inaach.htm>

Bermuda Genealogical Web Project <www.rootsweb.com/~bmuwgw/bermuda.htm>

10.8.5 Guides to the archives

Rowe, *Guide to the Records of Bermuda*

10.8.6 Further reading

Green, *Monumental Inscriptions*
Hallett, *Bermuda Index*
Hallett, *Early Bermuda Wills*
Hallett, *Early Bermudan Records*
Mercer, *Bermuda Settlers*
Stranack, *The Andrew and the Onions*

10.9 British Virgin Islands

Tortola was the first of the Virgin Islands to be settled by the Dutch in 1648. The English expelled the Dutch from many of the islands in 1666 and Tortola in 1672, when the islands were included in the Leeward Islands group. When the federation broke up in 1816 the Virgin Islands formed a separate government with Nevis, St Christopher and Anguilla. In 1833 they were reunited under one governor in chief and in 1871 the Leeward Islands federation was reconstituted. The islands continued to be administered by the Leeward Islands until 1960 when the Virgin Islands became a separate colony. The British Virgin Islands are a British Dependent Territory.

10.9.1 Colonial Office series

See also Leeward Islands (**10.16**) and St Christopher (**10.19**).

Original Correspondence	1711–1872	CO 314
	1816–1853	CO 239
	1874–1951	CO 152
Registers of Correspondence	1850–1951	CO 354
Acts	1774–1965	CO 315
Sessional Papers	1773–1965	CO 316
Miscellanea	1784–1896	CO 317
Registers of Out-letters	1872–1926	CO 507

10.9.2 Nominal censuses

1716	CO 152/11, no. 6(vi)	Account of householders for Spanish Town, Beef Island, Tortola and Widdows
1716	CO 152/11, no. 45(iv)	List of households for Spanish Town and Beef Island
1717	CO 152/12/2, no. 67 (vi and viii)	List of households for Spanish Town (vi) and Tortola (viii), includes nationality. CO 152/12/2, no. 67 (ix) contains a list of men able to bear arms and the number of slaves on Crabb Island

10.9.3 Slave registers and records of the Slave Compensation Commission

Slave registers, 1818, 1822, 1825, 1828, 1831, 1834	T 71/370–375
Valuers' returns	T 71/753
Register of claims	T 71/883
Index to claims	T 71/929
Claims and certificates, original	T 71/1040
Counter claims	T 71/1238–1240
Certificates for compensation and lists of awards	T 71/1341
Amended awards	T 71/1388
Parliamentary returns of awards	T 71/1409

10.9.4 Archives and other useful addresses

Library Services Department, Flemming St, Road Town, Tortola, British Virgin Islands, tel: (284) 494-3428

Registrar of Births, Deaths and Marriages, Government of the British Virgin Islands, Central Administration Complex, Road Town, Tortola, British Virgin Islands, tel: (284) 494-3701

British Virgin Islands Genealogical Project <www.britishislesgenweb.org/~bvi/>

10.9.5 Published guides to the archives

Baker, *Guide to Records in the Leeward Islands*

10.9.6 Further reading

Dookhan, *History of the British Virgin Islands*
Jenkins, *Tortola: A Quaker Experiment*
Titford, 'Settlers of the Old Empire: British Virgin Islands'

10.10 Cayman Islands

Christopher Columbus first discovered the Cayman Islands in 1503. The Cayman Islands were frequently visited by Spanish, English and French ships for revictualling, but it was not until 1670 that they were ceded to Britain by the Treaty of Madrid. In 1734 they were settled by colonists from Jamaica, and justices of the peace were appointed by the Governor of Jamaica to administer the affairs of the islands, which were loosely seen as part of Jamaica. However, it was not until 1863 that the relationship was recognized by an Act of British Parliament and the islands officially became a dependency of Jamaica. In 1957 the Cayman Islands, as a dependency of Jamaica, joined the Federation of the West Indies but this alliance was short-lived. In 1962, when Jamaica became independent, the Cayman Islands decided to remain as a dependent territory of the United Kingdom and this status continues today.

10.10.1 Colonial Office series

See also under Jamaica (**10.15**) and from 1951 see under West Indies general (**10.1**).

Acts	1898–1966	CO 650
Sessional Papers	1908–1965	CO 857
Government Gazettes	1956–1990	CO 1019
Miscellanea	1912–1947	CO 651

10.10.2 Nominal censuses

1802	CO 137/108, fos 265–272	Grand Cayman, 1802, general description of the island, together with (fos 269–271) list of head of households by location, broken down into white, free coloureds and free Blacks, with numbers in each household and number of slaves

10.10.3 Slave registers and records of the Slave Compensation Commission

Slave registers, 1834	T 71/243
Valuers' returns	T 71/734
Register of claims	T 71/875
Claims and certificates, original	T 71/1026
Certificates for compensation and lists of awards	T 71/1331

Other records are to be found under Jamaica (**10.15**).

10.10.4 Archives and other useful addresses

Cayman Islands National Archive, Government Administration Building, Grand Cayman, Cayman Islands. tel: (345) 949 9809, e-mail: CINA@gov.ky

Registrar of Births, Deaths and Marriages, General Registry Department, Tower Building, Grand Cayman. tel: (345) 244 3404

Cayman Islands Genealogical Web Project <www.britishislesgenweb.org/~cayman/>

Many records were destroyed by hurricanes in 1876 and 1932, and by a fire in the Government Administration Building in 1972. Also many Cayman Island records were lost in transit to Jamaica in the early 1900s.

10.10.5 Further reading

Hirst, *History of the Cayman Islands*
Williams, *History of the Cayman Islands*

10.11 Dominica

Dominica was in the possession of Caribs when it was settled by the French in 1632. In 1748 the Treaty of Aix-la-Chapelle made Dominica and the other Windward Islands neutral, to be left in the possession of the Caribs. However, the French still settled on the island. Dominica was captured by Britain in 1761 and ceded to her in 1763. French from Martinique recaptured Dominica in 1778, but it was restored to Britain in 1783. In 1763 Dominica was part of the Windward Islands and became a separate colony in 1771. In 1833 it formed part of the Leeward Islands federation but returned to the Windward Islands in 1940 until 1956, when the Windward Islands federation was dissolved. Between 1958 and 1962 Dominica was a member of the Federation of the West Indies. Dominica became independent on 3 November 1978 under the name of Commonwealth of Dominica.

10.11.1 Colonial Office series

See also under France (**11.4**), the Leeward Islands (**10.16**) and the Windward Islands (**10.25**); after 1951 see under West Indies general (**10.1**).

Original Correspondence	1730–1872	CO 71
	1872–1940	CO 152
	1940–1951	CO 321
Registers of Correspondence	1850–1940	CO 354
	1940–1951	CO 376
Entry Books	1770–1872	CO 72
Acts	1768–1965	CO 73
Sessional Papers	1767–1965	CO 74
Government Gazettes	1865–1975	CO 75
Miscellanea	1763–1940	CO 76
	1888–1939	CO 157
Registers of Out-letters	1872–1926	CO 507

10.11.2 Land records

1765–1766	CO 76/9	Dominica and St Vincent: Register of grants of land
1766	CO 101/1, fos 279–281	Docket register of plantation grants in the islands of Dominica, St Vincent and Tobago
1765–1767	CO 101/11, fos 219–222, 413	Docket register of plantation grants
1764–1797	CO 106/9–12	Sale of lands in the Ceded Islands
1766	T 1/453, fos 153–164	An account of lands granted on lease by the Commissioners to the French inhabitants of Dominica
1790–1803	CO 71/3	Includes returns of quit rents

10.11.3 Slave registers and records of the Slave Compensation Commission

Slave registers, 1817, 1820, 1823, 1826, 1829, 1832	T 71/337–363
Valuers' returns	T 71/748–750
Register of claims	T 71/881
Index to claims	T 71/927
Claims and certificates, original	T 71/1037
Counter claims	T 71/1233–1235
Certificates for compensation and lists of awards	T 71/1339
Amended awards	T 71/1386
Parliamentary returns of awards	T 71/1407

10.11.4 Archives and other useful addresses

National Documentation Centre, Government Headquarters, Roseau, Commonwealth of Dominica, tel: (767) 448-2401

General Registrar, Bay Front, Roseau, Commonwealth of Dominica, tel: (767) 448-2401

Dominica Genealogical Web Project <www.britishislesgenweb.org/~dominica/>

10.11.5 Guides to the archives

Baker, *Guide to Records in the Windward Islands*

10.11.6 Further reading

Baker, *Centring the Periphery*
Honychurch, *Dominica Story*
Honychurch and Aird, *Dominica: Island of Adventure*
Imperial Department of Agriculture in the West Indies, *Notes on Dominica.* Copy in CO 318/348 (Agriculture December 1919)
Kincaid, *Autobiography of My Mother*, a novel

10.12 Federation of the West Indies

The Federation of the West Indies was formed in January 1958 comprising the following territories and their dependencies: Barbados, Jamaica, Antigua, Montserrat, St Christopher-Nevis-Anguilla, Trinidad and Tobago, Grenada, Dominica, St Lucia and St Vincent. The federation was dissolved in 1962 with the loss of Jamaica (with the Cayman Islands and Turks and Caicos Islands) but was reformed in May 1962 although Trinidad and Tobago did not rejoin. The federation was finally abandoned in 1966.

Original correspondence	1958–1966	CO 1031
Government Gazettes	1958–1961	DO 136
Acts	1958–1962	DO 139

10.13 Grenada

Grenada was temporarily settled by the British in 1609, but in 1650 the governor of Martinique purchased the island and established a settlement. Captured by Britain in 1762 and ceded in 1763 under the Windward Islands. Grenada was recaptured by the French in 1779 and restored to the British in 1783. Between 1833 and 1956 Grenada was part of the Windward Islands federation and between 1958 and 1962 a member of the Federation of the West Indies. On 7 February 1974 Grenada became independent.

10.13.1 Colonial Office series

See also under France (**11.4**) and Windward Islands (**10.25**) and after 1951 see under West Indies general (**10.1**).

Original Correspondence	1747–1873	CO 101
	1874–1951	CO 321
Registers of Correspondence	1850–1951	CO 376
Entry Books	1763–1872	CO 102
Acts	1766–1965	CO 103
Sessional Papers	1777–1965	CO 104
Government Gazettes	1834–1975	CO 105
Miscellanea	1764–1938	CO 106
Registers of Out-letters	1872–1882	CO 504
	1883–1926	CO 377

10.13.2 Nominal censuses

| 1772 | CO 101/5, fos 147–151 | List of landholders, the numbers in the household, acreage, negroes, types of crops and mills |
| Carriacou, c.1767 | CO 101/11, fo 230 | Householder, number of English and French overseers, number of slaves, quantity of land, taxes |

10.13.3 Land grants

| 1762–1764 | CO 101/1, fos 245–246 | A list of sale of town lots in St George |
| 1764–1797 | CO 106/9–12 | Sale of lands in the Ceded Islands |

10.13.4 Miscellaneous lists

1763	CO 101/1, fos 18–31	Capitation Tax Rolls of people liable to pay tax on slaves
1821–1825	CO 101/66	Various slave returns including manumissions

10.13.5 Slave registers and records of the Slave Compensation Commission

Slave registers, 1817, annual 1819–1834	T71/264–336
Valuers' returns	T 71/744–747
Register of claims	T 71/880
Index to claims	T 71/926
Claims and certificates, original	T 71/1034–1036
Counter claims	T 71/1228–1232
Certificates for compensation and lists of awards	T 71/1337–1338
Amended awards	T 71/1385
Parliamentary returns of awards	T 71/1406

10.13.6 Archives and other useful addresses

Public Library/National Archives, 2 Carenage, St George's, Grenada, tel: (473) 440-2506
Registrar General, Church St, St George's, Grenada, tel: (473) 440-2030
National Museum, Young St, St George's, Grenada
Grenada Genealogical Web Project <www.britishislesgenweb.org/~grenada/>

10.13.7 Guides to the archives

Baker, *Guide to Records in the Windward Islands*
No records survive in Grenada before 1764, possibly having been removed by the French or destroyed during their occupations or in the several conflicts between the French and British. The governor's records were destroyed in a fire at St George's in 1771.

10.13.8 Further reading

Brizan, *Grenada: Island of Conflict*
Burgan, *Some West Indian Memorials*
Devas, *History of the Island of Grenada*
Titford, 'Settlers of the Old Empire: Grenada'

10.14 Guyana (formerly British Guiana)

The Dutch West India Company first settled the territories of Berbice, Essequibo and Demerara in 1580. These Dutch colonies were captured by Britain in 1796 but restored to the Dutch in 1802. The British recaptured the colonies in 1803, which were formally ceded to Britain in 1814. Gradually the administration of the three colonies was centralized; the legal and administrative unification of Demerara and Essequibo was effected in 1812. Finally the colony of British Guiana was created in 1831 when Demerara, Essequibo and Berbice were all combined and their administration conducted from Georgetown. British Guiana became independent on 26 May 1966 under the name Guyana.

10.14.1 Colonial Office series

Before 1803 see the Netherlands (**11.7**), although part of the records of the Dutch West India Company's administration, 1686–1792, were transferred to Britain in 1819 and are in CO 116; after 1951 see under West Indies general (**10.1**).

Original Correspondence	before 1814	WO 1
	1781–1951	CO 111
Registers of Correspondence	1850–1951	CO 345
Entry Books	1797–1872	CO 112
Acts	1837–1965	CO 113
Sessional Papers	1805–1965	CO 114
Government Gazettes	1838–1975	CO 115
Miscellanea	1681–1943	CO 116
Registers of Out-letters	1872–1926	CO 502

10.14.2 Land records

1819	CO 111/28	Lists of Dutch proprietors of plantations in Demerara, Essequibo and Berbice [in Dutch]
1735–1755	CO 116/73, 75, 76	Berbice: grants of land [in Dutch]
1737–1763	CO 116/78	Berbice: mortgages [in Dutch]

10.14.3 Miscellaneous

1811–1818	T 89/1	Records of the Berbice Commission
1764–1793	CO 116/106–117	Berbice: records of the court of policy and criminal justice [in Dutch]

1765–1794	CO 116/128–135	Berbice: Taxation returns – poll tax, church tax etc [in Dutch]
1826–1834	CO 116/143–153, 156–163	Reports of Protectors of Slaves: punishments, criminal cases, births, deaths, marriages, free baptisms, and manumissions, for: 1. Berbice: CO 116/143–153 2. Demerara and Essequibo: CO 116/156–163

Several of the reports were published in the British *Parliamentary Papers*: session 1829 (335), vol. XXV.255 (mfm 31.153–155) and session 1830–31 (262) vol. XV.1 (mfm 33.87–95).

10.14.4 Slave registers and records of the Slave Compensation Commission

Slave registers:

Demerara, 1817, 1820, 1823, 1826, 1829, 1832	T 71/391–436
Berbice, 1818, 1819, 1822, 1825, 1828, 1831, 1834	T 71/437–446
Valuers' returns	T 71/757–765
Register of claims	T 71/885–887
Index to claims	T 71/931–933
Claims and certificates, original	T 71/1045–1057
Counter claims	T 71/1252–1260
Certificates for compensation and lists of awards	T 71/1343–1347
Amended awards	T 71/1390
Parliamentary returns of awards	T 71/1411

10.14.5 Archives and other useful addresses

National Archives of Guyana, 26 Main Street, Georgetown, Guyana, tel: (592) 227-7687, e-mail: narchivesguyana@yahoo.com

General Register Office, GPO Building, Robb Street, Georgetown, Guyana, tel: (592) 225-7561

National Library, 76/77 Church & Main Streets, Georgetown, Guyana <www.natlib.gov.gy>

Guyana Heritage Museum, 17 Kastev, Meten-Meer-Zorg, West Coast, Demerara, Guyana <www.sdnp.org.gy/ghm/>

Guyana Genealogical Web Project <www.rootsweb.com/~guywgw/>

10.14.6 Guides to the archives

Gropp, *Guide to Libraries*
On 23 February 1945 a fire destroyed a substantial part of Georgetown including the library, the natural history museum, the post office and savings bank and a number of other government buildings.

10.14.7 Further reading

Viotti, *Crowns of Glory*

10.15 Jamaica

First settled by Spaniards from 1494, Jamaica was captured by Britain in 1655. Among the immigrants Jamaica received were: rebels and other criminals from Britain; 1500 people from Nevis and adjoining islands; Bermudans; New Englanders; Quakers from Barbados; and a large number of Jews. Planters were evacuated to Jamaica from Surinam in 1675, and survivors from the ill-fated Scottish colony of Darien settled in 1699. Jamaica became independent on 6 August 1962.

10.15.1 Colonial Office series

Before 1655 see under Spain (**11.9**) and after 1951 see under West Indies general (**10.1**).

Original Correspondence	1689–1951	CO 137
Registers of Correspondence	1850–1951	CO 351
Entry Books	1661–1872	CO 138
Acts	1662–1962	CO 139
Sessional Papers	1661–1965	CO 140
Government Gazettes	1794–1968	CO 141
Miscellanea	1658–1945	CO 142
Registers of Out-letters	1872–1926	CO 494

10.15.2 Colonial Office returns of baptisms etc

1821–1825	CO 137/162	March. Returns of slave marriages in Portland, St James, St Catherine, Kingston and Manchester

10.15.3 Nominal censuses

1670	CO 138/1, pp. 61–82	Survey of Jamaica, listing under parish owner and then number of acres (printed in *Calendar of State Papers, Colonial, America and West Indies, 1669–1674*, pp. 99–104)
1680	CO 1/45, fos 96–109	Inhabitants of Port Royal and St John's
1754	CO 137/28, pp. 191–196	St Andrews' parish. Plantation, landholder, nos acres, types of crops, livestock etc, nos slaves
1754	CO 142/31	List of landholders with number of acres, taken from the Quit Rent Books
1831	CO 140/121, pp. 353–378	Return of maroons of Moore-town, Charlestown, Scot's Hall and Accompong. The information includes name and age, and some entries give colour and comments (such as son of. . .), and a return of slaves belonging to the maroons

10.15.4 Land grants

1735–1754	CO 137/28, pp. 197–203, 225–249	Return of land grants
1805–1824	CO 137/162, Jan	Return of land grants

10.15.5 Miscellaneous documents

1675	CO 1/35, fos 178–185	A list of His Majesty's subjects and slaves transported in HM hired ship *Hercules* from Surinam to Jamaica
1740–1751	CO 324/55	Foreign Protestants naturalized in American colonies, including Jamaica. Printed in Guiseppi, *Naturalization of Foreign Protestants*, Huguenot Society, vol. 24
1802	WO 1/352	Return of Nova Scotians and maroons in Sierra Leone. The maroons had been transported from Jamaica to Nova Scotia in 1796 following the Maroon War; in 1800 they migrated to Sierra Leone
c.1800–1817	CO 137/144, fos 156–225	Correspondence and returns on the number of slave baptised into the Church

		of England. Including nominal returns of slave baptisms by Edmund Pope for St Elizabeth, Vere and Claredon parishes, 1815–1817 (fos 166–175) and by Thomas Stewart for St Elizabeth, 1815–1817 (fos 177–179)
1821–1825	CO 137/162, March	Various slave returns including a return of paupers, a return of people committed to the workhouse and manumissions. The return of manumissions has been transcribed by Edward Crawford at </www.rootsweb.com/~jamwgw/manum.htm>
1831	CO 137/179	Return of people confined to Kingston workhouse (fos 333–338), and list of negroes convicted in the parish of St Anne (fo 341)
1831	CO 137/181	List of people that have been confined in St Andrews Workhouse claiming their freedom
1825–1831	CO 137/181 (fos 145–148)	A list of convicts in the St James' Workhouse condemned to hard labour for life, 1788–1831 (fo 411)
1917	CO 137/720 (24 Feb 1917)	Petition of 909 signatures for the repeal of Estate Duty Law, 1916, with name, address/village and occupation

10.15.6 Slave registers and records of the Slave Compensation Commission

Slave registers, 1817, 1820, 1823, 1826, 1829 and 1832	T 71/1–242
Valuers' returns	T 71/685–733
Register of claims	T 71/852–876
Index to claims	T 71/915–922
Claims and certificates, original	T 71/943–1025
Counter claims	T 71/1174–1218
Certificates for compensation and lists of awards	T 71/1310–1332, 1371–1374
Amended awards	T 71/1381
Parliamentary returns of awards	T 71/1400–1402

10.15.7 Archives and other useful addresses

Jamaica Archives, Spanish Town, Jamaica, tel: (876) 984–2581
The Registrar General, Vital Records Information, Twickenham Park, Spanish Town, Jamaica
  , tel: (876) 984-3041-5, e-mail: information@rgd.gov.jm
National Library of Jamaica, 12 East Street, Kingston, Jamaica, West Indies <www.nlj.org.ja>
Jamaica Historical Society, c/o National Library of Jamaica, 12 East Street, Kingston 10, Jamaica
Genealogy of Jamaica <www.rootsweb.com/~jamwgw/index.htm>, by Madeleine E Mitchell
Madeleine Mitchell, Family history of Jamaica <users.pullman.com/mitchelm/jamaica.htm>
Jamaican family history: genealogical research library

10.15.8 Guides to the archives

Ingram, *Sources for Jamaican History*
Ingram, *Sources for West Indian Studies*
Port Royal, the old capital, was destroyed by an earthquake on 7 June 1692 and in 1907 an
  earthquake destroyed most of Kingston including the court house.

10.15.9 Further reading

Higman, *Jamaica Surveyed*
Higman, *Slave Population and Economy in Jamaica*
Livingston, *Sketch Pedigrees*
Mitchell, *Jamaican Ancestry*
Patterson, *Sociology of Slavery*
Porter, *Jamaican Records: Research Manual*
Robertson, 'Jamaican archival resources'
Soares, 'Jamaican research in Britain'
Wright, 'Materials for family history in Jamaica'
Wright, *Monumental Inscriptions of Jamaica*

10.16 Leeward Islands

A group of islands under one federal government until 1956 comprising Antigua, Barbuda, Montserrat, St Christopher, Nevis, Anguilla, the British Virgin Islands and, between 1833 and 1940, Dominica. The Leeward Islands temporarily broke up in 1816 and formed two authorities: Antigua, Barbuda and Montserrat, and the other St Christopher, Nevis, Anguilla and the British Virgin Islands. In 1833 the Leeward Islands government was re-established and included Dominica. In 1871 the federal legislature was revived with each colony having an administrator or commissioner responsible to the governor whose administrative office was in Antigua. In 1956 the federation was abolished.

10.16.1 Colonial Office series

See also under the individual territories; after 1951 see under West Indies general (**10.1**).

Original Correspondence	1689–1951	CO 152
Registers of Correspondence	1850–1951	CO 354
Entry Books	1670–1816	CO 153
Acts	1644–1956	CO 154
Sessional Papers	1680–1956	CO 155
Government Gazettes	1872–1965	CO 156
Miscellanea	1683–1945	CO 157
Registers of Out-letters	1872–1926	CO 507

10.16.2 Further reading

Baker, *Guide to Records in the Leeward Islands*

10.17 Montserrat

Montserrat was discovered by Christopher Columbus in November 1493 and named after the Abbey of Montserrat near Barcelona. Montserrat could be considered an Irish colony: the island is known as the Emerald Isle of the Caribbean and a green shamrock is its national logo. English and Irish from St Christopher first settled Montserrat in 1632. Further Irish immigrants arrived during the seventeenth century from Virginia, and from Ireland following Cromwell's victory at Drogheda in 1649.

The island was taken by the French in 1664 and 1667 but was restored to England in 1668 by the Treaty of Breda. The French raided Montserrat in 1712 and destroyed much of the island and most of the records. In 1782 Montserrat was again captured by the French but was returned to Britain in 1783 under the Treaty of Versailles.

Between 1671 and 1816 Montserrat formed part of the Leeward Islands federation. When the federation broke up in 1816 Montserrat formed a separate government with Antigua until 1871, when the Leeward Islands federation was reformed. The federation was finally dissolved in 1956 and Montserrat became a separate colony; for a short time between 1958 and 1962 it formed part of the Federation of the West Indies. Montserrat is now a British Dependent Territory.

10.17.1 Colonial Office series

See also Leeward Islands (**10.16**) and after 1951 see West Indies general (**10.1**).

Original Correspondence	1702–1872	CO 7
	1726–1872	CO 175
	1872–1951	CO 152
Registers of Correspondence	1850–1951	CO 354
Entry Books	1816–1872	CO 393
Acts	1668–1960	CO 176
Sessional Papers	1704–1965	CO 177
Government Gazettes	1967–1989	FCO 6
Miscellanea	1666–1829	CO 10
	1829–1887	CO 178
	1683–1945	CO 157
Registers of Out-letters	1872–1926	CO 507

10.17.2 Colonial Office returns of baptisms etc

1721–1729	CO 152/18	Baptisms and burials: St Anthony, 1723–1729 (fos 51–57), St George (fos 57–61) and St Peter (fos 61–63). Marriages: St Patrick (to 63), St Anthony (fos 64–65), St George (fos 65–66), and St Peter (fos 66–67)
1739–1745	CO 152/25	Baptisms and burials: various parishes (fo 137)

10.17.3 Nominal censuses

1677/8	CO 1/42, fos 218–228	Indicates whether English, Irish, Scottish, French or Dutch. Printed in Oliver's *Caribbeana*, vol. 2, p. 318
1729	EXT 1/258 (extracted from CO 152/18)	Printed in Oliver's *Caribbeana*, vol. 4, p. 302

10.17.4 Miscellaneous

1727	CO 152/16, fo 148–151	Account of losses sustained by the attack by the French under Cassart in 1712

10.17.5 Slave registers and records of the Slave Compensation Commission

Slave registers, 1817, 1821, 1824, 1828, 1831	T 71/447–451
Valuers' returns	T 71/766
Register of claims	T 71/888
Index to claims	T 71/934
Claims and certificates, original	T 71/1058
Counter claims	T 71/1261
Certificates for compensation and lists of awards	T 71/1348
Amended awards	T 71/1391
Parliamentary returns of awards	T 71/1412

10.17.6 Archives and other useful addresses

Montserrat Public Library, Government Headquarters, Plymouth, Montserrat, tel: (664) 491-4706, e-mail: publiclibrary@candw.ag

Registrar General, PO Box 22, Plymouth, Montserrat, tel: (664) 491-2129

The Montserrat National Trust, PO Box 393 Olveston, Montserrat <montserrat-natltrust.com> holds some photographs and documents relating to history of Montserrat.

Montserrat Genealogical Web Project <www.britishislesgenweb.org/caribbean/montserrat>

10.17.7 Published guides to the archives

Baker, *Guide to Records in the Leeward Islands*

In 1712 Governor John Hart reported that all the Montserrat laws and records had been burnt by the French during their invasion that year (*Calendar of State Papers, Colonial, America and West Indies, 1724–1725*, no. 91, p. 66, also *CSP, Col*, 1719–1920, no. 173, p. 86 and no. 241, p. 121). The 1928 hurricane and earthquakes between 1933–1935 damaged the court house including many of the records held there. In 1972 a fire in the new Court House destroyed most records held there.

10.17.8 Further reading

W. G. Annanen's condensed history of Montserrat <innanen.com/montserrat/history/>

Titford, 'Settlers of the Old Empire: Montserrat'

10.18 Nevis

Nevis was first colonized by British from St Christopher in 1628. Between 1671 and 1816 it formed part of the Leeward Islands federation. When the federation broke up in 1816 Nevis formed a separate government with St Christopher and the Virgin Islands until 1871, when the Leeward Islands federation was reformed. In 1882 Nevis joined with St Christopher and Anguilla to form a single presidency.

The Leeward Islands federation was finally dissolved in 1956 and St Christopher-Nevis-Anguilla became a separate colony with the capital in St Christopher. For a short time between 1958 and 1962 it formed part of the Federation of the West Indies. In 1971 Britain assumed administrative responsibility for Anguilla and in 1980 Anguilla was formally separated from St Christopher and Nevis. St Christopher and Nevis became independent on 19 September 1983.

10.18.1 Colonial Office series

See also under St Christopher (**10.19**) and Leeward Islands (**10.16**). After 1951 see West Indies general (**10.1**).

Original Correspondence	1689–1951	CO 152
	1703–1872	CO 184
	1816–1853	CO 239
Registers of Correspondence	1850–1951	CO 354
Acts	1664–1882	CO 185
	1882–1972	CO 240
Sessional Papers	1721–1882	CO 186
	1882–1960	CO 241
Government Gazettes	1879–1975	CO 242
Miscellanea	1704–1882	CO 187
	1704–1887	CO 243
Registers of Out-letters	1872–1926	CO 507

10.18.2 Colonial Office returns of baptisms etc

1726–1727	CO 152/16	Baptisms and burials: St Paul (fo 341)
1733–1734	CO 152/21	Baptisms and burials: St John (fo 163), St Thomas (fos 163–164), and St George (fo 164)
1740–1745	CO 152/25	Baptisms and burials: St James (fos 114–115)

10.18.3 Nominal censuses

1677/8	CO 1/42, fos 201–217	Indicates whether English, Irish, Scottish, French or Dutch. Printed in Oliver's *Caribbeana*, vol. 3, p. 27
1707/8	CO 152/6, no. 47 (vi)	
1707	CO 152/7, fo 47	Printed in *Caribbeana*, vol. 3, p. 255

10.18.4 Slave registers and records of the Slave Compensation Commission

Slave registers, 1817, 1822, 1825, 1828, 1831, 1834	T 71/364–369
Valuers' returns	T 71/751–752
Register of claims	T 71/882
Index to claims	T 71/928
Claims and certificates, original	T 71/1038–1039
Counter claims	T 71/1236–1237
Certificates for compensation and lists of awards	T 71/1340
Amended awards	T 71/1387
Parliamentary returns of awards	T 71/1408

10.18.5 Archives and other useful addresses

National Archives, Government Headquarters, Church St, Box 186, Basseterre, St Kitts, West Indies, tel: (869) 465-2521

Registrar General, PO Box 236, Basseterre, St Kitts, West Indies, tel: (869) 465-5251

Nevis Archives and Library, Nevis Historical and Conservation Society, Nelson Museum, Bellevue, Charlestown, Nevis, West Indies, tel: (869) 469-0408, e-mail: archives-library@nevis-nhcs.org

Nevis Historical and Conservation Society, PO Box 563, Charlestown, Nevis, West Indies <www.nevis-nhcs.org>

St Christopher and Nevis genealogical project <www.tc.umn.edu/~terre011/genhome.html>

Frank Goodwill's St Kitts-Nevis History Page <website.lineone.net/~stkittsnevis>

10.18.6 Guides to the archives

Baker, *Guide to Records in the Leeward Islands*

In 1706 many public records were damaged or destroyed by the French (*Calendar of State Papers, Colonial, America and West Indies*, 1721–1722, no. 204, XX and XXIV, pp. 120 & 122). Nevis joined with St Christopher in 1882 and most Nevis records have since been transferred to St Christopher. In 1982 a fire at the Court House in St Christopher destroyed many documents.

Many Nevis records described in Baker as being in the Archives Room, Basseterre, St Christopher, may have been destroyed by that fire.

10.18.7 Further reading

Hubbard, *Swords, Ships and Sugar: A History of Nevis*
Titford, 'Settlers of the Old Empire: Nevis'
Titford, 'Transcripts of 18th century registers'

10.19 St Christopher (St Kitts)

Settled by the English in 1623, and by the French in 1624 under d'Esnambuc. The island was divided, with the French having the two ends of the island and the English the middle. The English and French used St Christopher as a base to settle the other islands in the Leeward Islands group. In 1702 Britain took the French portions, which were ceded to Britain in 1713. St Christopher was recaptured by the French in 1782 but was restored to Britain in 1783.

Between 1671 and 1816 St Christopher formed part of the Leeward Islands federation. When the federation broke up in 1816 St Christopher formed a separate government with Nevis, Anguilla and the Virgin Islands until 1871, when the Leeward Islands federation was reformed. In 1882 St Christopher joined with Nevis and Anguilla to form a single presidency. The Leeward Islands was finally dissolved in 1956 and St Christopher-Nevis-Anguilla became a separate colony with the capital in St Christopher. For a short time between 1958 and 1962 it formed part of the Federation of the West Indies. In 1971 Britain assumed administrative responsibility for Anguilla and in 1980 it was formally separated from St Christopher and Nevis. St Christopher and Nevis became independent on 19 September 1983.

10.19.1 Colonial Office series

Before 1783 see also under France (**11.4**), see also under Leeward Islands (**10.16**) and from 1951 under West Indies general (**10.1**).

Original Correspondence	1689–1951	CO 152
	1702–1872	CO 239
Registers of Correspondence	1850–1951	CO 354
Entry Books	1816–1872	CO 407
Acts	1672–1972	CO 240
Sessional Papers	1704–1960	CO 241

Government Gazettes	1879–1975	CO 242
Miscellanea	1704–1887	CO 243
	1683–1945	CO 157
Registers of Out-letters	1872–1926	CO 507

10.19.2 Colonial Office returns of baptisms etc

1721–1730	CO 152/18	Baptisms and burials: Christ Church Nichola Town (fos 25–27); St John, Cabosaterre (fo 34); and St Mary Cayon (fos 36–38)
1733–1734	CO 152/18	Baptisms and burials: Christ Church, Nichola Town (fos 132, 134); St Mary Cayon (fos 133, 135); St George, Basseterre (fos 136–143); St Ann, Sandy Point (fos 143–144, 147–148)
1738–1745	CO 152/25	Baptisms, marriages and burials: St Mary Cayon (fos 118–121). Baptisms and burials: St George, Basseterre, 1743–1745 (fos 123–136)

The British Library (see **Useful addresses**) holds some transcriptions of population and tax records for the French part of St Christopher, 1776–1780, and parish registers, 1730–1823. The Society of Genealogists (see **Useful addresses**) holds transcripts of parish registers, 1730–1823, compiled by V. L. Oliver.

10.19.3 Nominal censuses

1674	CO 1/31, fos 7–21	Various lists of French proprietors living in or possessing land in the English quarters
1677/8	CO 1/42, fos 195–200	Indicates whether English, Irish, Scottish, French or Dutch. Printed in Oliver's *Caribbeana*, vol. 2, p. 68
1707	CO 152/7, fo 47	Includes age of head of household. Printed in *Caribbeana*, vol. 3, p. 132
1707/8	CO 152/6, no 47 (iv and v)	
1711	CO 152/9, fos 305–315	

10.19.4 Land records

1712–1716	CO 152/11, no. 6 (iii)	Account of grants of land in the former French part of St Christopher, noting grantee, by whom granted, quality of land, date, for how long, location

| 1721 | CO 152/13, fos 253–256 | List of possessors of the French land in Basseterre and Cabesterre divisions |
| 1729 | T 1/275, fos 248–249 | A list of contracts made by the Commissioners for Sale of Lands in St Christopher that formerly belonged to the French |

10.19.5 Miscellaneous

1706	CO 243/2	Account of losses sustained by the proprietors and inhabitants of the island because of the invasion of the French (other returns are in CO 152/9, fos 250–251, and CO 243/3)
1712–1720	CO 243/4–5	Powers of attorney, together with a number of wills
1717–1718	CO 152/12/1–2	Several lists relating to the French and to French plantations

10.19.6 Slave registers and records of the Slave Compensation Commission

Slave registers, 1817, 1822, 1825, 1827/8, 1831, 1834	T 71/253–260
Valuers' returns	T 71/740–742
Register of claims	T 71/879
Index to claims	T 71/925
Claims and certificates, origina	T 71/1031–1032
Counter claims	T 71/1224–1227
Certificates for compensation and lists of awards	T 71/1336
Amended awards	T 71/1384
Parliamentary returns of awards	T 71/1405

10.19.7 Archives and other useful addresses

National Archives, Government Headquarters, Church St, Box 186, Basseterre, St Kitts, tel: (869) 465-2521

Registrar General, PO Box 236, Basseterre, St Kitts, tel: (869) 465-5251

St Christopher Heritage Society, PO Box 888, Basseterre, St Christopher <www.islandimage.com/schs/home.htm>

Nevis Historical and Conservation Society, PO Box 563, Charlestown, Nevis

Michelle Terrell's St Kitts-Nevis genealogy web site <www.tc.umn.edu/~terre011/genhome.html>

Frank Goodwill's St Kitts-Nevis History Page <website.lineone.net/~stkittsnevis/>

10.19.8 Guides to the archives

Baker, *Guide to Records in the Leeward Islands*
Many records were destroyed during the wars with the French, for example Governor
    Stapleton reported in 1674 that all records had been burnt or lost in the late war (*Calendar of
    State Papers, Colonial, 1669–1674*, p. 547). In 1867 a fire destroyed much of Basseterre and in
    1982 a fire at the court house destroyed many historic records. Those records that survived
    are split between the National Archives and the New Court House.

10.19.9 Further reading

Dyde, *St Kitts*
Généalogie et historie de la Caraïbe <members.aol.com/GHCaraibe/index.html>. Sources for
    researching in the French Caribbean, including St Christopher. This site includes a
    transcription of a 1671 census of St Christopher at <members.aol.com/GHCaraibe/doc/st-
    chr/1671ter/p00.html>
Oliver, *Registers of St Thomas*
John Titford, 'Settlers of the old empire: St Kitts'

10.20 St Lucia

Temporarily settled by the English in 1605, St Lucia was claimed by the French in
1635. Settlers from St Christopher and the Bermudas settled in 1638 but were driven
off by the Caribs in 1641. A treaty of peace was made between the French and the
Caribs in 1660. St Lucia was then occupied by the British from St Christopher from
1664 to 1667, when it was restored to France. France and Britain disputed claims over
the island, and in 1723 St Lucia was declared neutral. All settlers were to leave, and
the island returned to the Caribs. In 1743 France reoccupied St Lucia which was made
neutral again in 1748. France settled the island again in 1756. Between 1762 and 1803
St Lucia was frequently captured by Britain and restored to France. St Lucia was
finally captured by Britain in 1803 and ceded to her in 1814. St Lucia was a member of
the Windward Islands federation between 1838 and 1956, and a member of the
Federation of the West Indies between 1958 and 1962. St Lucia became independent
on 22 February 1979.

10.20.1 Colonial Office series

Before 1814 see under France (**11.4**), see also Windward Islands (**10.25**) and after 1951
see West Indies general (**10.1**).

Original Correspondence	1709–1873	CO 253
	1874–1951	CO 321
Registers of Correspondence	1850–1881	CO 367
	1882–1951	CO 376
Entry Books	1794–1872	CO 254
Acts	1818–1965	CO 255
Sessional Papers	1820–1965	CO 256
Government Gazettes	1857–1975	CO 257
Miscellanea	1722–1940	CO 258
Registers of Out-letters	1872–1882	CO 505
	1883–1926	CO 377

10.20.2 Nominal census

1811   CO 253/7 [in French]

10.20.3 Miscellaneous

1787	CO 884/4, no. 44	Description of St Lucia including names of landholders with amount of land and crops grown [in French]
1823	CO 253/17	Various slave returns including manumissions granted between 7 Nov 1818 and 25 August 1823
1831	CO 253/29	Various returns relating to slaves including manumissions granted between 1825 and 1830
1831	CO 253/30, fos 488–496A	Account of losses following hurricane of 11 August 1831. Quarter, names, name of plantation or property – with references to particulars in appendix. Unfortunately this letter is a duplicate and does not include the appendix
1833	T 1/4396 (paper 6312/36)	Claims following hurricane of 11 August 1831 distributed under West Indies Loans Act. Quarter, name, purpose, value, money paid
1821–1825	CO 253/17	Various slave returns including manumissions
1825–1830	CO 253/29	Various slave returns including manumissions

| 1826–1834 | CO 258/5–15 | Reports of Protectors of Slaves, information includes punishments, births, deaths, marriages, free baptisms, and manumissions. Some of these returns are published in the British *Parliamentary Papers*, session 1829 (335) vol. XXV.255 (mfm 31.153–155), and session 1830–31 (262) vol. XV.1 (mfm 33.87–95) |

10.20.4 Slave registers and records of the Slave Compensation Commission

The St Lucia slave registry was established by Order in Council, 24 September 1814 (PC 2/196).
Slave registers, 1815, 1819, 1822, 1825, 1828, 1831, 1834, T 71/376–390
Valuers' returns, T 71/754–756
Register of claims, T 71/884
Index to claims, T 71/930
Claims and certificates, original, T 71/1041–1044
Counter claims, T 71/1241–1251
Certificates for compensation and lists of awards, T 71/1342
Amended awards, T 71/1389
Parliamentary returns of awards, T 71/1410

10.20.5 Archives and other useful addresses

St Lucia National Archives, PO Box 3060, Clarke St, Vigie, Castries, St Lucia <www.geocities.
   com/sluarchives/index.html>, tel: (758) 452-1654, e-mail: stlunatarch_mt@candw.lc
Registrar of Civil Status, Peynier Street, Castries, St Lucia, tel: (758) 452-1257
St Lucia Archaeological & Historical Society, La Clery, Castries, St. Lucia
St. Lucia National Trust, P.O. Box 595, Castries, St. Lucia <www.slunatrust.org/profile.htm>
Central Library of St Lucia, Castries, St Lucia <www.education.gov.lc/lib/lib.htm>
St Lucia Genealogical Web Project <www.britishislesgenweb.org/~stlucia/>

10.20.6 Guides to the archives

Baker, *Guide to Records in the Windward Islands*
Few if any records survive from before 1800 following the bombardment of Castries during the
   British invasion in 1796. The fires of 1927 and 1948 destroyed much of Castries and St Lucia's
   records.

10.20.7 Further reading

Breen, *St Lucia: Historical, Statistical and Descriptive*
Jesse, *Outlines of St Lucia's History*
J. Titford, 'Settlers of the Old Empire: St Lucia'

10.21 St Vincent and the Grenadines

In 1660 Britain and France declared St Vincent neutral, but between 1672 and 1748 both disputed sovereignty and attempted to settle on the island. In 1748 St Vincent was again declared neutral by the Treaty of Aix-la-Chapelle and left to the Caribs. The island was captured by Britain in 1762, ceded to her in 1763, and settled. France captured St Vincent in 1779, but it was restored to Britain in 1783. From 1763 until 1776, and then from 1833 to 1956, St Vincent was a member of the Windward Islands. Between 1958 and 1962 it was a member of the Federation of the West Indies. On 27 October 1979 St Vincent and the Grenadines became independent.

10.21.1 Colonial Office series

Before 1783 see also under France (**11.4**), see also under Windward Islands (**10.25**) and from 1951 see under West Indies general (**10.1**).

Original Correspondence	1668–1873	CO 260
	1874–1951	CO 321
Registers of Correspondence	1850–1951	CO 376
Entry Books	1776–1872	CO 261
Acts	1768–1969	CO 262
Sessional Papers	1769–1965	CO 263
Government Gazettes	1831–1975	CO 264
Miscellanea	1763–1941	CO 265
Registers of Out-letters	1872–1882	CO 506
	1883–1926	CO 377

10.21.2 Land records

1765–1766	CO 76/9	Dominica and St Vincent: Register of grants of land
1766	CO 101/1, fos 279–281	Docket register of plantation grants in the islands of Dominica, St Vincent and Tobago

1765–1767	CO 101/11, fos 212–217, 411–415	Docket register of plantation grants
1764–1797	CO 106/9–12	Sales of lands in the Ceded Islands
1766	T 1/453, fo 164	Account of one-fourth crops reaped from estates of which temporary possession was granted by the Commissioners in 1765
1766	T 1/453, fos 168–170	Account of the French Inhabitants of St Vincent whose claims were allowed by the Commissioners and who paid their fines in May 1766

10.21.3 Miscellaneous

| 1832–1833 | T 1/4396 (paper 12856/33) | Claims following hurricane of 11 August 1831 distributed under West Indies Loans Act, 1832. Date of payment, claimant, purpose, parish, value and money paid |
| 1821–1825 | CO 260/42 | Various slave returns including manumissions effected by purchase, bequest or otherwise, slave marriages, runaways committed to gaol who claimed to be free, and slaves sold in the Marshal's Office for debt |

10.21.4 Slave registers and records of the Slave Compensation Commission

Slave registers, 1817, 1822, 1825, 1828, 1831, 1834	T 71/493–500
Valuers' returns	T 71/780–782
Register of claims	T 71/892
Index to claims	T 71/938
Claims and certificates, original	T 71/1066–1068
Counter claims	T 71/1265–1269
Certificates for compensation and lists of awards	T 71/1351
Amended awards	T 71/1395
Parliamentary returns of awards	T 71/1416

10.21.5 Archives and other useful addresses

Archives Department, Cotton Ginnery Compound, Frenches, Kingstown, St Vincent and the Grenadines, tel: (784) 456-1689, e-mail: document@caribsurf.com

Registrar General, Government Buildings, Kingstown, St Vincent and the Grenadines, tel: (784) 457–1424

Land and Surveys Department, Richmond Hill, Kingstown, St Vincent and the Grenadines, for maps and plans

Saint Vincent and the Grenadines Genealogy Project <www.rootsweb.com/~vctwgw/>

10.21.6 Guides to archives

Baker, *Guide to Records in the Windward Islands*

10.21.7 Further reading

Anderson and McDonald (eds), *Between Slavery and Freedom*
Fraser and Joseph, *St Vincent and the Grenadines*
Potter, *St Vincent and the Grenadines*
Shepard, *Historical Account of the Island of St Vincent*
Young, *Black Charaibs*

10.22 Tobago

British from Barbados first settled Tobago in 1625. The Dutch in 1632, and the Courlanders in 1642, attempted further settlements. From 1658 the Dutch, French and British occupied Tobago at different occasions. Tobago was declared neutral in 1748 but was captured by Britain in 1763. France captured Tobago in 1781 and it was ceded to her in 1783. Tobago was again captured by Britain in 1793 but was restored to France in 1802. Britain finally captured Tobago in 1803, and Tobago was formally ceded to her in 1814. Tobago was a member of the Windward Islands between 1763 and 1783 and from 1833 until 1889 when it merged with Trinidad. Between 1958 and 1962 Trinidad and Tobago was a member of the Federation of the West Indies. On 31 August 1962 Trinidad and Tobago became independent.

10.22.1 Colonial Office series

See also under France (**11.4**) and Windward Islands (**10.25**), after 1888 see under Trinidad and from 1951 see under West Indies general (**10.1**).

Original Correspondence	1700–1873	CO 285
	1874–1888	CO 321
Registers of Correspondence	1850–1888	CO 376

Entry Books	1793–1872	CO 286
Acts	1768–1898	CO 287
Sessional Papers	1768–1898	CO 288
Government Gazettes	1872–1898	CO 289
Miscellanea	1766–1892	CO 290
Registers of Out-letters	1872–1882	CO 498

10.22.2 Nominal censuses

1770	CO 101/14, fos 126–127.	
1751	CO 285/2, fos 77–78	List of French inhabitants of Little Tobago by P. Drummond of HMS *Tavistock*

10.22.3 Land grants

1766	CO 101/1, fos 279–281	Docket register of plantation grants in the islands of Dominica, St Vincent and Tobago
1765–1767	CO 101/11, fos 209, 413	Docket register of plantation grants
1764–1797	CO 106/9–12	Sale of lands in the Ceded Islands

10.22.4 Slave registers and records of the Slave Compensation Commission

Slave registers, annual 1819–1834	T 71/461–492
Valuers' returns	T 71/779
Register of claims	T 71/891
Index to claims	T 71/937
Claims and certificates, original	T 71/1064–1065
Counter claims	T 71/1263–1264
Certificates for compensation and lists of awards	T 71/1351
Amended awards	T 71/1394
Parliamentary returns of awards	T 71/1415

See Trinidad for useful addresses and guides to the archives of Trinidad and Tobago.

10.22.5 Further reading

English Protestant Church of Tobago, *Register of Baptisms, Marriages and Deaths*

10.23 Trinidad

Trinidad was gradually settled by Spain during the sixteenth century and retained by Spain until 1797 when she was captured by Britain. Tobago was united with Trinidad in 1889. Trinidad and Tobago was a member of the Federation of the West Indies between 1958 and 1962, and on 31 August 1962 Trinidad and Tobago became independent.

10.23.1 Colonial Office series

Before 1797 see under Spain (**11.9**) and between 1797 and 1801 see WO 1; after 1951 see under West Indies general (**10.1**).

Original Correspondence	1783–1951	CO 295
Registers of Correspondence	1850–1951	CO 372
Entry Books	1797–1872	CO 296
Acts	1832–1960	CO 297
Sessional Papers	1803–1965	CO 298
Government Gazettes	1833–1975	CO 299
Miscellanea	1804–1945	CO 300
Registers of Out-letters	1872–1926	CO 497
High Commission, Registered Files	1962– 1966	DO 227

10.23.2 Land grants

1814 CO 295/35. Abstract of all grants of land made by the Spanish government and all permissions of occupancy or petitions of grants from the Capitulation, 14 June 1813

10.23.3 Miscellaneous

1814–1815	CO 385/1	List of people allowed to remain in Trinidad
1824	CO 295/63, fos 284–285	List of freeborn men [missing from the volume but available on film]
1824–1834	CO 300/19–33	Reports of Protectors of Slaves: punishments, criminal cases, births, deaths, marriages, free baptisms, and manumissions. Several of the reports were published in the British *Parliamentary Papers*: session 1829 (335), vol. XXV.255 (mfm 31.153–155) and session 1830–31 (262), vol. XV.1 (mfm 33.87–95)

10.23.4 Slave registers and records of the Slave Compensation Commission

Slave registers, 1813, 1815, 1816, 1819, 1822, 1825, 1828, 1831, 1834	T 71/501–519
Valuers' returns	T 71/783–789
Register of claims	T 71/893–894
Index to claims	T 71/939
Claims and certificates, original	T 71/1069–1082
Counter claims	T 71/1270–1279
Certificates for compensation and lists of awards	T 71/1352–1355
Amended awards	T 71/1396
Parliamentary returns of awards	T 71/1417

10.23.5 Archives and other useful addresses

National Archives, PO Box 763, 105 St Vincent St, Port-of-Spain, Trinidad, tel: (868) 625-2689

Registrar General's Office, Registration House, South Quay, Port-of-Spain, Trinidad, tel: (868) 623-2450

Tobago Warden's Office, TIDCO Mall, Scarborough, Tobago, tel: (868) 639-2410

Tobago Registrar General's Office, Jerningham Street, Scarborough, Tobago, tel: (868) 639-3210

National Library and Information System Authority, 105 Abercromby Street, Port of Spain, Trinidad

Trinidad and Tobago Genealogical pages <www.rootsweb.com/~ttowgw/>

10.23.6 Guides to the archives

Gropp, *Guide to Libraries*

On 23 March 1903 the government building in Port of Spain was destroyed by fire. All court, legislative and survey office files and most administrative records were lost. Many records relating to Tobago had been transferred to the government building and were also destroyed.

10.23.7 Further reading

Brereton, *History of Modern Trinidad*

Carmichael, *History of the West Indian Islands of Trinidad and Tobago*

Hansib reference special, *Trinidad and Tobago*

John, *Plantation Slaves of Trinidad*

Ottley, *Story of Tobago*

Uddenberg and Vaucrosson, *Lists from the San Fernando Gazette: 1865–1896*. Also contact gazette@shaw.ca for further information

Williams, *History of the People of Trinidad and Tobago*
Woodcock, *History of Tobago*

10.24 Turks and Caicos Islands

The Turks and Caicos Islands were uninhabited until about 1678 when saltrakers from the Bermudas frequented the Grand Turk. The Spaniards expelled these settlers in 1710, but they soon returned and held the islands. During and after the American Revolution American Loyalists settled the Caicos Islands. Both these island groups were annexed to and administered from the Bahamas in 1799. In 1848 the Turks and Caicos Islands formed their own government under the governor of Jamaica, and in 1874 they became a dependency of Jamaica until 1959. Between 1958 and 1962 the islands were a member of the Federation of the West Indies. Between 1965 and 1973 the islands were governed by the Bahamas. The islands are a British Dependent Territory.

10.24.1 Colonial Office series

Before 1848 see under Bahamas (**10.4**) and after 1873 see under Jamaica (**10.15**). After 1951 see under West Indies general (**10.1**).

Original Correspondence	1799–1848	CO 23
	1848–1882	CO 301
	1874–1951	CO 137
Registers of Correspondence	1868–1882	CO 495
Entry Books	1849–1872	CO 409
Acts	1849–1965	CO 302
Sessional Papers	1849–1965	CO 303
Government Gazettes	1907–1965	CO 681
Miscellanea	1852–1947	CO 304
Registers of Out-letters	1872–1881	CO 496
	1882–1926	CO 494

Records of the slave registry and Slave Compensation Commission for the Turks and Caicos Islands are with the records for the Bahamas (**10.4**).

10.24.2 Archives and other useful addresses

Turks and Caicos National Museum, Guinep House, Front Street, PO Box 188, Grand Turk, Turks and Caicos, BWI <www.tcmuseum.org/>, tel: (649) 946-2160, e-mail: museum@tciway.tc

The Registrar's General Office, Front Street, Turks & Caicos Islands, British West Indies, tel: (649) 946-2800

Turks and Caicos Islands Genealogy Project <www.britishislesgenweb.org/caribbean/turks/>

There is no guide to the archives of the Turks and Caicos Islands although documents relating to the islands, held in the archives and other repositories in the Bahamas, Jamaica and the PRO, may be described in guides to their archives. Very few original records have survived on the islands, but it is possible that material may survive in Jamaica, the Bahamas or in the PRO (under Jamaica and the Bahamas).

Minor political disturbances in the early 1970s saw the archive attacked and colonial records destroyed or stolen. In 1997 the archives were moved from the Post Office, where they had suffered from regular flooding, to the prison and many were later moved to the museum. About 20% of the surviving records were in such a poor condition that they were destroyed. Microfilm copies of parish registers from the late 1700s and other material relating to the islands, from Jamaica and the PRO, and some original records are available in the museum.

10.25 Windward Islands

Following the Seven Years War, in 1763 the newly ceded islands of Grenada, St Vincent, Dominica and Tobago were united under a single government called the Southern Caribbee Islands. Dominica was separated in 1771 to form part of the Leeward Islands, St Vincent left in 1776 and Tobago in 1783. In 1833 Grenada, St Vincent, Tobago and Barbados formed the Windward Islands with a single governor based initially in Barbados and later in Grenada. St Lucia was added in 1838, Barbados left in 1885, Tobago left on its merger with Trinidad in 1889, and Dominica was added in 1940. The Windward Islands federation was dissolved in 1956.

10.25.1 Colonial Office series

See also under the individual territories, after 1951 see under West Indies general (**10.1**)

Original Correspondence	1874–1951	CO 321
Registers of Correspondence	1850–1951	CO 376
Registers of Out-letters	1883–1926	CO 377

10.25.2 Further reading

Baker, *Guide to Records in the Windward Islands*

11 | Records of the non-British West Indies

This chapter describes material for the study of the history of British West Indians in other Caribbean countries.

Most of the records of British subjects on non-British West Indian islands are to be found in the records of the Foreign Office (see **9.2.1**). These are predominantly official despatches between Britain's representatives abroad and the Foreign Office. The records are arranged by country or, for the period they were colonies, under the administrative country. For example, records of St Thomas are under Denmark (before 1917) and the United States of America (after 1917), and those for St Eustatius are under the Netherlands.

Many West Indian islands of other European powers were at times occupied and administered by Britain. Surinam was originally a British settlement. In Saint Domingue British forces joined with the French forces during the slave uprising from 1791, until both countries evacuated in 1803. Most islands, however, were invaded and administered by British forces during periods of war. During the Seven Years War, 1756–1763, Guadeloupe (1759–1763), Martinique (1762–1763) and Havana (1762–1763) were occupied. During the French Revolutionary and Napoleonic Wars, 1793–1815, Curaçao (1800–1802 and 1807–1814), Guadeloupe (1810–1813), Martinique (1794–1815), St Croix (1810–1815), St Eustatius (1807–1815), St Thomas (1807–1815), and Surinam (1799–1802 and 1804–1816) were occupied.

Records during these periods of occupation are in the records of the War Office, Colonial Office and the Treasury. Information recorded includes censuses, lists of government officials and plantation returns, and identified references are included here. During periods of occupation foreign troops were often taken into British service. The means of reference to the War Office records is through Public Record Office Lists and Indexes, vol. LIII (see **Bibliography**).

11.1 Cuba

Before 1898 see Spain (**11.9**).

General Correspondence before 1906	1901–1905	FO 108
Embassy and Consular archives		
Correspondence	1870–1957	FO 277

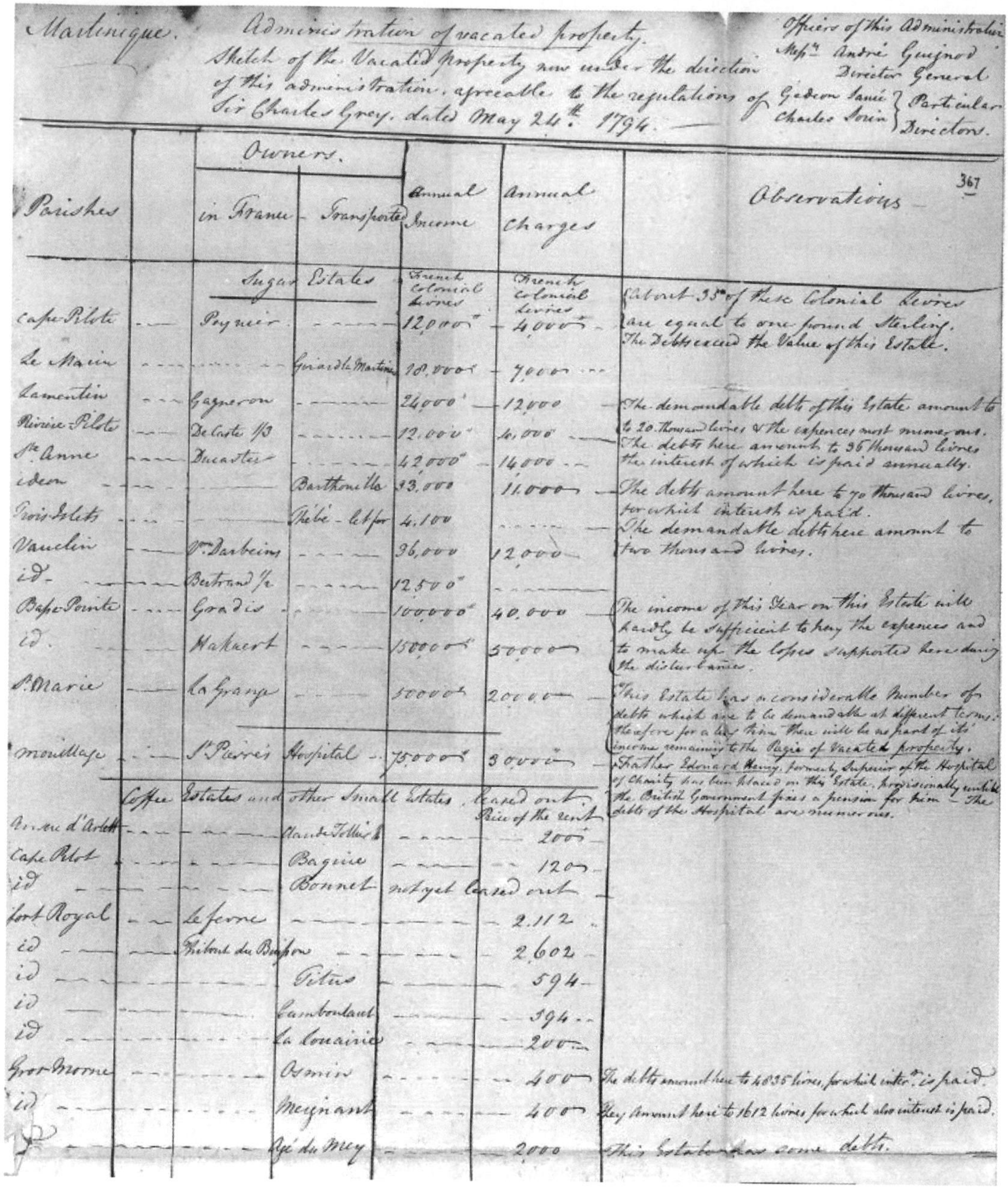

Martinique. Administration of vacated property.
Sketch of the Vacated Property now under the direction of this administration, agreeable to the regulations of Sir Charles Grey, dated May 24th. 1794.

Officers of this Administration
Messrs André Guignod — Director General
Gedeon Sanié, Charles Sorin — Particular Directors.

367

Parishes		Owners. in France	Transported	Annual Income	Annual Charges	Observations
		Sugar	Estates	French Colonial Livres	French Colonial Livres	
Cape Pilote	—	Poyneir	—	12,000	4,000	About 35 of these Colonial Livres are equal to one pound Sterling. The Debts exceed the Value of this Estate.
Le Marin	—	—	Girard le Martinie	18,000	7,000	
Lamentin	—	Gagneron	—	24,000	12,000	The demandable debt of this Estate amount to 20 thousand livres & the expences most numerous.
Rivière Pilote	—	De Laste ⅓	—	12,000	4,000	The debts here amount to 36 thousand livres the interest of which is paid annually.
Ste Anne	—	Ducastre	—	42,000	14,000	
idem	—	—	Barthonille	33,000	11,000	The debts amount here to 70 thousand livres, for which interest is paid.
Trois Islets	—	—	Thébé - lt for	4,100	—	The demandable debts here amount to two thousand livres.
Vauclin	—	Vve Darbeins	—	36,000	12,000	
id.	—	Bertrand ½	—	12,500	—	
Basse Pointe	—	Gradis	—	100,000	40,000	The income of this Year on this Estate will hardly be sufficient to pay the expences and to make up the losses supported here during the disturbance.
id.	—	Hakeert	—	150,000	50,000	
St Marie	—	La Grange	—	50,000	20,000	This Estate has a considerable Number of debts which are to be demandable at different terms: therefore for a long time there will be no part of its income remaining to the Regie of Vacated property.
Mouillage	—	St Pierre Hospital	—	75,000	30,000	Father Edouard Henry, formerly Superior of the Hospital of Charity has been placed on this Estate, provisionally untill the British Government fixes a pension for him — The debts of the Hospital are numerous.
	Coffee	Estates and	other Small Estates	leased out.	Price of the rent	
Anse d'Arlett	—	—	Claude Tellier	—	200	
Cape Pilot	—	—	Baguie	—	120	
id	—	—	Bonnet	not yet leased out		
Fort Royal	—	Le ferme	—	—	2,112	
id	—	Thibaut du Buisson	—	—	2,602	
id	—	—	Petus	—	594	
id	—	—	Cambonlaud	—	594	
id	—	—	La Louairie	—	200	
Gros Morne	—	—	Osmin	—	400	The debts amount here to 4035 livres, for which inter. is paid.
id	—	—	Meignant	—	400	They Amount here to 1612 livres for which also interest is paid.
[illegible]	—	—	Ayé du Mey	—	2,000	This Estate has some debts.

Figure 27 Martinique: list of vacated sugar estates, May 1794 (WO 1/31, p. 367).

	Registers of correspondence	1842–1939	FO 278
	Letter books	1877–1881	FO 279
	Miscellanea	1875–1914	FO 280
Havana:	Correspondence	1762–1763	CO 117
		1931–1948	FO 1001
	Registers of correspondence	1931–1936	FO 747
	Slave Trade Commission	1819–1869	FO 313
Santiago de Cuba:	Letter books	1832–1905	FO 453
	Registers of correspondence	1913–1935	FO 454
Nuevitas:	Register of correspondence	1926–1931	FO 455
Camaguey:	Register of correspondence	1925–1929	FO 456
Antilla:	Register of correspondence	1925–1932	FO 457

Archivo Nacional (National Archive), Compostela 906, San Isidro, Habana Vieja, 10100 La Habana, Cuba <www.cuba.cu/ciencia/citma/aid/archivo/>

Cuban genealogical web project

Carr, *Censos, Padrones y Matrículas de la Población de Cuba*
Carr, *Guide to Cuban Genealogical Research*

11.2 Denmark

Includes St Thomas, St John and St Croix. The Danish Virgin Islands were sold to the US in 1917. After 1917 see United States of America (**11.11**).

State Papers Foreign		1577–1780	SP 75
General Correspondence before 1906		1781–1905	FO 22
Embassy and Consular archives		1781–1957	FO 211
St Croix:	Correspondence etc	1808–1815	CO 244, WO 1
St Thomas:	Correspondence etc	1808–1815	CO 259, WO 1
	Danish emigrants	1796	FO 95/1/4, fo 258

Rigsarkivet (National Archives), Rigsdagsgården 9, 1218 København K, Denmark <www.sa.dk/ra/>

Computers in Genealogy Society of Denmark <dis-danmark.dk/indexuk.htm>

US Virgin Islands genealogical web project <www.rootsweb.com/~usvi/>

11.3 Dominican Republic (formerly Santo Domingo)

Before 1824 see under Spain (**11.9**), and between 1795 and 1844 see also under France (**11.4**) and Haiti (**11.5**).

General Correspondence before 1906	1848–1905	FO 23
Embassy and Consular archives	1848–1948	FO 140
Santo Domingo	1811–1932	FO 683

Archivo General de la Nacion, Calle M E Diaz, Santo Domingo, Dominican Republic

Dominican Republic genealogical web project <www.rootsweb.com/~domwgw/mhhbcgw.htm>

11.4 France

Includes Martinique, Guadeloupe, St Martin, St Barthélemy, and French Guiana (Guyane), and St Lucia (**10.20**), St Vincent (**10.21**), Tobago (**10.22**), Grenada (**10.13**), a portion of St Christopher (**10.19**) and Dominica (**10.11**) until these were ceded to Britain.

State Papers	1577–1780	SP 78
General Correspondence before 1906	1781–1905	FO 27
Embassy and Consular archives	1814–1957	FO 146
Martinique: Correspondence etc	1693–1815	CO 166, WO 1
Administration of vacated properties listing owners by parish	1794	WO 1/31, p. 367–397
Guadeloupe: Correspondence etc	1758–1816	CO 110, WO 1

Le Centre des Archives d'outre-mer, 29 chemin du Moulin-Detesta, 13090 Aix-en-Provence, France <www.archivesnationales.culture.gouv.fr/caom/fr/index.html>

Archives départementales de la Martinique, BP 649, 19 avenue Saint-John Perse, 97263 Fort-de-France, Cedex

Archives départementales de la Guadeloupe, BP 74, 97120 Basseterre, Cedex

Archives départementales de la Guyane, Place Leopold Heder, 97302 Cayenne, Cedex

Archives Nationales, *Guide des Sources de l'Histoire de l'Amerique Latine*

Archives Nationales, *Les Archives Nationales Etat General des Fonds*. Especially vol. 3 on overseas records

Généalogie et Histoire de la Caraïbe <users.aol.com/GHCaraibe/index.html>

France Genealogical Web Project <www.francegenweb.org>

11.5 Haiti (formerly Saint-Domingue)

Before 1824 see under France (**11.4**). Between 1795 and 1803 British troops occupied Saint-Domingue and records in the PRO often refer to Saint-Domingue as Santo Domingo; it is possible that they refer to the whole island. There is much correspondence relating to Saint-Domingue, between 1795–1808, in CO 137 (Jamaica).

General Correspondence before 1906	1693–1805	CO 245, WO 1
	1825–1905	FO 35
Embassy and Consular archives	1833–1963	FO 866
Aux Cayes consular archives	1870–1907	FO 376
Santo Domingo Claims Committee	1794–1812	T 81
Pay Lists and other documents concerning refugees	1780–1856	T 50
Accounts of Absentee estates	1794–1803	T 64/223–231

Archives nationales d'Haïti, BP 1299, Angle rues Borgella et Geffrard, Port-au-Prince, Haïti

Genealogy of Haiti and Saint-Domingue <www.rootsweb.com/~htiwgw/>

Haiti Genealogical Society

11.6 Honduras

Before 1821 see Spain (**11.9**). Between 1825 and 1838 Honduras was a member of the Federation of Central America, together with Costa Rica, El Salvador, Guatemala and Nicaragua.

General correspondence before 1906	1824–1905	FO 15
	1857–1905	FO 39
Embassy, legation and consulates	1825–1970	FO 252
Consular archives	1861–1948	FO 632

National Archives, Avenida Cristóbal Colón, Calle Salvador Mendieta, No. 1117, Tegucigalpa, M.D.C., Honduras <www.sdnhon.org.hn/miembros/cultura/archi.htm>

Honduras Genealogical Web Project <www.rootsweb.com/~hndwgw/honduras.html>

11.7 Netherlands

Includes the Netherlands Antilles (Aruba, Curaçao, St Eustatius, Saba, Bonair and St Maarten), Surinam (until 1975), and Berbice, Essequibo and Demerara until captured by Britain in 1803 (**10.14**). Documents relating to the Dutch West India Company administration of Berbice, Essequibo and Demerara are in CO 116.

State Papers	c.1560–1780	SP 84
General Correspondence before 1906	1781–1905	FO 37
	1967–1974	FCO 33
Embassy and Consular archives: Correspondence	1811–1956	FO 238
Registers of correspondence	1813–1894	FO 240
Miscellanea	1815–1908	FO 241

Netherlands Antilles registers of births, marriages and deaths for Curaçao, Aruba, Paramaribo and Surinam		1889–1966	FO 907
Curaçao:	Correspondence etc	1800–1816	CO 66, WO 1
St Eustatius	Correspondence etc	1779–1783	CO 246
	Lists of burghers	1781	CO 318/8, fos 60–86
Surinam:	Correspondence etc	1667–1832	CO 278, CO 111, WO 1
	Surinam Absentees Sequestered Property Commission	1813–1822	T 75
	Census	1811	CO 278/15–27
	List of people who have sugar works and plantations in Surinam with the number of slaves	c.1674	CO 1/31, fo 293
	List of plantation owners 1805		WO 1/149, p 307–357

General State Archives, Postal address PO Box 90520, 2509 LM, The Hague <www.archief.nl/rad/>

Landsarchiefdienst, Dockhiewg 18 A, Panamaribo, Suriname

Netherlands Antilles National Archives, Scharlooweg 77, Willemstad, Curaçao, Nederlandse Antillen <www.nationalarchives.an/htmls/index.html>

Netherlands Antilles Genealogical Web Project <www.rootsweb.com/~antwgw/>

Suriname Genealogical Web Project <www.geocities.com/surinamegenweb/index.html>

11.8 Panama

Before 1819 see under Spain (**11.9**). Between 1819 and 1903 Panama was a member of the Republic of Colombia and later the Republic of New Grenada. From the 1850s many West Indians worked on the construction of the trans-isthmian railway and later on the construction of the canal. Between 1906 and 1999 the Panama Canal Zone was under the jurisdiction of the United States of America, and vital records and census returns from 1920 are available in the United States (**11.11**).

General Correspondence before 1906	1835–1904	FO 55
	1904–1905	FO 110

Embassy and Consular archives

Colon:	General correspondence	1890–1948	FO 806
Panama:	General Correspondence	1828–1970	FO 288
	Letter Books	1827–1904	FO 289
	Registers of Correspondence	1860–1930	FO 290
Panama City:	General correspondence	1938–1947	FO 986

Archivo Nacional, Avenida Peru y Calle 31 y 32, Panama 5

Panama Genealogical web project <www.rootsweb.com/~panwgw/Panama_home. htm>

11.9 Spain

Includes Cuba (until 1898, **11.1**), Puerto Rico (until 1898, **11.11**) and Santo Domingo (until 1844, **11.3**), and to the Caribbean and Central and South America in general until other European powers settled Spanish possessions.

State Papers	1577–1780	SP 94
General Correspondence before 1906	1781–1905	FO 72
Embassy and Consular archives	1783–1962	FO 185

Archivo General de Indias, Avda. de la Constitución, 3, 41071 Sevilla <www.mcu.es/lab/ archivos/AGI.html>

Garcia (ed.), *Discovering the Americas: Archive of the Indies*
Tello, Menendez and Herrero, *Documentos Relativos a la Independencia de Norteamerica*
Spanish Genealogical Web Project <members.aol.com/balboanet/spain/index.html>

11.10 Sweden

St Bartholomew was Sweden's only Caribbean colony. It was purchased from France in 1784 and was sold back to France in 1878. Before 1784, and after 1878 see under France (**11.4**).

General correspondence	1784–1878	FO 73

Riksarkivet (National Archives) PO Box 125 41, SF-102 29 Stockholm <www.ra.se/index.html>

11.11 United States of America

Includes the US Virgin Islands of St John, St Thomas and St Croix (before 1917 see under Denmark, **11.2**) and Puerto Rico (before 1898 see under Spain, **11.9**). Between 1906 and 1999 the United States of America had jurisdiction over the Panama Canal Zone (**11.8**).

Embassy and Consulates archives

Correspondence	1791–1956	FO 115
Registers of correspondence	1816–1929	FO 117

National Archives and Records Administration, 700 Pennsylvania Avenue, NW, Washington, DC 20408 <www.archives.gov>

St Croix Landmarks Society, 52 Estate Whim, Frederiksted, St. Croix VI 00840 <www.stcroixlandmarks.org/library.html>

Genealogy of Puerto Rico <www.rootsweb.com/~prwgw/index.html>

US Virgin Islands genealogical web project <www.rootsweb.com/~usvi/>

US Genealogical Web Project <www.usgenweb.org>

Useful addresses

Addresses for West Indian archives, register offices and other useful addresses can be found under the relevant country in **Chapter 10** (for British Caribbean countries) and **Chapter 11** (for non-British Caribbean countries).

Archives of Canada, 395 Wellington Street, Ottawa, Ontario, K1A 0N3, tel: (613) 947 0391, <www.archives.ca>

British Library, 96 Euston Rd, London NW1 2DB, tel: 020 7412 7677, <www.bl.uk/>

British Library, Newspaper Library, Colindale Avenue, London NW9 5HE, 020 7412 7353, <wwwbl.uk/collections/newspapers.html>

British Library, Oriental and India Office Collections, 96 Euston Rd, London NW1 2DP, tel: 020 7412 7873, <www.bl.uk/collections/orientalandindian.html>

Commonwealth War Graves Commission, 2 Marlow Rd, Maidenhead, Berkshire SL6 7DX, tel: 01628 634221, <www.cwgc.org>

Family Records Centre, 1 Myddelton St, London EC1R 1UW, tel: 020 8392 5200, <www.pro.gov.uk> and <www.familyrecords.gov.uk>

Guildhall Library, Aldermanbury, London EC2P 2EJ, tel: 020 7332 1863, <www.history.ac.uk/gh/>

Home Office, Immigration and Nationality Directorate, 3rd Floor, India Buildings, Water St, Liverpool L2 0QN, tel: 0151 237 5200, <www.homeoffice.gov.uk> and <194.203.40.90>

Lambeth Palace Library, London, SE1 7JU, tel: 020 7898 1400, <www.lambeth palacelibrary.org>

Maritime History Archive, Memorial University of Newfoundland, St John's A1C 5S7, Newfoundland, Canada, tel: (709) 737 8428, <www.mun.ca/mha/>

Ministry of Defence, <www.mod.uk>

Army

Army Personnel Centre, Historic Disclosures, Mailpoint 400, Kentigern House, 65 Brown St, Glasgow, G2 8EX, tel: 0141 224 2023 and 0141 224 3303, email: apcsec@dial.pipex.com. For records of service for officers who left after 1922 and men who left after 1920

Army Medal Office, Government Buildings, Worcestershire Road, Droitwich Spa, Worcestershire WR9 8AU

Royal Navy

Naval Secretary (OMOBS), Room 169, Victory Building, HM Naval Base, Portsmouth, Hampshire PO1 3LS. For Royal Navy officers under 60

DR 2a (Navy Search), Room 31, Bourne Avenue, Hayes, Middlesex UB3 1RF. For retired Royal Navy officers

Naval Records, CS(R)2a, Bourne Avenue, Hayes, Middlesex UB3 1RF. For Royal Navy ratings, 1923–1938

HMS Centurion, Grange Rd, Gosport, Hampshire PO13 9XA. For Royal Navy ratings who joined after 1938

Royal Navy Medal Office, Room 3103, HMS Centurion, Gosport, Hampshire PO13 9XA

Royal Marines

Drafting and Record Office, Royal Marines, HMS Centurion, Grange Road, Gosport, Hampshire PO13 9XA

Royal Air Force

PMA (CS) 2a(2), RAF Innsworth, Gloucestershire GL3 1EZ

National Archives and Records Administration, National Archives Building, 700 Pennsylvania Avenue, NW, Washington, DC 20408, USA, <www.archives.gov>

National Archives of India, Janpeth, New Delhi 110001, India, <nationalarchives. nic.in/vsnationalarchives>

Office of National Statistics, Certificate enquiries, PO Box 2, Southport, Merseyside PR8 2JD, tel: 0870 243 7788, <www.statistics.gov.uk>. Indexes to birth, marriage and death registers are available at the Family Records Centre, Church of Jesus Christ of

Latter-day Saints' Family History Centres, the PRO and many UK archives and libraries

Ordnance Survey, International Library, Romney Rd, Southampton SO16 4GU, tel: 023 8079 2912, <www.ordnancesurvey.co.uk/osi/>

Principal Registry of the Family Division, First Avenue House, 42–49 High Holborn, London WC1V 6NP, tel: 020 7947 7000, <www.courtservice.gov.uk>. Written enquiries are to be sent to the York Probate Sub-registry, First Floor, Castle Chambers, Clifford St, York YO1 7EA

Rhodes House Library, South Parks Rd, Oxford OX1 3RG, tel: 01865 270909, <www.bodley.ox.ac.uk/dept/rhl/>

Royal Commission on Historical Manuscripts, Quality House, Quality Court, Chancery Lane, London WC2A 1HP, tel: 020 7242 1198, <www.hmc.gov.uk>. From April 2003, the Commission will join the Public Record Office to form a single organisation, the National Archives, at the PRO's current address at Kew.

Society of Genealogists, 14 Charterhouse Buildings, Goswell Rd, London EC1M 7BA, tel: 020 7251 8799, <www.sog.org.uk>

Southampton Archive Service, Civic Centre, Southampton SO14 7LY, tel: 023 8083 2251, <www.Southampton.gov.uk/education/libraries/arch.htm>

Bibliography

Acts of the Privy Council, Colonial Series, 1613–1783, 6 volumes (London, 1908–12)

A. Anderson, *Caribbean Immigrants: A Socio-demographic Profile* (Canadian Scholars Press, 1993)

J. Anderson and R. A. McDonald (eds), *Between Slavery and Freedom: Special Magistrate John Anderson's Journal of St Vincent During the Apprenticeship* (University of Pennsylvania Press, 2001)

J. A. P. M. Andrade, *A Record of the Jews in Jamaica: From the English Conquest to the Present Time* (Jamaica, 1941)

C. M. Andrews, *Guide to Materials for American History to 1783 in the Public Record Office of Great Britain*, 2 vols (Carnegie Institution of Washington, 1912 and 1914)

Archives Nationales, *Les Archives Nationales Etat General des Fonds*, 3 vols (Archives Nationales, 1978–1980)

Archives Nationales, *Guide des Sources de l'Histoire de l'Amerique Latine et des Antilles dans les Archives Francaises* (Paris, 1984)

L. Atherton, 'Never complain, never explain'. *Records of the Foreign Office and State Paper Office, 1500–c. 1960* (Public Record Office, 1994)

C. T. Atkinson, 'Foreign regiments in the British army 1793–1802', in *Journal of the Society for Army Historical Research*, vol 22 1943/4.

E. C. Baker, *A Guide to Records in the Leeward Islands* (Basil Blackwell, 1965)

E. C. Baker, *A Guide to Records in the Windward Islands* (Basil Blackwell, 1968)

J. H. Baker, *An Introduction to Legal History*, 4th edn (Butterworths Law, 2002)

P. L. Baker, *Centring the Periphery: Chaos, Order and the Ethnohistory of Dominica* (McGill-Queens University Press, 1994)

O. T. Barck and H. T. Lefler, *Colonial America* (Collier, 1968)

D. Beasley, *Family Pride: The Complete Guide to Tracing African-American Genealogy* (Hungry Minds Inc., 1997)

H. Beckles, *A History of Barbados from Amerindian Settlement to Nation-state* (Cambridge University Press, 1990)

H. Beckles and V. Shepherd (eds), *Caribbean Slave Society and Economy: A Student Reader* (James Currey Publishers, 1993)

H. C. Bell and D. W. Parker, *Guide to British West Indian Archive Materials in London and in the Islands for the History of the United States* (Carnegie Institution of Washington, 1926)

A. Bertram, *The Colonial Service* (Cambridge University Press, 1930)

A. Bevan, *Tracing Your Ancestors in the Public Record Office* (Public Record Office, sixth revised edition, 2002)

R. Blatchford, *Family and Local History Handbook: Annual Directory*, 6th edn (G. R. Specialist Information Services, 2002)

O. N. Bolland, *The Formation of a Colonial Society: Belize, from Conquest to Crown Colony* (John Hopkins University Press, 1977)

B. Bousquet and C. Douglas, *West Indian Women at War: British Racism in World War II* (Lawrence and Wishart, 1991)

S. J. Braidwood, *Black Poor and White Philanthropists: London's Blacks and the Foundation of the Sierra Leone Settlement 1786–1791* (Liverpool University Press, 1994)

J. C. Brandow, *Genealogies of Barbados Families* (Genealogical Publishing Co., Inc., 1983)

J. C. Brandow, *Omitted Chapters from Hotten* (Genealogical Publishing Co., Inc., 1982)

H. H. Breen, *St Lucia: Historical, Statistical and Descriptive* (reprinted by Frank Cass, 1970)

B. Brereton, *A History of Modern Trinidad 1783–1962* (Heineman Educational Books, 1981)

British Museum, *List of Documents Relating to the Bahama Islands in the British Museum and Record Office, London* (Nassau, 1910)

G. Brizan, *Grenada, Island of Conflict: From Amerindians to People's Revolution 1498–1979* (Zed Books, 1984)

W. Brown, 'The American Loyalists in Jamaica', *Journal of Caribbean History*, vol. 26, no. 2, 1992, pp. 121–46

R. N. Buckley, *Slaves in Redcoats. The British West India Regiments, 1795–1815* (Yale University Press, 1979)

J. A. Burdon, *Archives of British Honduras*, 3 vols (Sifton Praed & Co., 1931)

W. G. L. Burgan, *Some West Indian Memorials: Being a Record of the Tablets in St George's Grenada, With Notes* (Grenada, 1917)

T. Burnard, 'Slave naming patterns: Onomastics and the taxonomy of race in eighteenth-century Jamaica', *Journal of Interdisciplinary History*, vol. XXXI no. 3, Winter 2001

T. Burroughs, *Black Roots: A Beginner's Guide to Tracing the African American Family Tree* (Fireside, 2001)

M. Byron, *Post-war Migration from the Caribbean to Britain: The Unfinished Cycle* (Avebury, 1994)

Calendar of State Papers, Colonial, America and West Indies, 1574–1739, 40 vols (HMSO, 1860–1993). Published on CD-ROM, with obsolete references modernised, by Routledge in association with the PRO (2000)

Calendar of State Papers, Domestic, 1547–1704, 90 vols (HMSO, 1856–1972)

Calendar of Treasury Books, 1660–1718, 32 vols (HMSO, 1904–1962)

Calendar of Treasury Books and Papers, 1729–1745, 5 vols (HMSO, 1898–1903)

Calendar of Treasury papers, 1557–1728, 6 vols (HMSO, 1868–1889)

A. J. Camp, 'Some West Indian sources in England', *Family Tree Magazine*, November 1987, p. 11

H. D. Carberry and D. Thompson, *A West Indian in England* (Central Office of Information, 1950)

Caribbean Historical and Genealogical Journal, TCI Genealogical Resources, PO Box 15839, San Luis, Obispo, California 93406, USA

G. Carmichael, *The History of the West Indian Islands of Trinidad and Tobago 1498–1900* (Alvin Redman, 1961)

P. E. Carr, *Censos, Padrones y Matrículas de la Población de Cuba*, siglos 16, 17 y 18 (TCI Genealogical Resources, 1995)

P. E. Carr, *Guide to Cuban Genealogical Research* (Clearfield Co., 2000)

P. Cash, S. Gordon and G. Saunders, *Sources for Bahamian History* (Macmillan Publishing, 1991)

M. Chamberlain, *Narratives of Exile and Return* (Caribbean Publishing, 1997) – about Barbadian migration

M. Chamberlain (ed.), *Caribbean Migration* (Routledge, 1998)

M. Chandler, *A Guide to Sources in Barbados* (Basil Blackwell, 1965)

C. Chapman, *Tracing Your British Ancestors* (Genealogical Publishing Co., 1996)

P. Christian, *The Genealogist's Internet* (Public Record Office, 2001)

P. Clark and D. Souden, *Migration and Society in Early Modern England* (Hutchinson, 1987)

P. W. Coldham, *American Loyalist Claims* (National Genealogical Society, 1992)

P. W. Coldham, *American Wills and Administrations in the Prerogative Court of Canterbury 1610–1857* (Genealogical Publishing Co. Inc., 1989)

P. W. Coldham, *American Wills Proved in London 1611–1775* (Genealogical Publishing Co. Inc., 1992)

P. W. Coldham, *Bonded Passengers to America*, 3 vols (Genealogical Publishing Co. Inc., 1983)

P. W. Coldham, *The Bristol Registers of Servants Sent to Foreign Plantations, 1654–1686* (Genealogical Publishing Co. Inc., 1988)

P. W. Coldham, *The Complete Book of Emigrants, 1607–1776*, 4 vols (Genealogical Publishing Co. Inc., 1987–93)

P. W. Coldham, *The Complete Book of Emigrants in Bondage, 1614–1775* (Genealogical Publishing Co. Inc., 1988)

P. W. Coldham, *Emigrants from England to the American Colonies* (Genealogical Publishing Co. Inc., 1983)

P. W. Coldham, *Emigrants in Chains* (Genealogical Publishing Co. Inc., 1992)

J. Cole, *Tracing Your Family Tree* (Countryside Books, 2000)

Colonial Office List, annual publication 1862–1966

S. Colwell, *Dictionary of Genealogical Sources in the Public Record Office* (Weidenfeld and Nicolson, 1992)

S. Colwell, *The Family Records Centre* (Public Record Office, 2002)

S. Colwell, *Family Roots: Discovering the Past in the Public Record Office* (Weidenfeld and Nicolson, 1991)

S. Colwell, *Teach Yourself Tracing Your Family History* (Hodder and Stoughton, 1997)

J. Cox, *New to Kew?* (Public Record Office, 1997)

J. Cox, *Wills, Inventories and Death Duties: The Records of the Prerogative Court of Canterbury and the Estate Duty Office: A Provisional Guide* (Public Record Office, 1988)

M. Craton, *A History of the Bahamas* (Collins, 1962)

M. Craton, 'Changing patterns of slave families in the British West Indies', *Journal of Interdisciplinary History*, vol. 10, 1979

M. Craton and G. Saunders, *Islanders in the Stream: A History of the Bahamian People*, 2 vols (University of Georgia Press, 1992 and 1998)

D. Crewe, *Yellow Jack and the Worm: British Naval Administration in the West Indies, 1739–1748* (Liverpool University Press, 1993)

P. Crooks, *Ancestors* (Black Amber, 2002)

E. P. Crowe, *Genealogy Online* (McGraw Hill, 2000)

I. M. Cumpston, *Indians Overseas in British Territories, 1834–1854* (Oxford University Press, 1953)

F. Cundall, *Jamaica's Part in the Great War, 1914–1918* (Institute of Jamaica, 1925)

P. D. Curtin, *The Atlantic Slave Trade: A Census* (University of Winsconsin Press, 1969)

Current Guide to the Holdings of the PRO

D. Dabydeen and B. Samaroo (eds), *Across the Dark Waters: Ethnicity and Indian Identity in the Caribbean* (Macmillan, 1996)

R. P. Devas, *A History of the Island of Grenada, 1498–1796: With Some Notes and Comments on Carriacou and Events of Later Years* (Grenada, 1974)

I. Diamond and S. Clarke, 'Demographic patterns among Britain's ethnic groups', in *The Changing Population of Britain*, (ed.) Heather Joshi (Basil Blackwell, 1989)

D. Dobson, *Directory of Scots Banished to the American Plantations: 1650–1775* (Clearfield Co, 2001)

D. Dobson, *Directory of Scottish Settlers in North America, 1625–1825*, 6 vols (Genealogical Publishing Co., Inc., 1984–86)

D. Dobson, *The Original Scots Colonists of Early America, 1612–1783* (Genealogical Publishing Co. Inc., 1999)

N. Dobson, *A History of Belize* (Longman Caribbean, 1973)

E. Donnan, *Documents Illustrative of the History of the Slave Trade to America*, 4 vols (Carnegie Institution, 1930–1935)

I. Dookhan, *A History of the British Virgin Islands* (Caribbean Universities Press, 1975)

R. S. Dunn, *Sugar and Slaves: The Rise of the Planter Class in the English West Indies, 1624–1713* (WW Norton & Company, 1973)

B. Dyde, *Antigua and Barbuda: Heart of the Caribbean*, 2nd edn (Macmillan Caribbean, 1993)

B. Dyde, *The Caribbean Companion* (Caribbean Publishing, 1992)

B. Dyde, *The Empty Sleeve: The Story of the West India Regiments of the British Army* (Hansib Publications, 1998)

B. Dyde, *A History of Antigua: The Unsuspecting Isle* (Macmillan Caribbean, 2000)

B. Dyde, *St Kitts: Cradle of the Caribbean* (Caribbean Publishing, 1999)

B. Edwards, *The History of the British West Indies*, 5th edn, five vols (London, 1819)

J. Ellis, 'George Rose: An exemplary soldier', *Black and Asian Studies Association Newsletter*, no. 31, September 2001

D. Eltis, *The Rise of Atlantic Slavery in the Americas* (Cambridge University Press, 2000)

D. Eltis, 'The traffic in slaves between the British West Indian colonies, 1807–1833', *Economic History Review*, 2nd series, vol. 25, 1972

D. Eltis, S. D. Behrendt, D. Richardson and H. S. Klein, *The Transatlantic Slave Trade: A Database on CD-ROM* (EH.NET, 2000)

English Protestant Church of Tobago, *Register of Baptisms, Marriages and Deaths from 1781 to 1817* (Trinidad and Tobago, 1936)

J. D. Fage, *A History of Africa* (Hutchinson, 1986)

Family Tree Magazine, Family Tree Magazine, 61 Great Whyte, Ramsey, Huntingdon, Cambridgeshire, PE17 1HL <www.familytreemagazine.com>

P. L. Fermor, *The Travellers' Tree: A Journey through the Caribbean Islands* (Penguin Books, 1984)

G. Fiddes, *The Dominions and Colonial Offices* (G. P. Putnam's Sons, 1926).

P. W. Filby and M. K. Meyer (eds), *Passenger and Immigration Lists Index*, 3 vols and annual supplements (Gale Research Company, 1981–2002)

N. File and C. Power, *Black Settlers in Britain 1555–1958* (Heinemann Educational Books, 1981)

N. Foner, *Islands in the City: West Indian Immigration to New York* (University of California Press, 2001)

N. Foner, *Jamaica Farewell: Jamaican Migrants in London* (Routledge, 1979)

N. Foner (ed.), *New Immigrants in New York* (Columbia University Press, 2001)

S. Fowler, *The Joys of Family History* (Public Record Office, 2001)

S. Fowler, P. Elliot, R. C. Nesbit, and C. Goulter, *RAF Records in the PRO* (Public Record Office, 1994)

S. Fowler and W. Spencer, *Army Records for Family Historians*, 2nd edn (Public Record Office, 1998)

V. Francis, *With Hope in Their Eyes* (X Press, 1998)

A. Fraser and K. Joseph, *Our Country: St Vincent and the Grenadines* (Caribbean Publishing, 1998)

P. Fryer, *The Politics of Windrush* (Index Books, 1999)

P. Fryer, *Staying Power: The History of Black People in Britain* (Pluto Press, 1984)

D. Galenson, *White Servitude and Colonial America* (Cambridge University Press, 1981)

E. Galford, *The Essential Guide to Genealogy* (Marshall Editions, 2001)

A. Games, *Migration and the Origins of the English Atlantic World* (Harvard University Press, 1999)

P. G. Garcia (ed.), *Discovering the Americas: the Archive of the Indies* (Vendome Press, 1997)

Genealogists' Magazine, Society of Genealogists, 14 Charterhouse Buildings, Goswell Rd, London EC1M 7BA <www.sog.org.uk>

General Register Office, *Abstract of Arrangements Respecting Registration of Birth, Marriages and Deaths in the United Kingdom and the Other Countries of the British Commonwealth and in the Republic of Ireland* (HMSO, 1952)

J. S. W. Gibson, *Probate Jurisdictions: Where to Look for Wills*, 5th edn (Federation of Family History Societies, 2002)

G. Gmelch, *Double Passage: The Lives of Caribbean Migrants Abroad and Back Home* (University of Michigan Press, 1993)

K. Grannum, *Pocket Guide to Family History: Using Wills*, revised edn (Public Record Office, 2001)

C. H. Grant, *The Making of Modern Belize: Politics, Society and British Colonialism in Central America* (Cambridge Commonwealth Series, 1991)

T. H Green, *Monumental Inscriptions of the Royal Naval Cemetery, Ireland Island*, Bermuda (typescript, 1983)

R. Greenwood, S. Hamber and B. Dyde, *Caribbean Certificate History Book 1: Amerindians to Africans* (Macmillan Education, 2001)

R.Greenwood, S. Hamber and B. Dyde, *Caribbean Certificate History Book 2: Emancipation to Emigration* (Macmillan Education, 2002)

R. Greenwood, S. Hamber and B. Dyde, *Caribbean Certificate History Book 3: Decolonisation and Development* (Macmillan Education, 2001)

V. D. Greenwood, *The Researcher's Guide to American Genealogy*, 2nd edn (Genealogical Publishing Co. Inc., 1990)

J. Grenham, *Tracing Your Irish Ancestors* (Gill and Macmillan, 1999)

A. E. Gropp, *Guide to Libraries and Archives in Central America and the West Indies, Panama, Bermuda and British Guiana* (New Orleans, 1941)

Guildhall Library, *The British Overseas: A Guide to Records of Their Births, Baptisms, Marriages, Deaths and Burials Available in the United Kingdom*, 3rd edn (Guildhall Library, 1994)

H. Gutman, *The Black Family in Slavery and Freedom, 1750–1925* (Basil Blackwell, 1976)

A. C. H. Hallett, *Early Bermudan Records, 1619–1826: A Guide to the Parish and Clergy Registers with Some Assessment Lists and Petitions* (Juniperhill Press, 1991)

C. F. E. H. Hallett, *Early Bermuda Wills 1629–1835* (Juniperhill Press, 1993)

C. F. E. H. Hallett, *Bermuda Index, 1784–1914: An Index of Births, Marriages, and Deaths as Recorded in Bermudan Newspapers, 2 vols* (Juniperhill Press, 1989)

J. S Handler, *Guide to Source Materials for the Study of Barbados History, 1627–1834* (South Illinois University Press, 1971)

J. S. Handler, *Supplement to a Guide to Source Material for the Study of Barbados History, 1627–1834* (The John Carter Brown Library, 1991)

J. S. Handler, 'Slave manumissions and freedmen in Seventeenth century Barbados', in *The William and Mary Quarterly*, vol. 41, 1984, pp. 390–408

J. S. Handler, R. Hughes, and E. M. Wiltshire, *Freedmen of Barbados: Names and Notes for Genealogical and Family History Research* (Friends of the Barbados Archives, 1999)

J. S. Handler, F. W. Lange and R. V. Riordan, *Plantation Slavery in Barbados: An Archeological and Historical Investigation* (Replica Books, 2002)

J. S. Handler and J. Jacoby, 'Slave names and naming in Barbados, 1650–1830' in *The William and Mary Quarterly*, 3rd series, vol. 53, no. 4, October 1996

Hansib reference special, *Trinidad and Tobago* (Hansib, 2000)

S. Harney, *Nationalism and Identity: Culture and Imagination in a Caribbean Diaspora* (Zed Books, 1996)

D. Hawgood, *Internet for Genealogy* (David Hawgood, 1996)

D. T. Hawkings, *Criminal Ancestors: A Guide to Historical Criminal Records in England and Wales* (Sutton Publishing, 1996)

M. S. Healy, 'Colour, climate, and combat: The Caribbean Regiment in the Second World War', *The International History Review*, vol. XXII, March 2000, pp. 65–85

A. L. Helm and M. L. Helm, *Genealogy Online for Dummies*, 3rd edn (Hungry Minds Inc., 2001)

M. D. Herber, *Ancestral Trails* (Sutton Publishing, 2000)

D. Hey, *The Oxford Guide to Family History* (Oxford Paperbacks, 1998)

B. W. Higman, *Jamaica Surveyed: Plantation Maps and Plans of the Eighteenth and Nineteenth Centuries* (Institute of Jamaican Publishers, 1988)

B. W. Higman, *Slave Population and Economy in Jamaica, 1807–1834* (Cambridge University Press, 1976; University of the West Indies, 1995)

B. W. Higman, *Slave Populations of the British Caribbean, 1807–1834* (John Hopkins University Press, 1988)

B. W. Higman (ed.), *General History of the Caribbean, Volume VI: Methodology and Historiography of the Caribbean* (Caribbean Publishing, 1999)

G. S. S. Hirst, *Notes on the History of the Cayman Islands* (Jamaica, 1910)

F. Holmes, *The Bahamas During the Great War* (Nassau, 1924)

L. Honychurch, *The Dominica Story: A History of the Island*, 3rd edn (Macmillan, 1998)

L. Honychurch and G. Aird, *Dominica: Island of Adventure*, 3rd edn (Caribbean Publishing, 1998)

H. Horwitz, *Chancery Equity Records and Proceedings, 1600–1800*, PRO handbook no. 27 (Public Record Office, 1998)

H. Horwitz, *Exchequer Equity Records and Proceedings, 1649–1841*, PRO handbook no. 32 (Public Record Office, 2001)

T. Hoskins, *Black People in Britain 1650–1850* (Macmillan Education, 1984)

J. C. Hotten, *The Original Lists of People of Quality... and Others Who Went from Great Britain to the American Plantations 1600–1700* (Genealogical Publishing Co. Inc., 1980)

G. Howe, *West Indians and World War I: A Social History of the British West Indies Regiment* (University of the West Indies, 1994)

B. T. Howell, *How to Trace Your African-American Roots: Discovering Your Unique History* (Citadel Press, 1999)

R. Howell, *The Royal Navy and the Slave Trade* (Croom Helm, 1987)

F. A. Hoyos, *Barbados: A History from Amerindians to Independence* (Macmillan Press, 1992)

V. K. Hubbard, *Swords, Ships and Sugar: A History of Nevis to 1900* (Premier Editions, 1997)

Huguenot Society, *Guiseppi, Naturalization of Foreign Protestants in the American Colonies*, vol.24 (Huguenot Society, 1921)

R. A. Humphries, *The Diplomatic History of British Honduras, 1638–1901* (Oxford University Press, 1961)

Imperial Department of Agriculture in the West Indies, *Notes on Dominica and Hints to Intending Settlers* (1919)

Imperial War Museum, *Tracing Your Family History: Army* (Trustees of the Imperial War Museum, 1999)

Imperial War Museum, *Tracing Your Family History: Merchant Navy* (Trustees of the Imperial War Museum, 2000)

Imperial War Museum, *Tracing Your Family History: Navy* (Trustees of the Imperial War Museum, 1999)

J. M. Ingham, *Defence Not Defiance: A History of the Bermuda Volunteer Rifle Corps* (Bermuda, 1992)

K. E.. N. Ingram, *Manuscripts Relating to Commonwealth Caribbean Countries in the United States and Canadian Repositories* (Caribbean Universities Press, 1975)

K. E. N. Ingram, *Manuscript Sources for the History of the West Indies* (University of the West Indies, 2000)

K. E. N. Ingram, *Sources for Jamaican History 1655–1838: A Bibliographical Survey with Particular Reference to Manuscript Sources* (Inter Documentation Co., 1976)

K. E. N. Ingram, *Sources for West Indian Studies: A Supplementary Listing, with Particular Reference to Manuscript Sources* (Inter Documentation Co., 1983)

S. L. Jamison, *Finding Your People: An African-American Guide to Discovering Your Roots* (Pedigree, 1999)

C. Jeffries, *The Colonial Empire and its Civil Service* (Cambridge University Press, 1938)

C. Jeffries, *Whitehall and the Colonial Service: An Administrative Memoir, 1939–1956* (The Athlone Press, 1972)

C. F. Jenkins, *Tortola: A Quaker Experiment of Long Ago in the Tropics* (1923, reprinted with a forward by H. F. Durham in 1971)

C. Jesse, *Outlines of St Lucia's History* (St Lucia Archaeological and Historical Society, 1964)

A. M. John, *The Plantation Slaves of Trinidad, 1783–1816* (Cambridge University Press, 1989)

A. E. Johnson, A. M. Cooper, R. Rosen, *A Student's Guide to African American Genealogy* (Oryx Press, 1995)

F. C. Johnson and C. F. E. H. Hallett (eds), *Early Colonists of the Bahamas: A Selection of Records* (Juniperhill Press, c.1996)

S. B. Jones, *Annals of Anguilla* (St Christopher Printery, 1937)

C. L. Joseph, 'The British West Indies Regiment 1914–1918', *Journal of Caribbean History*, vol. II, May 1971, pp. 94–124

Journals of the Board of Trade and Plantations, 1704–1782, 14 vols (HMSO, 1920–38).

J. and M. Kaminkow, *A List of Emigrants from England to America, 1718–1759* (Magna Charta Book Co., 1964)

T. J. Kemp, *International Vital Records Handbook*, 4th edn (Genealogical Publishing Co. Inc., 2000)

T. J. Kemp, *Virtual Roots* (Scholarly Resources, 2002)

D. L. Kent, *Barbados and America* (Carol M. Kent, 1980)

R. Kershaw, *Emigrants and Expats: A Guide to Sources on UK Emigration and Residents Overseas* (Public Record Office, 2002)

R. Kershaw and M. Pearsall, *Immigrants and Aliens: A Guide to Sources on UK Immigration and Citizenship* (Public Record Office, 2000)

B. L. Kieran, *The Lawless Caymanas: A Story of Slavery, Freedom and the West India Regiment* (Bourne Press, 1992).

J. Kincaid, *The Autobiography of My Mother* (Plume, 1997)

J. Kincaid, *A Small Place* (Farrar Straus & Giroux, 2000)

A. H. M. Kirk-Greene, *A Biographical Dictionary of the British Colonial Service 1939–1966* (Hans Zell Publishers, 1991)

A. H. M. Kirk-Greene, *British Imperial Administrators 1858–1966* (Macmillan, 2000)

J. M. Kitzmiller, *In Search of the 'Forlorn Hope': A Comprehensive Guide to Locating British Regiments and Their Records (1640–WWI)*, 2 vols (Manuscript Publishing Foundation, 1988).

H. S. Klein, *The Atlantic Slave Trade* (Cambridge University Press, 1999)

R. R. Kuczynski, *Demographic Survey of the British Colonial Empire. Volume 3: West Indian and American Territories* (Oxford University Press, 1953)

W. L. Lai, *The Chinese in the West Indies 1806–1995: A Documentary History* (University of the West Indies Press, 1998)

Mrs Lannigan, *Antigua and the Antiguans*, 2 vols (Saunders & Otley, 1844; reprinted by Macmillan Education, 1991)

J. H. Lawrence-Archer, *Monumental Inscriptions of the British West Indies* (Chatto and Windus, 1875)

Z. Layton-Henry, *The Politics of Immigration: Immigration, Race and Race Relations in Post-war Britain* (Blackwell, 1992)

N. B. Livingston, *Sketch Pedigrees of Some of the Early Settlers in Jamaica* (Jamaica, 1909)

C. C. Lloyd, *The Navy and the Slave Trade: Suppression of the African Slave Trade in the Nineteenth Century*, (Longmans, Green and Co., 1949)

P. E. Lovejoy, *Transformations in Slavery: A History of Slavery in Africa* (Cambridge University Press, 1983)

W. R. Louise (general editor), *The Oxford History of the British Empire*, five volumes (Oxford University Press, 1998–9)

C. P. Lucas, *Historical Geography of the British Colonies: Volume 2: The West Indies* (Clarendon Press, 1890)

R. R. McClure and S. L. Wilcox, *The Complete Idiot's Guide to Online Genealogy* (Alpha Books, 2002)

H. Malcolm, *Historical Documents Relating to the Bahama Islands* (Nassau, 1910)

W. Manross, *The Fulham Papers in the Lambeth Palace Library: American Colonial Section Calendar and Indexes* (Oxford, 1965)

S. I. Martin, *Incomparable World* (Quartet Books, 1996)

J. E. Mercer, *Bermuda Settlers of the 17th century: Genealogical Notes from Bermuda* (Genealogical Publishing Co. Inc., 1982)

M. E. Mitchell, *Jamaican Ancestry: How to Find Out More* (Heritage Books, 1998)

R. N. Murray, *Lest We Forget: The Experiences of World War II Westindian Ex-service Personnel* (Hansib Publications, 1996)

W. Oldham, *Britain's Convicts to the Colonies* (Library of Australian History, 1990)

V. L. Oliver (ed.), *Caribbeana*, 6 vols (1910–1919). Reprinted by James Lynch by subscription in 2000 <www.candoo.com/olivers/caribbeana.html>

V. L. Oliver, *History of the Island of Antigua*, 3 vols (1894–1899). Reprinted by James Lynch in 1999 (see <www.candoo.com/olivers/caribbeana.html>)

V. L. Oliver, *The Monumental Inscriptions of the British West Indies* (The Friary Press, 1927)

V. L. Oliver (ed.), *Monumental Inscriptions in Barbados* (1915)

V. L. Oliver (ed.), *The Registers of St Thomas, Middle Island, St Kitts 1729–1832* (London, 1915)

C. R. Ottley, *The Story of Tobago* (Longman, 1973)

P. Panayi, *Racial Violence in Britain, 1840–1950* (Leicester University Press, 1993)

B. Pappalardo, *Tracing Your Naval Ancestors* (Public Record Office, 2002)

O. Patterson, *The Sociology of Slavery: An Analysis of the Origins, Development, and Structure of Negro Slave Society in Jamaica* (Associated University Press, 1969)

C. Peacock, *The Good Web Guide to Genealogy* (The Good Web Guide, 2002)

G. Pelling and P. Litton, *Beginning Your Family History*, 5th edn (Federation of Family History Societies, 1998)

P. A. Penfold (ed.), *Maps and Plans in the Public Record Office, Volume 2: America and West Indies* (HMSO, 1974)

C. Phillips, *The Final Passage* (Faber and Faber, 1989)

M. Phillips and T. Phillips, *Windrush. The Irresistible Rise of Multi-racial Britain* (Harper Collins, 1998)

S. D. Porter, *Jamaican Records: A Research Manual: A Two Part Guide to Genealogical and Historical Research Using Repositories in Jamaica and England* (Stephen D. Porter, 1999)

R. B. Potter, *St Vincent and the Grenadines* (ABC Clio Reference Books, 1992)

Public Record Office Lists and Indexes, Volume LIII: An Alphabetical Guide to Certain War Office and Other Military Records Preserved in the Public Record Office (HMSO, 1931, reprinted by Kraus Reprint Corporation, 1963)

Public Record Office, *Supplement to the Guide to the Records of the Commonwealth of the Bahamas* (Commonwealth of the Bahamas, 1980)

R. B. Pugh, *The Records of the Colonial and Dominions Offices*, PRO handbook no. 3, updated by Thurston (HMSO, 1964)

L. J. Ragatz, *A Guide to the Official Correspondence of the Governors of the British West India Colonies with the Secretary of State, 1763–1833* (The Bryan Edwards Press, 1923)

R. Ramdin, *Arising from Bondage: A History of the Indo-Caribbean People* (New York University Press, 2000)

Reader's Digest, *Explore Your Family's Past* (Reader's Digest, 2000)

J. Redington and R. A. Roberts (eds) *Calendar of Home Office Papers of the Reign of George III*, 4 volumes (London, 1878–99)

J. Robertson, 'Jamaican archival resources for seventeenth and eighteenth century Atlantic history', *Slavery and Abolition*, vol. 22, no. 3, December 2001, pp. 109–140

N. A. M. Rodger, *Naval Records for Genealogists*, 2nd edn, PRO handbook no. 22 (HMSO, 1998)

M. Roper, *The Records of the Foreign Office, 1782–1969* (Public Record Office, 2002)

M. Roper, *The Records of the War Office and Related Departments 1660–1964*, (Public Record Office, 1998)

C. Rose and K. G. Ingalls, *The Complete Idiot's Guide to Genealogy* (Macmillan Publishing Company, 1997)

J. Rose, *Black Genesis* (Gale Research Co., 1978)

H. Rowe, *A Guide to the Records of Bermuda* (The Bermuda Archives, 1980)

Royal Commission on Public Records, vol II, 1914, 'Memorandum on official records in the West Indies', pp. 115–120

P. Saha, *Emigration of Indian Labour, 1834–1900* (New Delhi, People Publishing House, 1970)

L. E. Salazar, *Love Child: A Genealogist's Guide to the Social History of Barbados* (L. E. Salazar, 2001) <www.candoo.com/projects/lovechild.html>

J. M. Sanders, *Barbados Records: Baptisms 1637–1800* (Genealogical Publishing Co Inc, 1984)

J. M. Sanders, *Barbados Records: Marriages 1643–1800*, 2 vols (Sanders Historical Publications, 1982)

J. M. Sanders, *Barbados Records: Wills and Administrations 1647–1725*, 3 vols (Sanders Historical Publications, 1981)

D. G. Saunders, and E. A. Carson, *A Guide to the Records of the Bahamas* (Nassau, 1973)

K. Saunders (ed.), *Indentured Labour in the British Empire, 1834–1920* (Croom Helm, 1984)

Scottish Record Office, *Tracing Your Scottish Ancestors* (HMSO, 1993)

The Second World War Army Roll of Honour WO 304, published on CD-ROM (Naval and Military Press, 2000)

S. Selvon, *The Lonely Londoners* (Longman, 1979)

T. Sewell, *Keep on Moving: The Windrush Legacy* (The Voice, 1998)

C. Shepard, *An Historical Account of the Island of St Vincent* (reprinted by Frank Cass, 1997)

M. Sherwood, *Many Struggles: West Indian Workers and Service Personnel in Britain, 1939–45* (Karia Press, 1985)

M. Sherwood and M. Spafford, *Whose Freedom Were Africans, Caribbeans and Indians Defending in World War II?* (Savannah Press, 2000)

E. M. Shilstone, *Monumental Inscriptions in the Burial Ground of the Jewish Synagogue at Bridgetown, Barbados* (Jewish Historical Society of England, 1956)

F. Shyllon, *Black People in Britain 1555–1833* (Oxford University Press, 1977)

C. Sinclair, *Tracing Your Scottish Ancestors* (The Mercat Press, 1997)

K. Smith, C. T. Watts and M. J. Watts, *Records of Merchant Shipping and Seamen* (Public Record Office, 1998)

C. Soares, 'Jamaican research in Britain', *Family Tree Magazine*, April 1991, p. 35

Soldiers Died in the Great War, first published in 1921, available on CD-ROM (Naval and Military Press, 2000)

W. Spencer, *Air Force Records for Family Historians* (Public Record Office, 2000)

W. Spencer, *Army Service Records of the First World War*, 3rd edn (Public Record Office, 2001)

N. L. Staff, *African-American Genealogy Workbook: Finding Your Roots*, 3rd edn (Legacy Publishing Co., 1994)

C. J. Stanford, 'Genealogical sources in Barbados', *The Genealogists' Magazine*, vol. 17, March 1974, pp. 489–498

D. Steel, *No Entry: The Background and Implications of the Commonwealth Immigrants Act, 1968* (C. Hurst and Co., 1969)

L. R. Stephenson, *The Complete Idiot's Guide to Writing Your Family History* (Alpha Books, 2000)

I. Stranack, *The Andrew and the Onions: The Story of the Royal Navy in Bermuda 1795–1975*, 2nd edn (Bermuda Maritime Museum Press, 1990)

D. H. Streets, *Slave Genealogy: A Research Guide with Case Studies* (Heritage Books Inc., 1986)

D. Syrett and R. L. DiNardo (eds), *The Commissioned Sea Officers of the Royal Navy 1660–1815: Occasional Publications of the Navy Records Society, Vol. 1* (Navy Records Society, 1994)

N. Tattersfield and J. Fowles, *The Forgotten Trade* (Pimlico, 1998)

P. L. Tello, C. Menendez and C. Herrero, *Documentos Relativos a la Independencia de Norteamerica Existentes en Archivos Espanoles* (Madrid, 1976)

M. Tepper, *Passengers to America* (Genealogical Publishing Co Inc, 1988)

G. Thomas, *Records of the Militia from 1757*, PRO readers' guide no. 3 (Public Record Office, 1993)

G. Thomas, *Records of the Royal Marines*, PRO readers' guide no. 10 (Public Record Office, 1994)

H. Thomas, *The Slave Trade* (Macmillan, 1998)

T. N. Thomas, *Indians Overseas: A Guide to Source Materials in the India Office Records for the Study of Indian Emigration, 1830–1950* (British Library, 1985)

A. Thurston, *Records of the Colonial Office, Dominions Office, Commonwealth Relations Office and Commonwealth Office* (The Stationery Office, 1997)

H. Tinker, *A New System of Slavery: The Export of Indian Labour Overseas, 1830–1920* (Oxford University Press, 1974)

J. Titford, *Succeeding in Family History* (Countryside Books, 2001)

J. Titford, 'Settlers of the Old Empire: The West Indies: Anguilla', *Family Tree Magazine*, June 2000, pp. 25–27

J. Titford, 'Settlers of the Old Empire: The West Indies: Antigua', 2 parts, *Family Tree Magazine*, June 2001 and September 2001

J. Titford, 'Settlers of the Old Empire: The West Indies: British Virgin Islands', *Family Tree Magazine*, September 2000

J. Titford, 'Settlers of the Old Empire. The West Indies: Grenada', 2 parts, *Family Tree Magazine*, December 2001 and March 2002

J. Titford, 'Settlers of the Old Empire: The West Indies manuscript sources', 2 parts, *Family Tree Magazine*, November 1998 and January 1999

J. Titford, 'Settlers of the Old Empire: The West Indies: Montserrat', 2 parts in *Family Tree Magazine*, December 2000 and March 2001

J. Titford, 'Settlers of the Old Empire. The West Indies: Nevis', 2 parts, *Family Tree Magazine*, September 1999 and November 1999

J. Titford, 'Settlers of the Old Empire: The West Indies: St Kitts', 2 parts in *Family Tree Magazine*, May 1999 and July 1999

J. Titford, 'Settlers of the Old Empire: The West Indies: St Lucia', *Family Tree Magazine*, June 2002, pp. 12–14

J. Titford, 'Transcripts of 18th century registers for St George Gingerland', *Family Tree Magazine*, January 2000 and March 2000

G. F. Tyson, *A Guide to Manuscript Sources in United States and West Indian Depositories Relating to the British West Indies During the Era of the American Revolution* (Scholarly Resources Inc., 1978)

T. Uddenberg and K. Vaucrosson, *Lists from the San Fernando Gazette: 1865–1896* (Uddenberg and Vaucrosson, 2002; contact gazette@shaw.ca for further information)

M. Vickerman, *Crosscurrents: West Indian Immigrants and Race* (Oxford University Press, 1999)

E. Viotti, *Crowns of Glory, Tears of Blood* (Oxford University Press, 1997)

J. W. StG. Walker, *The Black Loyalists: The Search for a Promised Land in Nova Scotia and Sierra Leone, 1783–1870* (Longman and Dalhousie University Press, 1976)

P. Walne (ed.), *A Guide to Manuscript Sources for the History of Latin America and the Caribbean in the British Isles* (Oxford University Press, 1973)

J. Walvin, *Black and White: The Negro and English Society 1555–1945* (Penguin Press, 1973)

J. Walvin, *Black Ivory: A History of British Slave Trade*, 2nd edn (Blackwell Publishers, 2001)

J. Walvin, *Britain's Slave Empire* (Tempus Publishing, 2000)

J. Walvin, *Passage to Britain* (Penguin Books, 1984)

J. Walvin, *The Slave Trade* (Sutton Publishing, 1999)

W. E. F. Ward, *The Royal Navy and the Slavers: The Suppression of the Atlantic Slave Trade* (Allen and Unwin, 1969)

M. C. Waters, *West Indian Immigrant Dreams and American Realities* (Harvard University Press, 1999)

I. Watkins-Owen, *Blood Relations: Caribbean Immigrants and the Harlem Community, 1900–1930* (Indiana University Press, 1996)

E. Watson, *The Carib Regiment of World War II* (New York, 1964)

C. T. Watts and M. J. Watts, *My Ancestor Was in the British Army* (Society of Genealogists, 1992)

C. T. Watts and M. J. Watts, *My Ancestor Was a Merchant Seaman: How Can I Find Out More About Him?*, 2nd edn (Society of Genealogists, 2002)

J. McNish Weiss, *The Merikens: Free Black American Settlers in Trinidad, 1815–1816*, 2nd edn (McNish and Weiss, 2002)

J. McNish Weiss, 'The corps of Colonial Marines 1814–16: A summary' in *Immigrants and Minorities*, vol. 15, no. 1, April 1996

R. V. Wells, *The Population of the British Colonies in America before 1776* (Princeton University Press, 1975

J. Western, *A Passage to England: Barbadian Londoners Speak of Home* (University of Minnesota Press, 1992)

D. E. Westlake, *Under an English Heaven*, (Hodder and Stoughton, 1973)

E. H. Whittleton, 'Family history in the Bahamas', *The Genealogists' Magazine*, vol. 18, December 1975, pp. 187–191

E. Williams, *History of the People of Trinidad and Tobago* (new edition, A & B Publishers Group, 1996)

N. Williams, *A History of the Cayman Islands* (Government of the Cayman Islands, 1970)

H. I. Woodcock, *History of Tobago* (Frank Cass, 1971)

D. Woodtor, *Finding a Place Called Home: A Guide to African-American Genealogy and Historical Identity* (Random House, 1999)

P. Wright, *Monumental Inscriptions of Jamaica* (Society of Genealogists, 1966)

P. Wright, 'Materials for family history in Jamaica', *The Genealogists' Magazine*, vol. 15, September 1966, pp. 239–250

T. M. Young, *Afro-American Genealogy Source Book* (Garland Publishing Inc., 1987)

W. Young, *Account of the Black Charaibs in the Island of St Vincent's* (reprinted by Frank Cass, 1971)

Index

abolition of the slave trade 1807, 39, 40, 68
abolition of slavery 1834, 12, 89, 90, 111
Access to Archives (A2A), 57, 110
Admiralty, 40
    see also Royal Navy
aerial photographs, 55
Africa and Africans, 4, 6, 10, 34
    in UK, 105
    see also Liberated Africans, slaves
African companies, 39, 124
American Loyalists, 13, 43, 44, 126
Amerindians, 3, 9, 17, 95, 137, 156, 159
Anglo-American War 1812, 68, 81
    black American refugees, 81
Anguilla, 147, 151, 154
    resources, 121–123
    see also Leeward Islands, Nevis,
      St Christopher
Antigua, 59
    dockyard musters, 79
    manumissions, 93
    resources, 123–125
    see also Leeward Islands
army, 40, 51, 60, 61–76, 102
    birth, marriage and death registers, 66–67
    foreign regiments, 61
    medal rolls, 66, 74
    service records, 62–64, 73
    war diaries, 67, 73, 75
    wills, 51, 66
    see also regiments (named)
Aruba *see* Netherlands
Asians *see* Indians (Asian), Chinese
Bahamas, 47
    American Loyalists in, 43, 126
    Bishop of London registers, 45
    in WWI, 71
    resources, 125–128
baptisms *see* births and baptisms
Barbados, 13, 45, 46, 47, 50, 57, 66, 89, 111
    Barbados Citizens' Contingent WWI, 64, 81
    dockyard musters, 79
      in WWI, 71
    manumissions, 93
    resources, 128–130
Barbuda *see* Antigua

Bay Islands, 131
    see also Belize, Honduras, Jamaica
Belgium soldiers in West India Regiment, 68
Belize (*formerly* British Honduras)
    British Hondurans in UK, WWII, 105
    resources, 131–132
Berbice *see* Guyana, Netherlands
Bermuda, 12, 64, 71, 81, 89
    black American refugees, 81
    dockyard musters, 79
    Ireland Island, 38, 79, 133
    regiments *see* regiments (named)
    resources, 133–134
births and baptisms, 7, 8, 19, 20, 24, 26, 45–48,
    93, 118
    army, 62, 63, 66
    consular, 111, 114, 115
    Indian migrants, 41
    Royal Air Force, 84
    Royal Navy, 78
    slave, 11, 12, 46, 47, 93
Bishop of London, 45, 115
black loyalists, 43, 44
    see also Committee for the Relief of Poor
      Blacks
black soldiers, 61, 68, 71, 72
    colonial marines, 4, 81
    see also army, black loyalists, regiments
      (named)
Board of Trade, 23, 33
Bonair *see* Netherlands
Brazil, 3, 10
    Rio de Janeiro Mixed Commission
      Court, 40
British Guiana *see* Guyana
British Honduras *see* Belize
British Nationality and Status of Aliens
    Act 1914, 36
British Rail recruitment, 105
British Virgin Islands resources, 134–136
    see also Leeward Islands
burials *see* deaths and burials
Canada, 111, 114
    Canadian Overseas Expeditionary
      Force WWI, 66
Caribs *see* Amerindians

Cayman Islands resources, 136–137
    see also Jamaica
Ceded Islands see Dominica, Grenada,
    St Vincent, Tobago
censuses
    colonial, 24, 48–50, 93, 118
    UK, 20, 103, 105
Chinese labourers, 4, 6, 40
Church of Jesus Christ of Latter-day Saints, 7,
    17, 18–19, 46, 47, 51, 118
church records, 7, 11
civil registration, 7
civil servants (Colonial), 24, 25, 26, 97–101
Colonial Office records, 12, 23–32, 54, 57, 69,
    111, 113, 118–121
    see under individual countries
    acts, 25, 34, 95
    Blue Books of Statistics, 26, 48, 99
    entry books, 25
    government gazettes, 11, 26, 29, 33, 34,
        41, 47, 48, 50, 51, 54, 75, 99
        see also newspapers
    original correspondence, 24, 33, 34, 41, 50
    Naval Office returns, 29, 39
    sessional papers, 26, 34, 54, 95
    registers of correspondence, 29, 31
    registers of out-letters, 31
    relating to slaves, 92–95
Committee for the Relief of Poor Blacks, 44, 103
commonwealth immigrants acts, 105, 108
Commonwealth Office, 24, 111, 118, 120
Commonwealth War Graves Commission, 66,
    78, 87
Consular Marriages Act 1848, 114, 115
Costa Rica, 111, 171
court records
    assize, 38
    Chancery, 57
    Exchequer, 57
    High Court of Admiralty, 41
    local courts, 24, 26, 50–51, 95
    Mixed Commission Courts, 40
    quarter sessions, 38
    Vice-Admiralty courts, 24, 40
Creole, 11
Cuba, 111
    Havana Mixed Commission Court, 40
    recruiting depot for West India Regiment, 68
    resources, 167, 169
    see also Spain
Curaçao see Netherlands
customs returns, 29, 39, 41
deaths and burials, 7, 8, 19, 20, 24, 26, 45–48, 93,
    118
    army, 63, 66–67

consular returns, 111, 114, 115
    Indian migrants, 41
    merchant seamen, 87
    Royal Air Force, 81, 84
    Royal Navy, 78
    slave, 11, 12, 46, 47, 93
deeds, 11, 36, 57, 59, 93
    see also manumissions, mortgages,
        plantation records
departmental reports (colonial)
    see Colonial Office records: sessional
        papers
Demerara see Guyana, Netherlands
Denmark and the Danes, 3, 6
    Danish Virgin Islands (St Croix, St John,
        St Thomas), 167, 169
    resources, 169
    see also United States of America
Directorate of Overseas Surveys, 55
discrimination in armed services, 60
dockyards see Bermuda: Ireland Island, naval
    dockyards
Dominica, 3, 4, 8, 43, 54, 57
    resources, 137–139
    see also France, Leeward Islands,
        Windward Islands
Dominican Republic (formerly Santo Domingo),
    111
    resources, 169–170
    St Domingo Corps, 68, 72
    see also France, Haiti, Spain
Dominions Office, 111
East Florida Claims Commission, 43
East India Company, 43
East Indians see Indians (Asian)
emigration see migration
emigration departments (Colonial Office), 41
Essequibo see Guyana, Netherlands
executive councils see Colonial Office records:
    sessional papers
Family Records Centre, 20–22
Federation of West Indies
    resources, 139–140
Foreign and Commonwealth Office, 24, 99, 111,
    114, 118, 120
Foreign Office, 111, 113–115
    Slave Trade Department, 40, 102
France and the French, 3, 4, 6, 8, 41
    French colonies (Dominica, French
        Guiana, Grenada, Guadeloupe,
        Martinique, St Barthèlemy, St Christopher,
        Saint-Dominique, St Lucia, St Martin,
        St Vincent, Tobago), 167, 170
    Guadeloupe soldiers in West India
        Regiments, 68

in Carriacou, 140
in Leeward Islands, 124, 149, 152, 154
in St Christopher, 154–155
in St Vincent, 160
in Little Tobago, 162
lands in Dominica, 138
Martinique, 66, 68, 170
Martinique dockyard musters, 79
resources, 170
genealogy, 4, 7–10
Germans, 6, 41, 68, 126
Grenada, 4, 8, 50, 54, 55, 71, 72
manumissions, 93
resources, 140–141
see also France and Windward Islands
Guadeloupe *see* France
Guyana (*formerly* British Guiana), 4, 8, 34, 47, 54, 57, 111
reports of protectors of slaves, 93
resources, 142–144
WWI contingent, 69, 71
see also Netherlands
Guyane *see* France
Haiti (*formerly* Saint-Domingue)
dockyard musters, 79
resources, 170–171
see also France, Santo Domingo
Home Office, 36
Honduras resources, 171
see also Spain
immigration *see* migration
immigration departments (Colonial Office), 41
indentured servants, 37
India Office, 43
Indians (American) *see* Amerindians
Indians (Asian), 4, 6, 41–43
International Genealogical Index, 18, 19, 46
see also Church of Jesus Christ and Latter-Day Saints
Internet resources, 16–18
Irish in the Leeward Islands, 124, 149, 152, 154
Jamaica, 43, 50, 57, 59, 89, 95, 111
dockyard musters, 79
immigration of Liberated Africans, 40
in WWI, 64, 69, 71
Jamaican Defence Force, 68
manumissions, 93, 95
resources, 144–147
Santo Domingo references, 170
Kwéyòl, 8
Labour Gazette, 111
labour vouchers, 108
land records, 24, 25, 26, 54–59, 111
see also deeds, mortgages, plantation records
Lebanese, 6
Leeward Islands, 111

resources, 147–148
see also Anguilla, Antigua, British Virgin Islands, Montserrat, St Christopher
legislative councils *see* Colonial Office records: sessional papers
liberated Africans, 4, 16, 40–41, 68
see also Africa
licences, 26
licences to pass beyond the seas, 33
London Transport recruitment, 105
maps and plans, 55
maroons, 7, 44, 145
marriages, 7, 8, 19, 20, 24, 26, 45–48, 118
army, 63, 66
consular, 111, 114, 115
Royal Air Force, 84
Royal Navy, 78
slaves 46, 92, 93
Martinique *see* France
Mauritius, 68, 88
merchant navy, 39, 60, 78, 84–87, 102, 103, 105
agreements and crew lists, 87
deaths, 87
musters, 87
records of service, 84–85
Special Restriction (Coloured Alien Seamen) Order 1925, 105
migration
emigration to places outside the UK, 111–117
emigration to the UK, 102–111
immigration to the West Indies, 33–44
militia (colonial), 60, 61, 75
see also army
military personnel *see* army, militia, Royal Air Force, Royal Marines, Royal Navy
Ministry of Labour, 60, 103
Ministry of Pensions, 64, 69
Moffat, John
plantations in Jamaica, 59
Montserrat
resources 148–150
see also Leeward Islands
mortgages, 11, 54, 57, 59
see also deeds, land, plantation records
mulatto, 11
Mutiny Act, 68
names, 8
nationality acts (UK), 108
naturalization, 25, 26, 34, 36, 102, 108, 113, 114
naval dockyards, 79
Netherlands/the Dutch, 3, 4, 6, 8, 10, 40, 61, 134
Dutch colonies (Aruba, Berbice, Bonair, Curaçao, Demerara, Essequibo, Saba, St Eustatius, St Maarten, Surinam), 111, 167, 171–172

Dutch West India Company, 8, 142
garrison battalions, 61
in Leeward Islands, 124, 149, 152, 154
passports issued to Dutch colonists, 34
resources, 171–172
Surinam, 3, 34, 145, 172
Nevis, 51, 111, 121
Bishop of London registers, 45
resources, 151–153
see also Leeward Islands, St Christopher
newspapers, 11, 12, 24, 26, 29, 33, 47, 95
see also Colonial Office records:
government gazettes
Nicaragua, 111, 171
Nova Scotia, 43, 64, 145
Black American refugees in, 43, 44, 81
Ordnance Survey International, 55
Oxford Colonial Records Project, 101
Panama, 111, 114
Panama Canal Zone *see* United States
of America
resources, 172–173
see also Spain
parish records, 7, 46
passenger lists
to Canada, 114
to the UK, 103
to the United States, 114
to the West Indies, 26, 33, 40, 114
passports, 34, 108, 113, 114
pensioners
army, 62, 64, 68, 69, 72
colonial, 26, 97, 99
Royal Navy, 77
petitions, 24, 25, 26, 39, 95
plantation records, 11, 13, 47, 55, 57–59
plantations (named)
Blenheim, 59
Cranbrooke, 59
Golden Vales, 59
port books, 33
Portugal and Portuguese, 3, 4, 6, 40, 41
Prerogative Court of Canterbury, 20, 51, 53
see also wills and administrations
prisoners, 24
see also transportation
Privy Council, 23, 33, 88, 99
probate *see* Prerogative Court of Canterbury,
wills and administrations
Public Record Office, 20–22
Puerto Rico *see* Spain, United States of America
race riots 1919 (UK), 103, 105
regiments (named)
Bahamas Garrison Company, 72, 73
Barbados Rangers, 72

Bermuda Contingent, Royal Garrison
Artillery, 74
Bermuda Garrison Company, 64
Bermuda Volunteer Rifles, 64, 75
Bourbon Regiment, 68
British West Indies Regiment, 64, 66, 68–71,
73, 74, 75
Caribbean Regiment, 71, 75
Carolina Black Corps, 67
Corps of Military Labourers, 68, 72, 73
Devonshire Regiment, 64
London Regiment, 64
Royal African corps, 40
Royal Artillery, 71
St Helena Corps, 72
Santo Domingo Corps, 68, 72
South American Rangers, 72
West India Rangers, 72, 73
West India Regiment, 4, 40, 66–68, 71,
72, 73, 74
York Light Infantry Volunteers, 61, 72, 73
registration of citizenship of UK and colonies,
36, 108
Royal Air Force, 60, 64, 81–84, 105
births, marriages and deaths, 84
records of service, 82
war diaries, 84
Royal Commission on Historical Manuscripts,
57, 99
Royal Flying Corps *see* Royal Air Force
Royal Hospital Chelsea, 63
see also army
Royal Marines, 80–81
colonial marines, 4, 81
medal rolls, 80
records of service, 80
Royal Naval Air Service *see* Royal Air Force
Royal Naval Reserve, 78
Royal Naval Volunteer Reserve, 78–79
Royal Navy, 40, 51, 60, 76–79, 102
births, marriages and deaths, 78
medal rolls, 78
records of service, 76–77
ship's logs, 77
wills, 51, 78
Saba *see* Netherlands
St Bartholomew *see* France, Sweden
St Christopher, 4, 51, 54, 111, 121, 122, 123
resources, 153–156
see also France, Leeward Islands
St Croix *see* Denmark, United States of America
Saint-Dominque *see* Haiti
St Eustatius *see* Netherlands
St John *see* Denmark, United States of America
St Lucia, 4, 8, 12, 13, 50, 57, 66, 89

immigration of Liberated Africans, 40
manumissions, 93
reports of protectors of slaves, 93
resources, 156–159
slave registry, 88
see also France, Windward Islands
St Maarten *see* Netherlands
St Martin *see* France
St Thomas *see* Denmark, United States of
   America
St Vincent and the Grenadines, 4, 8, 50, 54, 57
manumissions, 93
resources, 159–161
see also France, Windward Islands
Santo Domingo *see* Domican Republic
Scottish Archives Network (SCAN), 57
Scots in the Leeward Islands, 124, 149, 152, 154
ships and shipping, 26, 29, 39, 40, 41
   see also merchant navy, passenger lists
ships (named)
   Agnes, 40
   Albion (HMS), 81
   Amity, 40
   Balantia, 71
   Danube, 69, 71
   Empire Windrush, 105
   Etheldred, 40
   Hercules (HMS), 145
   Morayshire, 40
   Quillata, 71
   Santille, 105
   Severn (HMS), 81
   Tavistock (HMS), 162
   Una, 40
   Verdula, 69
Sierra Leone, 40, 41, 43, 44, 68, 145
   censuses, 40, 145
slave trade, 39, 40
slaves and slavery, 4, 8, 24, 26, 39, 40, 46, 47, 57,
   61, 67, 88–96
manumissions, 11, 12, 13, 24, 26, 92, 93, 95
protectors of slaves, 11, 12, 93, 95
Slave Compensation Commission, 11,
   90, 92, 118
slave registry, 11, 12, 47, 50, 88–89, 95, 118
surnames, 12–13, 16
tracing slave ancestry, 10–16
Spain and the Spanish, 3, 4, 6, 8, 40
resources, 173
Spanish colonies (Cuba, Puerto Rico,
   Santo Domingo), 167, 173
Special Restriction (Coloured Alien Seamen)
   Order 1925, 105

Surinam *see* Netherlands
surnames, 8, 12–13, 16
Sweden and the Swedes, 3
   St Bartholomew, 173
Tobago, 54
   resources, 161–163
   see also France, Trinidad, Windward
      Islands
tax lists, 24, 26, 54
transportation, 25, 38
   to Ireland Island, Bermuda, 79
Treasury, 38, 41, 57, 69
Trinidad, 4, 8, 12, 13, 41, 50, 54, 57, 66, 89
colonial marines settlement, 81
immigration of liberated Africans, 40
in WWII, 71
reports of protectors of slaves, 93
resources, 163–165
slave registry, 88
Trinidad Merchants' and Planters'
   Contingent WWI, 64, 69, 71, 81
Trinidad Royal Naval Volunteer Reserve, 79
see also Spain
Turks and Caicos Islands
resources, 165–166
see also Bahamas, Jamaica
United States of America, 6, 111
American overseas territories
   (Panama Canal Zone, Puerto Rico,
   St Croix, St John, St Thomas), 172, 174
      Ellis Island passenger lists, 114
refugee slaves, 68, 81
resources, 173–174
see also American Loyalists, Anglo-
   American War 1812
Venezuela, 114
Virgin Islands
see British Virgin Islands, Denmark, United
   States of America
West Indian Hurricane Relief Commission, 57
West Indian Incumbered Estates Commission,
   57, 59
West Indians, 6
West Indies resources, 119–121
wills and administrations, 11, 13, 19, 26, 45,
   50–53, 95, 103, 113, 114
army, 51, 66
Royal Navy, 51, 78
see also Prerogative Court of Canterbury
Windward Islands
resources 166
see also Barbados, Dominica, Grenada,
   St Lucia, St Vincent, Tobago